HR
to the
RESCUE

IMPROVING
HUMAN
PERFORMANCE
SERIES

HR
to the
RESCUE

Case Studies of HR Solutions to Business Challenges

Edward M. Mone and Manuel London, Ph.D., Editors

Gulf Publishing Company
Houston, Texas

HR to the Rescue

Case Studies of HR Solutions to Business Challenges

Gulf Publishing Company
Book Division
P.O. Box 2608 □ Houston, Texas 77252-2608

10   9   8   7   6   5   4   3   2   1

Library of Congress Cataloging-in-Publication Data

HR to the rescue : case studies of HR solutions to business
challenges / Edward M. Mone and Manuel London,
editors.
    p. cm.
Includes bibliographical references and index.
ISBN 0-88415-397-5 (alk. paper)
    1. Personnel management—Case studies.
2. Organizational change—Case studies.   3. Human
capital—Case studies.
I. Mone, Edward M.   II. London, Manuel.
HF5549.H658   1998
658.3—dc21   98-20775
                                        CIP

Printed on acid-free (∞) paper.

Contents

Acknowledgments

This book evolved as a result of discussions between the editors about the state of HR practice today, a time when the terms *change agent* and *organization transformation* are being widely discussed in the field's literature, as well as in the hallways outside most HR departments. HR professionals today are, more often than not, struggling with these concepts and how they relate to their own evolving roles and practice. As a result, we believed that there was value to be gained by providing a forum for real-world practitioners to tell their stories about how they have dealt with the thorny issues of being change agents faced with the challenge of driving and supporting organization transformation in today's environment. We hope our readers will find these stories both affirming and educational.

We owe a heartfelt thanks to many people, but only a few can be mentioned here: First, the chapter authors, for their honesty, insight, and courage, and for their belief in the editors' vision of this book; second, Victoria Marsick, for providing the editors with reactions to their ideas and steering them in the direction of Jack Phillips, the series editor, who graciously embraced the concept for this book and was supportive throughout the entire process; third, Sharon Williams, who always provided the lead editor with a supportive climate for developing his professional skills and testing his ideas; fourth, Kelly Perkins, our editor at Gulf, whose skill and enthusiasm was often needed and well appreciated; finally, our families, Marilyn, David, and Jared London, and Ceil Mone, for always being loving and extremely supportive.

Contributors

Dennis J. Adsit, Ph.D., received his undergraduate degree in mathematics and psychology, summa cum laude, from Bowling Green State University in Ohio. He received his master's and doctoral degrees from the University of Minnesota in industrial and organizational psychology. Currently, Adsit is a vice president at the consulting firm of Rath & Strong, a division of Aon Corporation. He offers consulting in culture realignment, large system change management, conflict resolution, and globalization to presidents and senior executives. Adsit's previous work experience includes serving as director of human resources for a large, French-owned high-tech multinational company. He also served as its manager of organization development. As an adjunct faculty member of Northeastern University's Human Resource Management Department, Adsit teaches leadership and human resource management courses in the Evening MBA and High-Tech MBA programs. He is also an associate editor and a member of the executive advisory panel for the Academy of Management's publication *Executive*.

Jill Conner is the director of people development at Colgate-Palmolive. In this role, she is responsible for leadership development, performance development, workforce planning, and HR capability. She has an MBA from the University of Georgia and a BA in psychology from the University of Miami. She is currently working on her doctorate in human resource development at George Washington University.

Thomas Diamante, Ph.D., consults with a variety of *Fortune* 500 organizations to produce desired organizational change, resolve conflict, and improve management effectiveness. A former human resource manager for a *Fortune* 10 company, Diamante's consultations reflect the perspective of an internal manager as well as his experience as an external organizational change consultant. He holds a doctorate in industrial and organizational psychology from the Graduate Center, City University of New York. His work appears in diverse publications, such as the *Journal of Business & Psychology, Psychological Reports, The Leadership & Organization Development Journal, Academic Emergency Medicine, The Journal of Management Development,* and *HR Magazine*. Diamante is an assistant professor at Dowling College's Graduate School of Business on Long Island, N.Y.

Carol Gorelick co-founded SOLUTIONS for Information and Management Services Inc., a management consulting company that specializes in implementing work-group and collaborative technologies for knowledge and document management applications. Before she founded SOLUTIONS, Carol held executive positions at Prudential Securities, American Express, American Airlines, Lufthansa, and AT&T. Carol has an MBA, with distinction, from the executive program at Pace University and a BA in economics from the State University of New York at Stony Brook. She has been an adjunct professor at Baruch College and Pace University, teaching management and data processing courses.

Stephen John, Ed.D., was Zurich-based global head of organizational learning and development for SBC Warburg. He has an MBA/CPA and a doctorate of education in adult and organizational learning from Columbia University. He is presently a principal at Arthur Andersen LLP specializing in human resource strategy development and implementation. He is particularly interested in designing and implementing technology-enabled organizational development interventions that significantly improve business results.

Henrik Holt Larsen is associate professor of human resource management at the Institute of Organization and Industrial Sociology, Copenhagen Business School. He has a master's degree in psychology and economics from the University of Copenhagen and a master's degree in organizational behavior from the University of Wisconsin. Larsen also holds a diploma in international economics from the College of Europe in Bruges, Belgium, and is completing his Ph.D. at the Copenhagen Business School. His major research interests are in the areas of (1) career, organization, and management development, (2) training, and (3) appraisal systems. He has authored numerous books and articles in these areas.

Manuel London, Ph.D., is professor and director of the Center for Human Resource Management in the Harriman School for Management and Policy, State University of New York at Stony Brook. After receiving his doctorate from Ohio State University, he taught for three years in the business school at the University of Illinois in Champaign-Urbana. He then held a variety of research and human resource management positions at AT&T. He moved to Stony Brook in 1989. His research interests are principally in employee and management development (including career motivation theory, performance evaluation and feedback, training, and retraining and job placement for displaced workers). His recent books include *Self and Interpersonal Insight: How Individuals Learn About Themselves and Others in Organizations* (Oxford, 1995) and *Jobs, Careers, and Economic Growth* (Jossey-Bass, 1995). He has been an associate editor of the *Academy of Management Journal* and on the editorial boards of the *Academy of Management Review,* the *Journal of Applied Psychology, Personnel Psychology,* and *Administrative Science Quarterly.* He is currently senior editor of the Society for Industrial and Organizational Psychology's Professional Practice series.

Stinne Madsen is a master's student in the human resources program at the Copenhagen Business School Institute for Industrial and Organizational Sociology. She has a BA in business law and has worked in both profit and not-for-profit organizations in Denmark and the United States.

Edward M. Mone has twenty years of experience in career, leadership, and organization development. Currently, he is director of people processes and systems at Booz•Allen & Hamilton Inc. Formerly HR division manager for strategic planning and development at AT&T, he has held a variety of human resource and organization development positions since 1982. Before that, he was a partner in an outplacement and career management firm based in New York City. He has also served as an adjunct faculty member at the Harriman School for Management and Policy, State University of New York at Stony Brook. He holds an MA in counseling psychology, has completed doctoral-level coursework in organization psychology, and is currently a doctorate-of-education candidate at Teachers College, Columbia University, where he researches individual, team, and organization learning. He has co-authored and co-edited books, book chapters, and articles in the areas of human resources and organization development. He also maintains a limited consulting practice.

Lilian Morgensen holds an MS in information technology and is the director for staff and management development at Den Danske Bank, where she has held a number of positions in information systems and human resource management. She frequently speaks at human resource conferences and has contributed to a number of publications in the field.

Tanya Rytterager Olsen holds a master's degree in human resource management from the Copenhagen Business School in Denmark and is now a research assistant at that institution.

James B. Shillaber, Psy.D., is director of organization development and training at Berlex Laboratories, a manufacturer and marketer of innovative pharmaceutical products in Montville, N.J. He has been using HR systems, programs, and processes to implement business strategy at Berlex since 1992. Prior to joining Berlex, Shillaber was a management consultant with Wm. Schiemann & Associates Inc. in Somerville, N.J. He received his bachelor's degree in psychology and human development from Hampshire College and his doctorate of psychology from Rutgers

University. He is a licensed psychologist and a licensed family therapist, and he has research and practice interests in community development.

Coleen A. Smith is the associate director of leadership development at Colgate-Palmolive. In this role, she is responsible for global succession planning, executive staffing, and high-potential management. She has also served as a human resource generalist for Colgate's international operations in Asia, the South Pacific, Central Europe, and Africa. She has a master's degree in labor relations from Cornell University and a BA in psychology from Villanova University.

Lyle Yorks, Ed.D., is chair of the Department of Business Administration and professor of management at Eastern Connecticut State University. He also serves on the executive development faculties at Louisiana State University and the University of Tennessee at Knoxville and as an adjunct faculty member in the adult education doctoral program at Teachers College, Columbia University. He regularly serves as a consultant for companies worldwide. Before coming to ECSU, he was a senior vice president of Drake Beam and Associates in New York City. He has also worked in the Corporate Management Systems Department at the Travelers Insurance companies. He has written several books, and his articles have appeared in the *Academy of Management Review*, the *California Management Review*, *Human Resource Development Quarterly*, the *Sloan Management Review*, and many other professional journals. He holds a BA from Tusculum College, an MA from Vanderbilt and Columbia universities, and a doctorate of education from Columbia University.

Preface

Today's CEOs and organization leaders are faced with competing under new and constantly changing rules, which regularly affect the global business landscape. Competition from around the world has forced executives with profit and loss responsibilities to develop a quality focus, think globally, shift core competencies, establish strategic alliances, downsize, and divest (or in the case of AT&T, trivest). These frame-breaking business initiatives need support to focus, motivate, develop, sustain, and reward the employee behavior necessary to ensure overall success. The cases in this book show how human resource professionals design and implement work processes and programs that contribute to organizational change and development.

Consider the need for employee development in the following situations:

- A quality-driven organization must employ people who understand and can manage a process-driven environment—one in which people work on projects and processes across functions, levels, and departments.

- An organization changes its business, perhaps by moving into new products or taking over sales and distribution functions previously handled by vendors, and it needs employees to learn new skills and functions.

- Two companies form a joint venture, requiring that employees develop a new spirit of cooperation and collaboration.
- A firm that downsized its staff to reduce costs and enhance efficiencies changes career opportunities for the remaining employees.
- An organization in the process of divesting units (for example, by spinning them off into separate corporations or by selling units to other companies) requires that remaining employees adopt a new sense of corporate identity and purpose.

This book is about transformation. Through case studies written by human resource practitioners engaged in organizational change, we describe a set of significant business challenges facing corporate leaders and human resource professionals. Our emphasis is on demonstrating how human resource development (HRD) principles, strategies, and programs can ensure the requisite business transformations to meet those challenges.

Many business leaders are realizing that HR practitioners can offer much more to the enterprise than maintaining personnel transactions such as payroll, benefits, and compensation. As important as these functions are, executives and HR practitioners alike increasingly recognize the transformational nature of HRD functions. Human resource development is a key component of successful organizational transformation. For example, HR personnel get involved in determining job requirements to make the business successful, in recruiting and hiring people who match the new and emerging skill demands, and in training these new employees and managers, as well as existing personnel to ensure they have the required knowledge and skills. Significant changes in how business is conducted entail concomitant changes in how employees are attracted, developed, maintained, and rewarded.

Our goal is to help readers learn from the experiences presented here by highlighting the human resource side of strategic business initiatives, some of which proved successful and some of which did not. This book should be of value to a wide audience, including the following: organizational leaders and managers who are interested in how HR helped other organizations' transformation efforts; human resource professionals, who will find practical ideas and strategies that they can use to develop and enhance their practices; and graduate students in HR or organizational behavior (OB) who are interested in how to actually bring theory into practice.

The cases provide a real-world perspective. They are not classical textbook cases of step-by-step approaches to transformation. Most practitioners live in imperfect worlds where things do not proceed by formula or standardized process. Some of the cases show that even partial solutions—those that focus on only one HR function, such as training—have significant impact when driven by the strategic needs of the business. In our view, these solutions or interventions (such as training to support new sales strategies) have value because they (a) are driven by business needs and (b) can often open doors to further HR intervention and change. We hope that the cases will expand the readers' horizons, affirming their experiences on one hand and providing challenge on the other.

Edward M. Mone
Manuel London, Ph.D.

I

Human Resource Development and Organizational Transformation

EDWARD M. MONE AND MANUEL LONDON, PH.D.

Human resource functions, such as selection, placement, and compensation, are essential ingredients to organizational success. Human resource development in relation to changing demands is vital for organizational growth. Employees and managers need to understand how their competencies match the organization's requirements and what competencies need to be strengthened (or new competencies acquired) to succeed in the future. Thus, individual and organization development support each other. Individual development contributes to maximizing the organization's capabilities, and changing organizational opportunities provide direction for individual development.

This book shows the supportive linkages between human resource and organization development. In particular, cases from a variety of organizations demonstrate how the human resource function in general, and human resource development in particular, contributes to organization transformations that allow the organization to thrive in an ever-changing, continuously demanding environment. Human resource development is a significant and necessary tool for supporting organization change.

The Strategic Role of Human Resources

People sometimes think of human resource functions in the abstract—as stand-alone policies and programs that are not driven by changing organizational needs. Indeed transactional aspects of human resources, such as managing the payroll and benefits systems, are fairly stable. Sometimes human resource functions follow from regulatory requirements, such as equal employment opportunity legislation and judicial rulings. Other human-resource-related initiatives, such as methods for task design, group functioning, and quality improvement, arise because they support new technologies. Companies adopt these programs because other companies are using them, not because of a profound belief that the programs can meet the organizations' specific needs.

However, an organization can tailor its transactional, regulated, and popular functions and programs to meet its strategies. For example, it can tie its compensation system to organizational goals and team functioning or can create a heterogeneous work force because it is good business, not because it meets the letter of the law. Total quality management or re-engineering can be designed in a way that incorporates best practices from other organizations and meets the specific current needs of the organization.

Human resource management must be transformational and strategic. Human resource managers' value to the organization derives from helping make the organization successful. Human resource managers are likely to be successful when they keep abreast of where the business wants to go by paying attention to the strategies set by top executives, the emergence of new technologies, and evolving market conditions. To understand where the business wants to go, HR managers must carefully analyze strategic business objectives and determine how human resource functions operate in relation to each other to support those objectives. These steps will ensure an integrated, systemic approach to human resource management.

On the other hand, human resource managers who work as if they are in a vacuum are likely to be disappointed when the company does not adopt their ideas or their programs have a minimal life. Human resource programs that are developed independently of other human resource functions and separately from organizational objectives are likely to fall flat and waste valuable resources. To guard against this, human resource functions may need to be redesigned in recognition of changing business goals and the need to have mutually supportive HR functions.

An example will help explain this philosophy. If businesses are moving to a process-quality environment, what are the implications for human resources? A process environment means people across departments work on interrelated functions in support of a business process, such as order tracking. The generic goal of any process is to provide service to customers in a way that is responsive to the customers' needs rather than to the corporate structure. So the needs of the customers drive the business. Human resource managers give careful thought to the best ways HR functions and processes can support process management. They should think about how the organization sets goals, what kinds of performance feedback systems they should put into place, what skills would be important as a basis for selecting new employees and developing all employees (such as skills needed to lead and participate in a quality improvement team process), and how to reward group as well as individual performance.

The Changing Nature of Work

Ilgen and Pulakos identified the following eight major changes in how organizations structure and accomplish work [1]. The following list considers and analyzes the implications of each of these changes for individual behaviors and skills, group characteristics and activities, and organization strategies and change.

1. Employees increasingly work in process teams. As a result, individuals will need to hone such skills as listening, group problem solving, resolving conflict, negotiating, leading a group, and cooperating. They will need to move from one team to another and serve in different roles, such as team leader, member, and/or facilitator. Organizations will need to give attention to team composition, structure, and development (effective and efficient teamwork). Teams will need to develop alliances with other teams, integrate newcomers, and focus on improving ·member interaction to minimize or overcome process losses because of member incompatibility. To be competitive and adaptable, organizations will need to identify their customers and their customers' needs, invest in quality improvement teams, empower individuals and teams to learn and develop, promote team interaction with outside constituencies, and measure and reward performance at the team level as well as individual level.

2. Companies organize jobs around projects, not functions. As a consequence, employees and managers must understand customer-supplier relationships. Work groups need flexible roles, effective and efficient work flows, and highly flexible structures. These groups need to encourage opportunities for participation, allegiance to team and work process as well as function, and the pursuit of a consensus after an argument. Organizations need flexible organization structures not tied to functions (such as matrix designs).

3. Companies are integrating new technologies. Individuals must know of, manage, and use diverse information; apply technolo-

gy to control and monitor work processes; use technology to learn (gain information, observe others, and learn through simulated exercises); and communicate through a variety of technological media. Groups can use technologies to track their performance, share information within groups and with other groups, and do their work (for instance, by participating in remote group interaction through computer networks next door or around the world). The organization can benefit from simultaneous direct communication with all organization members as well as goal setting and feedback though technological media. All employees can receive timely information simultaneously. Systems designers can create, manage, and make data bases available organization-wide.

4. Higher performance standards and complexity is another trend. Individuals need feedback so they can compare themselves to standards. They need to understand performance dimensions (such as timeliness, quality, cost, and efficiency) and expected performance requirements. Groups require standards for performance. Members need to understand how they contribute to their groups' performance. The organization must ensure it communicates changing standards along with the reasons for the changes (for example, shifting customer demands). The organization must identify multiple constituencies and track their needs and level of satisfaction.

5. Today's performance includes preparing for tomorrow. Employees need to do the following: seek information to identify skill gaps, recognize areas in need of performance improvement, keep up with advances in the profession, and anticipate how changes elsewhere in the firm and the industry may affect work demands and skill requirements. Groups can seek benchmark information from other organizations and groups to develop more competitive standards of excellence. Groups can also foster teamwork for continuous quality improvement, through participative, highly involving processes based on information about customer needs and team capabilities. The organization

(that is, the organization's human resource function) needs to communicate changing opportunities for learning and career development, assess changing skill requirements for different types of jobs and at different levels of the management hierarchy (such as comparing the changing roles of low-, middle-, and high-level managers), revise curricula, and design new programs for development based on changing organizational needs.

6. Multiple constituencies have different expectations. This suggests employees have to balance diverse time demands and have to do more to manage themselves, including developing themselves in relation to the expectations of different constituencies as well as self-management and self-regulation skills. Also, they need to resolve role conflict and ambiguity, and seek and integrate feedback information from multiple sources. Groups need to develop intergroup networks and alliances and to value diversity within and between groups. Organizations need multiple strategies and multiple measures of effectiveness in relation to different customers. Moreover, they need to clarify their expectations to suppliers.

7. Leaders serve as facilitators, coaches, and developers. Managers need to transition from the roles of monitor and director to coach, developer, and facilitator. Groups need to use facilitation to enhance the work process. Organizations need to recognize that managing people plays an important part in the managerial role. Organizations need to ensure that they evaluate managers against these evolving roles and that effective managers receive rewards for their contributions as facilitators, coaches, and developers.

8. More opportunities exist for temporary and part-time workers. Such workers will have to adapt to changing environments. Similar to full-time workers, temporary and part-time workers can use self-assessment and self-management to take advantage of work changes and temporary job opportunities. Within the

organization, groups need contingent and temporary work structures that are reformulated to fit changing work processes. Teams must become dynamic (fluid) structures that can integrate new members and remove old members as required with minimal process losses. Organizations will have to invest in assessment processes that ensure that temporary and part-time people fit the organizations' needs. Also, organizations need to develop welcoming, challenging, and rewarding cultures to attract contingent workers.

Challenges for Human Resource Professionals

The changing nature of work and the subsequent implications for individuals, groups, and organizations suggests directions for human resource management. Some examples include the challenge to . . .

☐ Communicate new corporate strategies so employees understand the strategies and realize how the strategies contribute to making the organization successful

☐ Decide what human resource strategies and policies to continue, discontinue, and adapt

☐ Involve employees in the change process by benefiting from their expertise, increasing their understanding of the change, and enhancing their commitment to the change

☐ Determine the most effective and efficient work processes

☐ Build work teams that have cohesiveness, a sense of purpose, and the capacity to learn

☐ Establish cooperative work relationships between units within the organization

☐ Develop a sense of corporate identity, gain employees' commitment to the new identity, and communicate it to outside constituencies

☐ Overcome employees' cynicism about applying management programs, such as continuous quality improvement, to the new enterprise

☐ Ensure that employees do not view programs for improved organization effectiveness and customer satisfaction as synonyms for cutting costs and people

☐ Overcome employees' fears and distrust about their job security

☐ Ensure that people have the competencies needed for today and the future

☐ Support employee growth and development while struggling to establish new corporate strategies

☐ Motivate the survivors of organizational change so that they become enthusiastic supporters of change and contributors to organizational success rather than doubters and naysayers

☐ Help managers continually diagnose the business situation so that they know when to hold the course or shift directions

☐ Recognize when commitments to courses of action are productive and when they are counterproductive

☐ Hold leaders and managers accountable for success and failures

☐ Integrate management programs so that they are mutually supportive—they work together for the same goals rather than clashing with each other.

In short, human resource managers will need to evaluate organization needs, assess employees' competencies, and develop methods to train and motivate employees. As such, they will help develop the operating policies of the organization, communicate organizational and human resource strategies, and implement organizational change strategies. In the process, HR managers will develop processes and systems that empower employees' self-determination and commitment, design challenging and effective task- and work-group structures, and establish appropriate and effective reward systems that hold employees accountable for their performance. HR managers will design and implement compelling and cohesive organization interventions for improved operations, and they will formulate integrated human performance systems that link human resource functions so they build on and support each other.

Evaluation of organizational and individual needs. Human resource managers will help ensure that employees have the competencies needed for today and the future. This responsibility does not lie solely with the Human Resource Department. Immediate supervisors, department managers, and unit executives will participate actively in the process as will employees. Human resource professionals will prompt managers and executives to think about upcoming organizational needs. They will develop and administer assessment instruments (sometimes self-assessment measures) to evaluate the skills and knowledge resident in the organization for comparison to estimates of future needs. They will help managers and employees recognize competency gaps, and they will design cost-effective training programs to close the gaps. In addition, they will establish ongoing program evaluation for continuous organization learning and refinement of development processes to meet changing organizational requirements.

Understanding individual needs and motivation. The assessments described above require that human resource professionals understand critical skills and knowledge areas. Also, the assessments require that they understand motivational processes and how environmental conditions support motivation. The concept of career motivation may explain an employee's desire to participate in continuous education. Generally, motivation consists of three components: career insight (the spark that initiates behavior), career identity (the sense of direction and purpose), and career resilience (the will to persist even in the face of barriers) [2].

Understanding organizational change. HR programs are evolutionary in that they develop over time to fit the changing needs of the business. The program that works today must be revised or supplanted by new approaches to meet tomorrow's business needs. Also, HR programs are not designed by rigid adherence to standard guidelines and procedures. Although such guidelines are valuable and necessary to ensure HR's effectiveness, HR professionals must learn to apply these guidelines under less than ideal circumstances. The HR professional often works in a changing and confusing world with multiple constituencies and high expectations and demands. Being an expert in one HR function and concentrating on that function alone is no longer effective and may not even be possible. HR functions fit together and evolve, sometimes in haphazard ways, to meet business needs.

Human Resource Policy and Programs Development

   Corporate executives turn to human resource professionals for recommendations about which human resource strategies and policies to start, continue, discontinue, and adapt. As stated above, human resource managers need to be aware of organizational strategies and be able to identify human resource initiatives that contribute to the accomplishment of those strategies. The ability to do this does not just depend on insight and creativity. Human resource managers need to have information about the effectiveness of programs. Criteria for effectiveness include whether the program does what it is intended to do. For example, HR managers need to know whether managers completing a training program designed to improve their negotiation skills have a better understanding of negotiation processes and are able to demonstrate those skills in classroom exercises. Criteria that are harder to come by include whether the program affects job behavior and performance. Still more distal criteria are evidence of whether the program affects organizational performance and contributes to organizational goals. Human resource managers need research designs that allow them to evaluate the programs they institute. Corporate executives hesitate to invest in initiatives that do not have demonstrable value. Ultimately, the question arises: why should companies employ human resource professionals if they cannot demonstrate their value?

One role for human resource managers is to help corporate executives communicate organizational goals and strategies to the rest of the company. Human resource programs can provide a way to communicate and reinforce organizational strategies. HR professionals can convey such information by direct announcements in company bulletins, videos, and memos. They can also incorporate the information into human resource programs and processes. The corporate strategies should drive the types of people the company hires, the performance expectations the company imposes on these employees, how employees are developed, criteria for performance reviews, and how the company rewards positive outcomes. These types of programs and processes convey which behaviors the organization considers important—essentially, how executives want to manage the business. It's easy to convey the wrong message, for example, by not rewarding desired performance, not offering training on new required competencies, retaining people who are not meeting expectations, and not encouraging executives to model desired management strategies.

The changing nature of work presents challenges to human resource managers not only to design and implement programs that meet changing organizational requirements but to do so in stressful times. For instance, how can the organization support employee growth and development while struggling to establish new corporate strategies? How can the organization motivate the survivors of organizational downsizing and restructuring so that they enthusiastically support change and contribute to organizational success rather than doubting and naysaying? No easy answers to these questions exist other than a continued effort to work with the organization's executives and managers to bring about change while recognizing the principles and values to which these executives and managers want to adhere in running the enterprise.

Human resource managers also contribute to designing effective task- and work-group structures as organizational needs change. They advise managers, teams, and executives in analyzing work flows and processes, and help to conceptualize new organizational structures and reconfigure jobs and workgroups.

Human resource managers will also need to understand individual differences, group dynamics, and organizational behavior. These areas of expertise come together in new work methods and processes that are attuned to changing organizational objectives. A prime example is the movement toward total quality management (TQM) programs. A principle of these programs is that organizations will be competitive and successful as long as they satisfy customers. Quality is defined in terms of customer satisfaction. Another principle of TQM is that employees from different departments and with different job functions and levels of expertise can work together to make improvements that enhance customer satisfaction. Human resource professionals contribute to TQM programs by helping to design the programs, communicate goals to employees, train team leaders and members, and facilitate group processes. Such programs are not just jumping on the bandwagon of a corporate fad but developing the organization to make it better now and ready for additional changes as technologies, the marketplace, and the economy evolve.

Holding Employees Accountable

Human resource managers also face the challenge of how to establish an empowering environment and gain commitment for new programs and work processes in a way that holds employees accountable for their behaviors and performance. London, Smither, and Adsit [3] outlined a model of the components of accountability. Accountability means accepting and meeting one's personal responsibilities, being and/or feeling obligated to someone else or oneself, or having to justify one's actions to others about whom one cares. Accountability may be imposed by oneself, others (such as one's supervisor), the social situation and norms (for example, peer pressure), organizational policies, or task requirements. Individuals must know what behaviors the company expects of them. The power or force behind an individual's feelings of accountability may be internal or external to the individual. External forces include financial or other positive or negative outcomes (such as job security) that are under the discretion of the source. Internal forces include feelings of morality, the desire for approval, and the internalized goal to meet an obligation. People regulate their own accountability by virtue of their motivation for high performance, sensitivity to others' views, and wanting to conform to others' wishes. Supervisors institute accountability by means of rewards, control of work processes, and friendship with subordinates. Human resource programs can be designed to train supervisors in ways to institute accountability forces. Also, human resource programs can create environments that encourage individuals to recognize what they are accountable for and to increase self-management.

Integrating Human Resource Functions

Human resource managers must integrate management programs with each other so that they work together for the same goals. As stated above, corporate strategies should drive selection, development, goal setting, training, performance review, and compensation. As organizational directions and goals shift, HR professionals need to revise or redesign the HR system—not just one individual program. HR professionals also need to fine-tune this system continuously to ensure each does what it should do in relation to the other components. Some components compensate for others by design. So, for instance, the organization may emphasize retraining employees to meet changing skill requirements rather than firing employees with outdated skills and hiring new people. The organization may pay employees more money when they acquire multiple skills because they are then more valuable. Members of a quality improvement team may share in the financial gains from the improvements instituted by their team. Performance review methods may collect evaluations from multiple constituencies (customers, peers, subordinates, and supervisors), recognizing the diversity of views needed by managers to assess their performance. This book focuses on such examples.

Supporting Individual and Organizational Change

The processes of individual and organization development are integrated and occur in parallel. This is a critical point, not to be taken lightly. It is the fundamental reason why human resource programs work to support both individual and organizational growth and vitality.

Individuals, for example, process information to analyze their strengths and development needs and to interpret the environment in which they function. Organizations directly or indirectly provide this information, as well as the programs and systems individuals need for processing, so that individuals can establish learning goals, track their progress, and ultimately enhance their performance.

Organizations develop similarly. They constantly seek environmental information and data that tell the organizations how well they are functioning. They scrutinize their processes and, when necessary, determine the nature and extent of the necessary changes to those processes to enhance overall performance.

Human resource initiatives, then, when strategically driven, come from the need to make changes in organizational function and performance. Human resource initiatives attempt to ensure that those changes take place by providing individuals with the necessary programs, processes, and tools, as well as the rationale for them. In this way, HR initiatives contribute to both individual and organizational growth and development. Readers should keep this framework in mind for understanding the evolution and success of the HR initiatives discussed in the cases in this book.

Following is a brief description of how this overall process works. The description provides an example of a company that designed its human resource programs to support new organizational strategies and to show how those programs evolved as the organizational strategies changed. This example focuses on initiatives that helped retrain employees in light of shifting career opportunities.

The Evolution of a Human Resource System

London and Mone [4] described the evolution of such a process in one company as a vehicle for enhancing performance excellence and managing marginal performance. This company's HR Department published and distributed a performance management model and supporting human resource programs to all organization managers in a series of booklets called the Managing for Excellence Library. The company intended to support a new type of management to match the increasingly competitive environment. Recognizing the changing nature of work, the model specified a limited set of critical management competencies: designing meaningful jobs and effective work structures, facilitating teamwork, building networks and alliances between work groups, and ensuring positive performance outcomes. The HR Department supported these materials with orientation workshops, facilitators, self-evaluation tools, new criteria for performance appraisal, training, and a new compensation system that rewarded people for new behaviors. A new training curriculum offered courses associated with the new competencies. For example, courses were developed in interpersonal communication, and management of a diverse work force, and an orientation for new managers addressed understanding people and improving communication. A course catalog outlined the key competencies and described the new courses. Other material in the Managing for Excellence Library offered guidance for self-assessment on the competencies.

Two to three years later, the company's goal was to ensure that all managers, regardless of department or function, were up-to-date on the firm's products and services as well as the management strategies needed to keep the firm competitive. In the form of another set of booklets and supporting guidelines and courses, this professional development program for managers re-stated the firm's standards and its expectation that all managers understand the roles they play in quality management and enhancement, technological design and implementation, customer satisfaction, people management, and general business acumen. Materials distributed to managers contained descriptions of relevant skills and knowledge, self-assessment and supervisory assessment instruments, a list of required experiences to demonstrate mastery in a specific area, recommended training courses designed by the Training Department (for purposes of the program) to prepare for mastery, supplemental learning methods (ways to gain additional knowledge through readings, job aids, videotapes, audiotapes, and other courses and seminars), and a discussion guide to facilitate conversations with the managers' supervisors who would be responsible for reviewing progress. Managers assigned to serve as professional development coordinators were trained by the HR Department to introduce, facilitate, and monitor the program. New performance appraisal forms required supervisors to record each subordinate's progress in the program.

Five to six years after the introduction of the first model, the company needed to help managers understand how to behave and lead in a process-focused world. This new model recognized that performance demands were increasing and that skills such as leadership, empowerment, conflict resolution, negotiation, and teamwork were important to the company. The process approach to work transcended departmental lines, often with employees assigned to one or more process teams. Managers needed to balance the multiple expectations that came from leading process teams, being a member of a process team, or supporting those employees who reported to them and served on multiple process teams. Employees needed to be responsive to multiple process team leaders, to balance work load responsibilities, and to be held accountable for meeting the performance obligations of each work process. The model introduced in a training session accompanied new procedures for employee development, performance management, appraisal, and compensation. The introductory training emphasized that managers should get involved in setting individual and group goals and should apply a participative, negotiatory style of management.

HR Professionalism

Human resource managers must stay attuned to continuous learning, just as any professional must in today's fast-paced organizations. Support programs that foster continuous learning encourage employees to enhance their professionalism and maintain performance excellence in their areas of expertise. These support programs start with benchmark analyses to determine best professional practices in other firms as a guideline. Generally, the HR professionals work together, often with a consultant, to establish professional standards, expected areas of competence and knowledge, and criteria for excellence. The HR Department may specify courses and job experiences as part of a mastery path to certification and continued development.

The Cases

The cases in this book describe human resource interventions that transform organizations. These mostly large-scale, strategically-linked interventions are critically important to the organization's future success.

Each case describes a different transformational experience. Each was written by an HR professional or professionals who typically had hands-on experience leading the HR effort that supported the business transformation. Each case includes the following: (1) a description of the business challenge and the need for change; (2) the circumstances in the organization and any overarching and concurrent change processes under way (such as a merger or downsizing); (3) how the HR professionals appraised the situation, developed action strategies, and revised these strategies as the needs emerged and became clearer and as the situation changed; and (4) an evaluation of the effort—an assessment of what worked, what didn't work, and why and how the case demonstrates the role of HR in support of a business transformation.

Diagnostic Questions

The following questions help in understanding the cases and applying their ideas.

☐ What was supposed to be transformed?

☐ Did the HR Department evaluate organization and individual needs before designing the intervention(s)? Were the organizational circumstances clear? How complex were they?

☐ Did the HR Department evaluate current human resource policies and programs to understand their operation and success relative to changing needs?

☐ At what point did the organization involve human resource executives and managers in establishing business strategies? Did the organization bring these people in after the strategies had been decided? Did HR executives and managers help formulate the strategies by providing insight into human resource capabilities?

☐ What were the central goals of the intervention(s) (for example, to empower employees to take responsibility for their own development)?

☐ Did the HR managers take into account underlying psychological, social, and organizational processes (such as employees' insight into their abilities, employees' performance relative to job requirements, work group dynamics, and interorganizational relationships)?

☐ What roles did human resource professionals play in the organization? Educators? Facilitators? Visionary leaders?

☐ Did the HR managers identify multiple human resource leverage points? Did the interventions address and link these leverage points in a systematic way?

☐ How did the organization hold managers and employees accountable for development and performance outcomes? What accountability forces and mechanisms did the organization rely on? How did it establish and enhance these forces and mechanisms?

☐ What steps did the organization take to evaluate the human resource intervention(s)?

☐ Did the interventions evolve over time to make themselves more effective and responsive to changing organizational needs?

☐ Were the initial transformational goals met? If the goals changed over time, did the intervention(s) contribute to organizational success?

☐ What problems occurred? Were there internal problems, such as systems, processes, functions, or people unaccounted for (for example, critical players weren't involved or lacked commitment) or faulty design and/or implementation of the interventions? Were there external problems, such as intervening, uncontrollable events, changes in what the organization needed and expected, or new technologies or competitors?

Table 1-1 summarizes the cases and allows easy comparison of their central features. The rest of this chapter briefly describes each case.

(*text continued on page 29*)

TABLE 1-1.
KEY FEATURES OF THE CASES.

Author(s)	Yorks, L.
Industry	Industrial products
Business Problem(s)	Contain costs, 70% of which are related to procurement
Human Resource Challenge(s)	• To get people throughout the organization to think differently • To redesign the procurement function
Human Resource Processes	• Staffing • Compensation • Job redesign • Competency modeling
Change Strategy	• Utilized key stakeholders in a cross-functional structure design team • Extensive communication effort
Leader(s) of Change Effort	• Company president • Vice president of finance
Role(s) of HR Professional	Consultant
Major Lessons Learned by HR Professionals	• Work collaboratively with senior management during periods of strategically driven change. • Recognize transformational change and its impact on the organization. • Ensure leaders are visible and engaged. • Build commitment to the change in other parts of the organization. • Form partnership between business managers, HR, and external consultants. • Utilize a holistic and integrated approach to the change process.

TABLE 1-1 (CONTINUED).
KEY FEATURES OF THE CASES.

Author(s)	Adsit, D.
Industry	High technology
Business Problem(s)	• Losing business • Continuous erosion of market share
Human Resource Challenge(s)	• To improve the quality of management • To give more voice to employees • To establish a culture that supports adaptability and decision making with the customer in mind
Human Resource Processes	• Survey and survey feedback processes • Upward appraisal component • Compensation linkage
Change Strategy	Emphasized feedback through survey processes
Leader(s) of Change Effort	Senior management
Role(s) of HR Professional	Lead survey design and development process
Major Lessons Learned by HR Professionals	• Use models to guide the development of survey and overall change processes. • Feedback needs to get to those who can make the changes. • Be flexible when introducing a new process. • Focus on the end result, not the survey.

continued on next page

TABLE 1-1 (CONTINUED).
KEY FEATURES OF THE CASES.

Author(s)	Diamante, T.
Industry	Consumer products
Business Problem(s)	• Market share eroding • Changes in regulatory environment • Changes in consumer behavior and values
Human Resource Challenge(s)	• To transform culture from bureaucratic to organic • To align HR practices with the new business direction
Human Resource Processes	• Performance management • Competency identification and 360° feedback • College relations program • Coaching
Change Strategy	Off-site team building led to a variety of strategic business and HR initiatives, including a change management workshop
Leader(s) of Change Effort	Senior business unit leadership
Role(s) of HR Professional	Support the people side of the resultant changes in business direction
Major Lessons Learned by HR Professionals	• Include a communication phase before launching each initiative. • Establish initiatives that target personal change necessary to improve performance and well-being. • Involve the Employee Assistance Program as a supporting organization. • Involve HR in planning the change strategy. • HR needs to play the role of business partner. • Educate business partners on the competency of consultants. • Educate people on the true rationale and intent of initiatives. • Collaborate with external consultants who have been brought in.

TABLE 1-1 (CONTINUED).
KEY FEATURES OF THE CASES.

Author(s)	Conner, J.; Smith, C.
Industry	Consumer products
Business Problem(s)	Support ongoing, global expansion of the business
Human Resource Challenge(s)	To provide a pipeline of people with the requisite skills and talents to assume international general-management positions
Human Resource Processes	• Succession planning • Executive staffing • Training and development
Change Strategy	Engaged senior management to introduce and integrate a new initiative into the culture
Leader(s) of Change Effort	Partnership between HR and senior leadership
Role(s) of HR Professional	• Engage senior leadership in the process • Develop strategy and processes
Major Lessons Learned by HR Professionals	• Involve the people in the organization who are most critical to the operating success of the initiative. • Ensure leadership strategy is aligned with other HR practices. • Establish uniform criteria for identifying high-potential people. • Reward the high-performers in the organization. • Ensure that a tracking mechanism is in place to monitor effective operation. • Build synergy with other events.

continued on next page

TABLE 1-1 (CONTINUED).
KEY FEATURES OF THE CASES.

Author(s)	John, S.
Industry	Investment banking
Business Problem(s)	Become a Top 5 investment bank—make fundamental change in the way it does business
Human Resource Challenge(s)	• To initiate transformational change to support business goal • To build a performance-based culture
Human Resource Processes	• Performance management based on contribution and competency • Formal executive and leadership development process
Change Strategy	Emphasized support on the individual level for performance and development
Leader(s) of Change Effort	Senior management team
Role(s) of HR Professional	• Design and develop new processes • Advocate change
Major Lessons Learned by HR Professionals	• Get agreement on the business model. • Embrace action learning. • Use technology to support HR efforts. • Facilitate development of global teams.

TABLE 1-1 (CONTINUED).
KEY FEATURES OF THE CASES.

Author(s)	John, S.; Gorelick, C.
Industry	Investment banking
Business Problem(s)	Operate in an increasingly global environment requiring teamwork, innovation, and cooperation across departments and functions located throughout the world
Human Resource Challenge(s)	To transform HR to operate effectively in a global environment—communicating, coordinating, and collaborating in new ways
Human Resource Processes	• Re-engineer all HR processes • Globalize the role of HR professionals • Develop a human resource information system
Change Strategy	Utilized groupware technology as the lever to support the HR Department's transformation from a regionally focused to a globally based function
Leader(s) of Change Effort	HR team
Role(s) of HR Professional	Design and implement a new model for working together in a global environment
Major Lessons Learned by HR Professionals	• Recognize that at whatever pace companies merge, cultures develop at a far slower pace because people tend to remain in their former companies' cultural mind-sets. • Maintain some degree of stability in roles when developing a collaborative team process within organizations. • Ensure standardized technology and support are available for the introduction of software-based initiatives. • Help people overcome their resistance to learning and using new technology.

continued on next page

TABLE 1-1 (CONTINUED).
KEY FEATURES OF THE CASES.

Author(s)	Larsen, H.; Morgensen, L.; Olsen, T.
Industry	Banking
Business Problem(s)	After a merger and downsizing, prepare employees for new environment
Human Resource Challenge(s)	To explain and help employees cope with changing demands and expectations
Human Resource Processes	• Career development • Training to match changing context
Change Strategy	• New, more flexible career opportunities • Total quality management program • New management development program
Leader(s) of Change Effort	HR director
Role(s) of HR Professional	• Communicate new goals and work demands • Design new career programs
Major Lessons Learned by HR Professionals	• Use HR programs to ensure employees' skills are aligned with the changing business needs. • Recognize that a merger and downsizing can lead to more and different opportunities; help employees recognize and take advantage of these opportunities. • Use HR to contribute to organization change and development in different ways (for example, through TQM programs as well as human resource development).

TABLE 1-1 (CONTINUED).
KEY FEATURES OF THE CASES.

Author(s)	Larsen, H.; Madsen, S.
Industry	Healthcare products
Business Problem(s)	Enhance competitiveness through quality, technology, and lower costs
Human Resource Challenge(s)	• To overcome inefficient bureaucratic structure • To use people's time and energy in a more flexible and efficient way
Human Resource Processes	• Organization redesign • Job redesign • Employee development
Change Strategy	• CEO announced planned changes and gave people time to understand the changes and adjust • New computers and office configurations were established
Leader(s) of Change Effort	CEO
Role(s) of HR Professional	• External consultant • Evaluators
Major Lessons Learned by HR Professionals	• Help the CEO become the HR leader. • Help awaken employees to new opportunities for learning and professional growth resulting from frame-breaking changes. • Recognize that employees can learn to appreciate the chance to be creative and contribute in many ways without being pigeonholed in specific jobs or places on the organizational hierarchy. • Recognize that some employees miss the structure and career paths with clear time frames and rewards, while others thrive on the flexibility and taking responsibility for their own learning and development.

continued on next page

TABLE 1-1 (CONTINUED).
KEY FEATURES OF THE CASES.

Author(s)	Shillaber, J.
Industry	Pharmaceutical
Business Problem(s)	Determine and operationalize a strategy to ensure company-wide success in an industry undergoing transformation
Human Resource Challenge(s)	To support strategic imperatives of opportunism and flexibility through a focus on building productive relationships
Human Resource Processes	• Management development curriculum • Performance management • Compensation • Recognition
Change Strategy	Emphasized support of employees and increasing organization capability through skills building and infrastructure support for sustaining behavior change
Leader(s) of Change Effort	Executive committee
Role(s) of HR Professional	• Lead the design, development, and implementation of HR strategy, programs, and initiatives • Transform HR organization
Major Lessons Learned by HR Professionals	• Support strategy over initiatives. • Lead whenever possible. • Make deep and broad changes in HR systems and programs. • Leverage efforts directly into line initiatives. • Recognize that change takes time.

(*text continued from page 19*)

Strategic Change at Thermo King (Chapter 2)

It was the president of the company who actually began thinking about the strategic change presented in this case by Yorks.

The president, an experienced champion of change, recognized that, for the company to maintain its industry leadership position, a major change was needed in how the company's purchasing department functioned. This change idea led to nothing less than a transformation in the strategy, function, organization design, and responsibilities of employees in the company's Procurement Department. And this transformation occurred while the business was experiencing a period of rapid growth in business volume!

The overall goal of the transformation was to build an organization that would create procurement strategies that would effectively utilize the company's supplier base as a key resource for distinct competitive advantage. This would require the people in the purchasing function to become more than just buyers. They would have to be partners to selling, engineering, and manufacturing in all the company's strategic planning and decision-making processes.

Yorks describes how the company worked with an external consulting firm to help design and manage the change, which was actually led by the vice president of finance; subsequently, internal HR also took part in the process, playing a key role in internal communication about the transformation.

Of particular note in this case is that a change management model, proprietary to the consulting firm, was utilized to guide the transformation process.

Finally, in a systemic way and from an HR initiatives perspective, Yorks describes the changes involved that led to achieving the strategic transformation of the procurement function. The changes were as follows: creating new positions for the function; identifying the necessary competencies for those positions; selecting people to fill the new positions; realigning the reward system to support the new expected behaviors; and creating new career development opportunities for people in the company.

Surveys and Survey Feedback As a Basis for Organizational Change (Chapter 3)

Adsit opens this case with an effective overview of the role of surveys in, and how they contribute to, organization change. He not only provides a rationale for the use of surveys in this instance but also provides an effective argument, in general, for practitioners to use when faced with possible resistance to a survey intervention.

The case description follows this overview and focuses on how necessary changes in management style and culture developed while the business itself was transforming and entering into new service areas.

These changes in management style and culture included improving the quality of management, giving more voice to employees, and breaking down the hierarchical, paternalistic top-down management style culture that was ham-stringing the organization. As Adsit describes, the organization's goal was to move toward a flatter, more participative operation. What makes the magnitude of the change in this particular case so great is that it focused on changing the attitudes and behaviors of long-service employees—employees who had seen so many attempts at change that they were skeptical.

Adsit focuses his attention in this case on the survey process and how to increase the effectiveness of survey interventions in organizations. He describes, for example, how the senior leadership and management helped shape the survey and how optional questions were included by each business to help the unit better understand its specific needs. A phone response system created the opportunity for rapid turnaround of results to manager. Adsit also describes a technique that ensured the reliability of a manager's survey results when job assignments changed.

Although progress halted after 2½ years into the process because of a merger, it is interesting to note how the survey, the survey process, and supporting HR initiatives evolved during the process to improve the effectiveness of the intervention. For example, in Round 2 of the survey's administration, modifications added impetus to the change effort, including a connection to compensation. Feedback and training helped in the later rounds, along with compensation, as ways to continue to improve the effectiveness of the intervention and to drive attitude and behavior change.

Transforming a Consumer Products Organization: A Multipronged HR Approach (Chapter 4)

This rule-oriented consumer products company, with its well-planned procedures, faced turmoil. After fifty years of predictable stability, it found itself in a turbulent environment. As Diamante puts it, competitors were attacking, market share was eroding, and brand equity was decaying. In addition, regulatory changes and changes in consumer buying behavior turned the company's products into devalued commodities. Something needed to be done, and done quickly.

Interestingly enough—but unfortunately—the HR initiatives described in the case were the result of leadership's recognition that people problems were getting in the way of the necessary business transformation. This mind-set probably accounts for the fact, as well, that HR's role merely supported the change rather than acting as a strategic partner alongside leadership and deciding together how to make changes happen in the company.

Specifically, human resources in this case assumed the role of helping transform the culture from bureaucratic to more flexible or adaptive. Although top management directed the changes, HR handled the people problems so the business could meet its objectives. Some of the supportive HR initiatives in this case included identifying key competencies, attracting the right people, developing managers' skills, creating a radically different performance management process, and nurturing performance and achievement.

Of particular note is how Diamante draws from his own experience, as well as the experiences of others in this case. For example, it is interesting to consider his notion of organization transformation as "strategically haphazard" and the implications for managing organization transformation that notion implies. He makes another point about what he frames as the concept of "organization delusions," which he defines as the mind-set that develops under conditions of forced change (driven strongly from power and political bases) in organizations when leadership begins to believe that everyone has accepted its vision because people are saying and doing the right things.

Developing the Next Generation of Leaders at Colgate-Palmolive (Chapter 5)

To be the best truly global consumer products company requires many things, not the least of which is effective leadership. This case tells about Colgate's needs and concerns regarding management development and what HR has done to ensure the availability of leaders, thus enabling Colgate to achieve its vision and business objectives. Senior management had concerns that a shortage of general managers would occur, making it difficult to support Colgate's planned global expansion.

Contributing to management's concern was its fear that other companies would recruit away its next generation of leaders as well as its expectation that managers would be reluctant to accept important overseas assignments—assignments critical to the business and to the development of future global leaders.

From a systemic perspective, HR's goal in this case was to integrate succession planning, executive staffing, training, and development activities in support of leadership development. Conner and Smith describe the integration of these processes, beginning with interviewing the Top 20 leaders in the business, who reveal their concerns about the development of future leaders. Enlisting, involving, and engaging senior leadership throughout this effort was a conscious strategy by the HR Department to ensure leadership's buy-in and the future success of HR's efforts to support leadership development at Colgate.

The interviews resulted in a composite of leadership qualities. The next step in the process was seeking commitment of the top tier of executives to change. The top tier needed to become more proactive about leadership development—and could no longer just wait for the cream to rise to the top. Conner and Smith accomplished this objective by developing a set of commitments leadership needed to make and then challenged the leadership to accept and act on them.

Conner and Smith continue descriptions of how HR put the overall leadership development process into place and, in particular, describe the development planning process and an extensive self-assessment tool kit that HR developed.

Finally, and worthy of consideration, Conner and Smith explain and plan for dealing with a range of potential obstacles they have yet to face.

SBC Warburg: Creating a Global World-Class Investment Bank (Chapter 6)

Swiss Bank Corporation Warburg (SBCW) was reeling from recent acquisitions. It needed to fundamentally change how it did business if it was to achieve its goal of becoming a Top 5 investment bank. Significant questions required critical answers: what the role of leadership should be, how the bank should form global teams, how it should identify the needed competencies and the individuals who possess them, and what technology platforms were necessary to support global teams.

Specifically, the transformation at SBCW required an approach to global investment banking conducted by cross-functional and

specialty teams led and managed by competent people. To compete globally, the bank needed highly specialized technical people
who could also be team players and demonstrate leadership, as
necessary; but generally, these technical people were used to being
independent contributors or, perhaps, only working with others
within their specialties. Senior management faced an equally
daunting task of learning how to create and foster a new environment that supported team and individual accomplishment. Fortunately, however, senior management did realize that it was essentially asking for a transformational change in how people worked
and how the company rewarded them for their efforts.

While the bank underwent this transformation and asked HR
for support, HR was itself moving from decentralized to central-
ized operations and emphasizing global responsibility for all HR
functions. (Chapter 7 discusses HR's attempt at transformation in
its own organization more fully.)

HR, in this case, played a role in supporting the change effort
initiated by the bank's leadership. HR ultimately succeeded in
bringing two major initiatives to the table, a new performance
management process and an executive leadership development
process, both of which required implementation within relatively
short time frames. John discusses the fact that the concurrent reorganization in HR influenced the effectiveness and support available for these two initiatives.

By the way, and not unusually, only after the initiatives got
under way did the senior leadership provide a strategic framework
to lend a degree of coherence to what was happening at the
bank—the shaping of a performance-based culture.

Transforming Human Resources to Create a Global World-Class Investment Bank (Chapter 7)

Chapter 6 tells how HR tried to support strategic transformation at Swiss Bank Corporation Warburg (SBCW) with the
launching of two major initiatives. In this case, John and Gorelick

address an approach to transforming *the human resource function* at SBCW to better support the strategic needs and direction of this investment bank.

HR recognized that the business of making deals was increasing in complexity. The bank was encountering global competitors, and capital was now readily available through worldwide sources. Technology was becoming faster and smarter—products and services could be designed anywhere, funded anywhere, and delivered anywhere in the world. HR recognized that these factors together would require transformational changes in the bank's business strategy and work processes. These changes, in turn, would require HR to take a strategic look at how it recruited, developed, retained, and rewarded technical talent. HR professionals would have to communicate, coordinate, and collaborate with each other in new ways.

HR also had specific feedback from its customers. Survey data suggested that HR needed to act as competent strategic business partners and change agents while flawlessly executing HR transactions in areas such as compensation, benefits, employee relocation, and staffing.

HR professionals, however, did not have the work processes or tools that would enable them to collaborate and communicate with each other, or employees, from anywhere in the world at any time. Nor did they have a central data base and work space that would ensure the integrity and confidentiality of employee data. Given this environment, John and Gorelick concluded that groupware, properly designed and implemented, had the potential to facilitate the globalization of the HR function. This would enable HR to provide the levels of service needed by employees and senior management as the company worked toward becoming a global world-class investment bank.

John and Gorelick discuss in this case how they tried to integrate the concepts of teamwork and a performance-based culture with an enabling technology. Their success would require that they could provide a well-designed and implemented infrastructure, both in technology as well as in work team processes, and a culture that supported individuals and teams in their work.

Clearly, in this case, HR's goal was to create a collaborative teamwork process within its own function that had a truly global purpose and operation, a model for working that could be shared within the bank, ultimately helping all bank employees to contribute to the overarching goal of becoming a global, world-class investment bank.

Management Development in a Large Danish Bank after a Merger and Downsizing (Chapter 8)

This book presents two international cases—both from Denmark but representing two extreme differences in organizational structure within the same national culture.

Denmark is a social welfare state. Yet private enterprise is highly competitive. Danish cultural work values emphasize interpersonal cooperation and power equalization [5]. Danish employees generally speak their minds, and they don't let differences in organizational level get in the way of doing business effectively. Danes also tend to say what's on their minds. However, large-scale organizational change, especially accompanied by downsizing, is new and threatening to Danish employees.

This case describes changes in a major bank in Denmark—Den Danske Bank (in English, "The Danish Bank"), a large, bureaucratic, traditional type of organization. Just as the banking industry in the United States has experienced increased competition, consolidation through mergers, and new business opportunities brought about by advancing technology, Danske Bank resulted from a merger and subsequent employee downsizing. The case describes changing career paths, a new conceptualization of the nature of job security, and what employees need to do to take responsibility for their own development. As such, U.S. practitioners will find the experiences and ideas in the case meaningful and useful.

Larsen, Morgensen, and Olsen describe how the Danske Bank HR Department introduced a number of creative programs for new and different career opportunities. The merger and subsequent staff reductions led to creating new corporate values and changing criteria for success and measurement. Leaders and managers needed to understand the following new expectations and demands: achieving business results; focusing on the customer; increasing customer satisfaction; achieving profitability in daily operations; and developing themselves, their people, and their own organizations, guided by the principles of respect for the individual and equality in dialogue. A comprehensive training and development program supported these emerging expectations. In addition, a total quality management program was instituted as a long-term organization development process to involve employees and customers in creating a more customer-focused organization. The bank wanted to make the offices (branches and staff offices) more customer-minded, making internal work processes in the individual departments and across the organization more effective, improving internal collaborative relations among specialists, increasing the employees' engagement and motivation, and creating a more visible and goal-oriented management.

Regarding career development, the case shows that the merger and the turbulence of recent years (including the layoffs) actually improved career development opportunities instead of curtailing them. New types of jobs emerged, and the rapid development of job tasks and working conditions made the daily work an intensive learning process. Interviews with employees indicate they feel they solve problems better because of the merger. While job and career opportunities at this firm have become more flexible, and structured career paths have disappeared, the firm still needed a management development program that targeted and developed top talent for future promotion.

Overall, the case shows the importance of the Human Resource Department in designing and managing special initiatives for organization development and career growth in a changing environment.

Career Development in a Spaghetti Organization (Chapter 9)

This case, also from Denmark, describes an organization with a structure diametrically opposed to that of the large Danish bank. This smaller organization (1,500 employees) has a flexible organization structure. Employees don't have rigid job descriptions or pursue structured career paths. They don't even have designated offices, but rather they use portable carts to move their computers and office supplies. They participate in project teams, working jointly with others to meet immediate business needs.

The case details the history of the firm Oticon, which makes high-technology hearing-aid equipment. The CEO instituted the firm's flexible, spaghetti-like organization design to increase Oticon's efficiency and customer responsiveness and to compete in cost, quality, and technological advancement.

Unlike the other organizations described throughout this book, Oticon does not have a Human Resource Department. Keeping with the flexible form and reduced overhead, the company's continued transformation and success rests on the CEO's idiosyncratic, much-admired leadership style. Personal interviews with twelve managers, including the CEO, show that the firm's managers recognize that the organization provides wonderful opportunities for learning and professional experience. Taking advantage of these opportunities is very much up to each individual. Few visible opportunities for advancement exist because of the flat organizational structure and because the CEO and a few close associates make compensation and limited promotion decisions. Some managers miss the structure, career development options, and advancement options available in large companies, and the few managers who missed those things the most left the firm.

The case shows that a CEO can drive organizational design and management philosophy. While some employees may long for the traditional hierarchy that lets them know where they stand career-wise at any given moment, others thrive on the excitement of change and the chance to contribute, unconstrained by reporting relationships and organizational structure. The Danish values of equality, willingness to take reasonable risks, and concern for others work well in this type of company. In any organization, part of the job of a manager is managing people. In this sense, every manager is a human resource manager. Similarly, every CEO is a human resource director in spirit, if not in title. Oticon demonstrates a new organizational form that may be more common in post-modern organizations with human-resource-type initiatives guided from the top. Human resource professionals may be consultants or, in the case of the authors of the chapter, evaluators of the change. In other such organizations, human resource managers may play a more direct role in designing and implementing the change.

Transformation in the Pharmaceutical Industry: HR's Prescription for Success (Chapter 10)

After having eyed and considered purchasing a new Porsche automobile for some time, do you think you could be persuaded to purchase its functional equivalent—virtually identical in every way—for about 50 percent of the price of a Porsche?

Shillaber poses this question to explain the impact of one of two major recent forces for change in the pharmaceutical industry: the introduction of generic drugs. The second major force, the increasing bargaining and buying power of larger and larger managed care organizations (MCOs), impacted not only the price at which pharmaceutical companies could sell their drugs but also which drugs MCO-participating physicians would prescribe.

These two and other smaller forces in healthcare have transformed the pharmaceutical industry. To be more competitive, some companies established their own MCOs, while others bundled their products together to offer value-added programs. Many companies, however, found their profit margins increasingly destroyed by these forces.

This case tells about the strategic choices one pharmaceutical company, Berlex Laboratories, made to compete in this turbulent marketplace. Although a subsidiary of a German chemical and pharmaceutical company, Berlex needed to form alliances and partnerships that met long-term needs. It needed to identify new drugs where no existing treatments were currently available.

Strategically, the imperatives for success became opportunism and flexibility. HR's role was to support and sustain these imperatives through the identified theme of "relationships." Relationship building, internally and externally, became critical to Berlex's success.

After a thorough organization analysis, HR was on its way. Working with senior executives and employees, Shillaber developed a strategic framework, called the Berlex Outcomes, which focused all subsequent efforts HR made to support transformation at Berlex.

Throughout this case, Shillaber notes how HR's model-driven approach to curriculum design for management development supported the theme of building productive work relationships, how HR transformed the performance appraisal process into an employee development process, how a compensation system gave managers the capability to allocate financial rewards, and how a recognition program further supported key Berlex Outcomes. Shillaber also notes how HR had to transform itself to be more effective in fulfilling its strategic role at Berlex.

References

1. Ilgen, D. R. and Pulakos, E. D. *The Changing Nature of Work Performance: Implications for Staffing, Personnel Actions, and Development.* San Francisco: Jossey-Bass, 1998.

2. London, M. *Developing Managers.* San Francisco: Jossey-Bass, 1985.

3. London, M., Smither, J. W., and Adsit, D. J. "Accountability: The Achilles Heel of Multi-source Feedback." *Group and Organization Management,* Vol. 22, No. 23, 1997, pp. 162–184.

4. London, M. and Mone, E. M. "Managing Marginal Performance in an Organization Striving for Excellence," in *Human Dilemmas in Work Organizations: Strategies for Resolution.* A. K. Lorman (Ed.), New York: Guilford, 1994.

5. Hofstede, G. *Cultures and Organizations: Software of the Mind.* London: Harper-Collins-Hill, 1991.

Applying Human Resource Technologies in Support of Strategically Driven Transformational Change at Thermo King

LYLE YORKS, ED.D.

Thermo King, a wholly owned subsidiary of Westinghouse, leads the industry in transport temperature control systems. Maintaining this position in today's highly competitive business world requires that the company sustain high standards of quality, while striving to contain costs. Successfully competing through providing high quality at minimum cost requires management to add value to the business through more effective utilization of resources, including human resources. This case describes how management added value to the business through reconceptualization of the purchasing strategy for its worldwide procurement function and the subsequent transformation of the corporate purchasing organization. Implementing this transformation required Thermo King to apply a number of human resource management methods in an integrated and coherent manner.

The company's success in executing this transformational change has been impressive. Through careful planning and implementation, the company saved more than $20 million in procurement activities in 1995. In that year, Thermo King delivered to the parent company a 30 percent increase in operating profit on a 21 percent increase in revenue. In this period of record demand, Thermo King needed to implement effective production strategies worldwide involving the procurement of materials for thirteen plants. Thermo King accomplished this implementation even as the purchasing function was transforming itself. As this chapter is being written in the fourth quarter of 1996, the company is running an operating profit of 10 percent higher than the previous year, even though sales volume has declined from 1995. A significant contribution to this financial result has been made by the procurement function, which has accomplished a 3 percent reduction on material costs.

Unfortunately, in many instances *transformation* is a code word for simple downsizing. This is not the case at Thermo King. The company accomplished the results cited above through a strategically driven realignment of the business. Making this change happen during a period of rapid growth in business volume proved challenging—a challenge that could only be met through the skillful application of human resource management methods. This chapter tells the story of how this transformation was accomplished at Thermo King, with a focus on the human resource management methods that were utilized. It is a story of a partnership between senior executives, members of the Human Resource Department working to orchestrate the change process, and external consultants.

Reconceptualizing Procurement in Strategic Terms

In the spring of 1994, Jim Watson, president of Thermo King, contemplated how to continue to enhance his company's position as a global competitor. His attention focused on Thermo King's purchasing organization, which functioned very traditionally. Buyers primarily staffed the supply organization. Their responsibilities typically involved locating vendors, negotiating contracts for orders required by one or more of the company's thirteen plants, placing the orders, and expediting the material shipments. These buyers spent 95 percent of their time expediting. Watson envisioned a more strategic role for the purchasing agents: a role that would require a sophisticated set of competencies and would significantly impact the financial performance of the company.

Watson believed Thermo King needed a world-class supply management organization that was a mirror image of the company's sales organization. He explained the business rationale for this belief in a company speech he gave in the spring of 1994:

> Our purchasing people have the ability to impact the bottom line as much if not more than the salespeople. Their strategies for buying and the global contracts that they can negotiate for materials and services for our thirteen manufacturing plants could have a huge impact on our profits. As far as I am concerned, they need to be as skilled in negotiating as our salespeople, with many of the same competencies. They should work with our suppliers as closely as our salespeople work with our customers to build lasting partnerships. The only difference between the two groups is that one does the buying and the other does the selling.

Watson arrived at this conclusion after reviewing an in-depth cost analysis of the company's operations. He continued:

Like most traditional purchasing groups, instead of participating up front in the decision-making process to help define cost-effective product designs and production processes, our purchasing group controls inventory and expedites product shortages. Yet, they control nearly three quarters of our costs. As I see it, they should work up front, as equal partners to sales, engineering, and manufacturing in the strategic planning and decision-making process.

Considerable potential existed for bottom-line impact, and Watson believed that realizing that potential was critical to Thermo King's long-term competitive success. In the same speech referenced above, Watson defined the business problem as follows:

To be a successful global competitor, you must contain costs. In our case, this is particularly important, since seventy percent of our costs are related to the procurement of materials and services.

As Watson's staff members thought about what it would take to implement the changes their boss envisioned, it became clear to them that this change would not be incremental. The Purchasing Department lacked the structure and stature it needed to drive strategic decisions within the organization. An assignment to work in Purchasing did not put an employee on a fast-track career. Up to this point, the employees in the Engineering Department had driven the decision-making process regarding materials by telling Purchasing, "We like this supplier, and here are our specifications." No one had ever required the people in Purchasing to conduct high-level negotiations.

Watson saw the challenge as getting people to move out of their traditional boxes and think about the purchasing function in a different way. So he asserted a new mission for the purchasing function: to build an organization that would create procurement strategies to effectively utilize the company's supplier base as a key resource for distinct competitive advantage. This mission required a completely different kind of organization, staffed with highly skilled professionals focused on implementing global procurement strategies. Watson chose Jim McNulty, vice president and chief financial officer, to spear-head the change effort, and Caea Sager, manager of internal communications, from Human Resources to deal with the challenge of getting people throughout the organization to think differently about the purchasing function. In Sager's words, Watson's vision amounted to "quantum change." To be effective, the whole organization would have to transform.

Human Resource Implications in Transforming the Purchasing Organization

A number of challenges had to be met by McNulty's team to create a procurement organization capable of realizing Watson's strategic vision. First, team members had to ensure the redesign of the organization to create a structure aligned with this vision. Second, everyone employed by Thermo King would have to understand and accept this new strategic role for procurement. The importance of this acceptance was three-fold. First, the new procurement strategy would shift the roles and responsibilities of the procurement people. In the new procurement organization, the manufacturing facilities would handle certain routine activities, such as expediting. Contracting and negotiating with suppliers would change, with the procurement staff gaining more influence and control. The people at the Thermo King organization would need to learn to interface with the procurement function in a new way. Under the new procurement strategy, the supply manager would become an important adviser to Engineering, Manufacturing, and Marketing. It was envisioned that an Engineering staff member would come to the supply manager and say, "Here are the specifications. What do you think?" Based on a range of considerations, including price, quality, reliability, and delivery, the supply manager might recommend, "We had better focus on ordering from these suppliers in Europe." The traditional buyers didn't have the background to give advice to these departments. Selection of people to fill the supply manager jobs was important because Engineering and Manufacturing had to believe that the people filling these new roles brought important information to the decision-making process.

A second reason acceptance by the rest of the organization was important related to staffing the redesigned function. As stated above, McNulty and his team understood that the new organization would have to be restaffed with people who had world-class negotiating skills as well as strong product and manufacturing knowledge. Many of the new staff members would be recruited from within Thermo King and Westinghouse as well as from the outside. Attracting candidates from a variety of backgrounds (marketing, sales, manufacturing, and engineering) would require those candidates to change their perceptions of the career implications of working for the purchasing organization.

The third reason acceptance was important related to helping employees understand that this reorganization was a strategically driven realignment, not a downsizing. People throughout the company would have to understand the rationale for the change and see it as strategically effective. Otherwise the word-of-mouth grapevine would divert attention and energy away from work throughout the organization as people began speculating about when this kind of change might happen to their departments.

In addition to redesigning the organization and gaining acceptance of the procurement function's new role, Thermo King also needed to position the proper people in the new purchasing organization to execute the strategy. This would require aligning reward systems, information systems, and career development opportunities with the new structure. The company would have to accomplish all of this during a period of the strongest product demand in Thermo King's history. The change must not disrupt the supply chain.

The enormous human resource implications included the following:

☐ Lead the organization through a well-managed process of organizational redesign

☐ Communicate effectively with the entire organization

☐ Create a fair and effective restaffing process

☐ Redesign the compensation system

☐ Manage the transition to the new procurement organization.

Making Change Happen Through Skillful Human Resource Management

McNulty took his first step in late June 1994 by forming a cross-
functional structure design team with employees from Marketing,
Engineering, Manufacturing, and Purchasing. How task forces like
the design team are staffed is important to their effectiveness [1].
Those employees selected for the design team knew how the purchasing function impacted the company and were respected and
influential, not only in their respective areas but in the company at
large. Their stature would play an important role in selling the new
structure and role of the purchasing function to the larger company. These people had the skills to build supportive linkages
between the design team and the rest of the organization.

The prior year, McNulty headed a similar design team charged
with redesigning Human Resources. The process for that redesign
effort had been provided by consultants from The Marshall
Group, a consulting firm specializing in transformational organization change. So Watson and McNulty asked Jim Krefft, one of
the consultants in that effort, to serve as lead consultant for this
procurement project. McNulty had been impressed with Krefft's
work with the previous design team and his understanding of both
organizational and human resource issues.

The Marshall Group worked within the context of a macro-
transformation model that emphasized working through strategy,
structure, staffing, and ultimately synergy (see Figure 2-1). A key
postulate of the model is that a strategic vision that defines how the

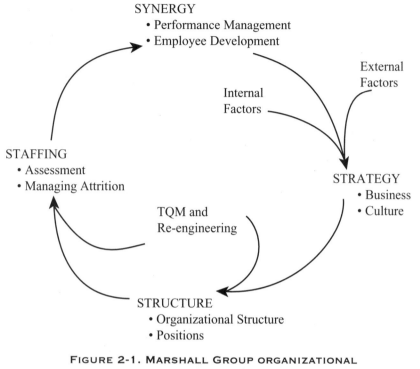

FIGURE 2-1. MARSHALL GROUP ORGANIZATIONAL TRANSFORMATION MODEL.

organization could effectively compete should drive transformative change, structural design, and in turn, the appropriate staffing levels. In short, companies should determine staffing levels by positioning the proper people in the proper jobs to yield profits and performance, not by selecting arbitrary targets for staffing cuts [2, 3].

This model supported Watson's emphasis that the change process under way was not a downsizing. Further, the model provided a context through which the design team could conceptualize its task. The globalization of the business and the 70 percent of the company's costs located in materials respectively served as the external and internal factors driving the strategy. The structure would be designed by the team to fit Watson's strategy and would involve a significant cultural change in how the company conducted its business. The structure would determine staffing requirements, in terms of both the necessary competencies and the necessary staffing levels.

The Structural Redesign Process

With McNulty as the team leader and Krefft as the coach, the design team embarked on its mission to think creatively in examining the current organizational structure and analyzing traditional purchasing processes and procedures. To facilitate this mission, Krefft enacted a four-phase process provided by The Marshall Group.

The first phase of the process was **disassembly and review.** The design team broke down the organization into discrete activities or products and services to thoroughly familiarize themselves with all aspects of the organization. Using data the team gathered from interviews with people familiar with the organization, the team then produced a set of work sheets listing the organization's major functions and activities, the products of these activities, and the customers of these activities.

The second phase of the process was **analysis**—extracting meaning from the data produced in the first phase. In this phase, the design team identified unnecessary work, or work not germane to the strategic mission of the organization. This became the starting point for the third phase, **synthesis and reassembly,** during which the design team tested observable patterns of organizational interaction for effectiveness alongside the organization's new direction and focus. Simply, the team looked at the current activities in the department and compared them to what was demanded by the new strategy. New activities suggested by the mission were also examined, as well as new insights on ways to enhance the work of the purchasing unit. This led to the final phase, **the development of the new structure.**

This highly fluid, iterative, and creative process called for task force members to brainstorm ideas, such as the creation of a supply manager position. After the group conceived the supply manager position, the new organizational structure began to fall into place. The authority and responsibility of the new position equaled that of a sales manager, and both positions have managerial responsibilities. Supply managers manage vendors and commodities, and sales managers manage customers and orders. In addition, both have authority over pricing. Supply managers approve vendor prices, and sales managers approve contract prices with customers. This new position was given broad authority to develop partnerships with suppliers prepared to work with supply managers to reduce costs.

The design team also developed a second position, the supply service representative, to support the supply manager. The group conceptualized supply service representatives as equal to customer service representatives, who support sales managers. The supply service representatives would assist the supply managers through activities such as gathering and analyzing data (for example, price, delivery, and quality) and so forth. The representatives would also respond to requests for information and resolve service issues. Placing, following, and expediting orders would now be the responsibility of the people in the local material organizations in the manufacturing plants. In an interview with the author in the fall of 1996, McNulty said:

> The local material organization does this better in support of production. Within the arrangements made by the supply manager, the local organization works with vendors to expedite orders. Vendors want to resolve problems locally. If a problem can't be resolved locally to the satisfaction of the local material organization, it gets bumped up to the supply manager. Vendors know that if the problem gets to the supply manager, the vendor has a big problem.

These two positions, supply manager and supply service representative, replaced the former structure of buyers, senior buyers,
and lead buyer.

The new structure took the shape of a wheel of tightly knit
teams, which replaced the multilayered organization and stream-
lined the decision-making process (see Figures 2-2 and 2-3). Five
of the teams focused on major procurement areas—engines and
motors; support team services (quality engineering, transportation,
general systems, and indirect services); metals and fabrications;
plastics and non-metals; electrical and electronics. Two teams
focused on geography—Europe and Asia Pacific. This structure
was put in place in two phases. The first five teams became operational during Phase 1. The two geographic teams became operational during the second phase.

PHASE 1

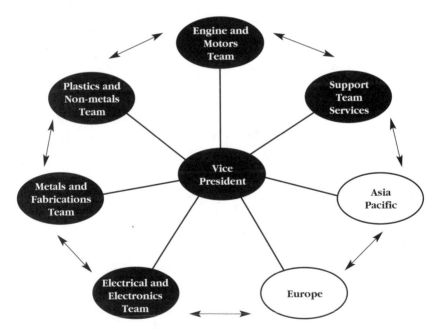

FIGURE 2-2. TEAM STRUCTURE OF THE PROCUREMENT ORGANIZATION.

PHASE 2

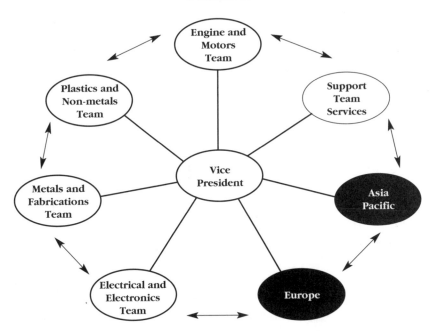

FIGURE 2-3. TEAM STRUCTURE OF THE PROCUREMENT ORGANIZATION.

The teams reported to a new role in the organization—vice president and general manager of supply management, who reported directly to the CEO. This gave a new level of status to the purchasing organization.

This design provided a flexible organization in which teams must cooperate with each other. For example, in some instances it may not have been possible to have a world contract for a particular commodity. China, for example, may have wanted to produce a certain amount of that commodity locally. In such a case, the teams organized around procurement areas would have to work collaboratively with the two geographically based teams. At other times supply managers who have overlapping interests in a particular supplier would have to work together to form an effective supply management strategy. In effect, the seven teams constitute a global procurement team. Members of the procurement organization can draw on the experience of the whole team. This team structure is appropriate for an organization that must function in a fluid way, drawing on diverse sets of skills and knowledge to simultaneously work globally and locally [4].

Working intensively, and following Watson's clear vision and mission for the new organization, it took the design team two weeks working full time to put together the framework for how the organization would work. The framework included a new charter for the organization and the creation of innovative organizational structure, the supply manager role, and the supply service representative role. Once the design team concluded the structure design process and defined the roles of supply managers and supply service representatives, it became apparent that the positions called for new and higher-level skills. So the work force team established a set of key competencies for the new positions. These competencies, in fact, compare to those required of sales managers and customer service representatives (see Table 2-1). Watson and his staff approved the new structure and announced it to the company in late August.

TABLE 2-1.
KEY COMPETENCIES: THE SUPPLY MANAGER POSITION.

Negotiation Skills	Interpersonal Skills
Professionalism	Problem-Solving/Decision-Making Skills
Teamwork	Leadership
Customer Focus	Communication Skills
Technical Expertise	Global Commodity Knowledge
Analytical Skills	Skills in Planning/Organizing

Communication Through Broad-based Participation in the Implementation Process

An effective communication strategy played a vital role in employees' acceptance of the new organization. Caea Sager, manager of internal communications in Human Resources, became increasingly central to the change effort by crafting communication and by selecting and applying human resource processes to restructure the purchasing organization. Part of her role as a human resource representative was to work with McNulty and Krefft to create a communication campaign to educate employees throughout the company about the value of the restructuring effort and about the potential of the new procurement strategy. "We had to have involvement of people from the organization who would be affected," she said in a fall 1996 interview with the author.

This process of communication through participation began by allowing people to help reconceptualize the organization by giving input into the redesign process. The communication continued through an organization-wide invitation for employees to interview for the new positions. Watson also engaged his employees in the selection of people to staff the new organization, ensuring that his leadership team had both accountability for and involvement in the change. In short, communication became critical to the implementation process—providing opportunities for involvement throughout the organization. The communication effort was more than printed announcements, video presentations, and official pronouncements. This widespread participation resulted in what Sager characterizes as "an awakening" in the organization about the new strategy for the purchasing function.

However, plenty of written and oral communication did support the process. Anyone interested in applying for positions in the new organization could pick up an information packet. These packets were widely publicized among engineers, product managers, production managers, sales managers, and production planners.

Both Watson and McNulty stayed very visible throughout the process as active change leaders, meeting with employees to articulate the new supply management philosophy. Watson visited the plants to talk about the change. He repeatedly emphasized that the change was being driven by business needs, highlighting the imbalance between the sales and purchasing functions and the percentage of cost controlled by purchasing. Watson believed it impossible to overcommunicate. In the words of Sager, "We did everything we could—a full court press."

Staffing the New Organization

Obviously Thermo King needed to restaff the organization with people who possessed the new competencies needed in the organization. This also meant Thermo King needed to build a new compensation system to attract, retain, and motivate these skilled people.

The design team took the lead to plan for restaffing the entire organization, and the team supported launching an aggressive search for highly qualified individuals to fill the positions. Candidates came from both inside and outside the company, with a variety of backgrounds.

Management had to accomplish this staffing process while the organization kept functioning. Indeed, as previously noted, the company was experiencing strong demand for its products. Procurement had to remain effective in this kind of year. This meant planning for continuity and fairness in the staffing process. Everyone could interview for the new jobs. Some qualified for the supply manager position, and others were offered the supply service representative position. Some did not qualify for either position. Thermo King needed to treat these people with respect. Thermo King, therefore, provided them with career transition training, severance packages, and outplacement support. Almost all these individuals left the company for positions elsewhere that better fit their experience and skills.

Maintaining morale during this time required that the company repeatedly communicate the logic and competitive need behind the change to those directly affected by the change and employees throughout the organization. Equally important was maintaining a perspective of fairness in the process. Thermo King enacted a process to allow people to say so if they felt mistreated. The fact that no one came forward to complain was seen by the leadership as a testimony of the fairness of the staffing process and how well it was communicated.

The first position filled was that of the vice president and general manager of supply management. A team from Watson's staff interviewed candidates and selected Jim McNulty, who had served as chief architect of the new structure. He immediately took a strong lead in the staffing process, working with Human Resources to involve managers from Sales, Marketing, Engineering, and Manufacturing in a team interview process.

Employees who previously held purchasing positions received first consideration for the new jobs. To help prepare them for the interview process, the Marshall consultants trained employees on how to effectively communicate their qualifications and coached them on interviewing techniques.

However, the process was highly selective. McNulty and Sager wanted to ensure that they put the right people in these jobs. Successful candidates had to have the right knowledge base and the ability to think strategically and tactically. McNulty and Sager planned to complete the staffing process in three months. In practice, it took close to nine months to fill all the jobs. In a fall 1996 interview with the author, Sager commented:

We didn't want to settle for just anyone. We sought highly talented people with specific competencies who could envision our worldwide procurement requirements and execute targeted strategies for measurable results in terms of product quality, reliability, pricing, and delivery. Some of the talent we wanted was unique—for example, a mix of plastics and automotive experience. We would have to ask, "Who knows best what we need?" In this case the answer might be to recruit from outside, in the auto industry. Candidates had to have a global perspective, think globally, and be able to arrange deals for a large number of plants.

At the conclusion of the staffing process, Thermo King replaced more than 60 percent of the people in the Purchasing Department. McNulty and members of the executive staff selected the new supply managers and representatives on the basis of the key competencies. These new employees came from a variety of backgrounds ranging from procurement to engineering, marketing, manufacturing, finance, and education. Several buyers did become supply managers. Others, of the 40 percent who remained, became supply representatives. In the end, the number of staff members in the new organization slightly increased.

Behavior-based Interviewing

Critical to the entire staffing process was ensuring that the right people were selected. So, to improve and enhance the effectiveness of the selection process, Sager and Krefft designed a behaviorally based interview process. McNulty told the author:

> In the beginning, our interviewing skills were weak at best. Questions like, "What did you do, when did you do it, and how long did you do it?" just didn't give much insight into what the candidates were capable of doing. We needed to learn how to identify their competencies and evaluate their proven performance capabilities.

To begin the process, the design team created job profiles. Following a format provided by Krefft, the profiles featured job accountabilities that correlated with specifically defined competencies, like negotiating skills, communication skills, and a broad business perspective. Then the Marshall consultants trained fifteen managers from across the company in behavioral interviewing techniques. On a rotating basis they teamed with McNulty and John Cobb from Human Resources to complete a series of team-based interviews of all of the candidates.

Significant advantages to the team-based interviewing process existed. First, by working in teams of four or five interviewers, managers could more effectively probe for specific behavioral examples of the candidates' proven capabilities. Working in teams provides more opportunity for more people to listen carefully and ask thoughtful questions. Strengths and weaknesses become much easier to identify. Behavioral-based interviewing gives the interviewers a chance to methodically evaluate candidates and their experiences on the basis of specific and detailed examples. It's like peeling back the layers of an onion to check for consistency in the layers.

Thermo King also gained another important advantage of team-based interviewing. By using a group of managers from Thermo King's marketing, manufacturing, and engineering organizations to assist in the interviewing process, these managers got a chance to clearly understand the potential value of re-engineering the supply management group, as well as the impact that this new organization could have in improving the performance of these managers' own departments. That helped promote not only the buy-in of these managers but also shared ownership in the success of the undertaking.

This interviewing process proved so effective that behavioral-based interviews are now standard practice throughout the organization for all professional- and management-level jobs.

Broad Compensation Bands

Thermo King used a new compensation strategy to attract quality candidates both from within the company and from the highly competitive marketplace. In the same fall 1996 interview with the author, McNulty explained:

> Traditionally, jobs in the purchasing arena have not been considered to be positioned to put people who had successful careers in areas like sales and marketing. So we created an innovative salary structure to make it attractive for top performers to move into procurement, positioning them to continue to progress at some point in the future into high-paying positions back in sales or marketing if they chose to in the future.

The company introduced a "broad-band" salary scale that provided top performers the opportunity to move to supply manager or representative positions without negatively impacting their pay or career progresion. This too sent a signal to the rest of the organization of supply management's new level of status.

Additionally, based on personal and group achievements, supply managers became eligible for incentives based on performance, on par with Sales and Marketing.

Ongoing Learning Support for the New Organization

Once Thermo King had staffed its new organization, attention turned to providing appropriate learning support, both for individuals and the organization as a whole. McNulty asked The Marshall Group to facilitate a full-day renewal workshop for the members of the new organization. At the start of the workshop, McNulty reclarified Thermo King's vision for the organization and asked the members of the new organization to define key challenges and obstacles to success.

Jane Foster, the workshop facilitator from The Marshall Group, worked with the new organization members to produce a detailed list of risk factors that could derail implementation of the strategy and impact performance outcomes. It was important to build a strategy to prevent anything from falling through the cracks in the delivery of materials and services to Thermo King's plants worldwide. So, the group presented its list of factors to McNulty to assure the successful completion of the transition. Reflecting on the workshop, McNulty told the author, "Although I had a pretty good understanding of our organizational issues, the list of recommendations that the teams came up with gave me a valuable working document to continuously refer to in understanding the new organization's needs."

Thermo King continues to invest in the development of its supply management organization in various ways. The company has provided extensive computer systems training and testing to ensure that the new team is fully capable of using computer technology to service the organization. A media expert came in to work with the supply managers to hone their presentation skills. They've even studied cultural issues to ensure success in working with suppliers worldwide. Sager commented to the author, "As the supply management [organization] strategies evolve, different learning requirements surface. The investment in continuous learning will be on-going, because it is key to keeping the supply management team on the leading edge in applying their procurement strategies."

Results of the Transformational Change Effort

The financial results of this effort were presented in the introduction to this chapter. These results come from the supply organization operating in a strategic fashion. What does this mean in practice? Sager said the new supply organization has "taken the philosophy of procurement to a new level" for Thermo King.

The supply organization itself has cross-functional vision by design, and the rest of the organization—including Marketing, Sales, Engineering, and Manufacturing—has begun to recognize the important contributions supply management can make to improving product designs as well as the flow and outcome of the manufacturing process. In the old environment, Purchasing received the requirements for materials and services from other departments. Now, supply managers sit at the table with managers from the rest of the organization throughout the decision-making process. As a result, they understand the requirements better. Plus, they can translate these needs more effectively to the suppliers to build partnerships that provide real savings, both in time and cost. Sager attributed part of the success of including the supply managers in the decision-making process to the success of the selection process. Managers from other departments took part in the interviewing process and consequently respect the expertise in the procurement function.

In fact, supply managers now carefully assess suppliers on criteria such as cost, quality, and delivery schedules. Suppliers may be asked to invest in the partnership with Thermo King for the long run. In some cases, suppliers have purchased new equipment to provide new, expanded services and deliverables for Thermo King, and they have negotiated creative, long-term contracts for enhanced performance and value.

The teams in the supply management organization don't just look externally for process improvements. They have discovered that it can be best to recommend that Thermo King manufacture its own parts for reasons such as demand and cost savings. At one point, a product required a service valve that Thermo King could guarantee was leak-free. The supply manager demonstrated it would be best to purchase the equipment and produce the valve in-house rather than to use an outside supplier. At the plant level, the local material purchasing organizations use a purchasing MasterCard. Plants can purchase low-value material directly at a cost savings using the cards. These and many other practices have been aggressively put in place and accepted by the company.

The company still has much to accomplish in realizing the full potential of Watson's strategic vision. Thermo King is in the process of implementing a new computer system that will provide mainframe forecasting for all plants worldwide. McNulty's people have upgraded their information system, and the next step is to link all the plants. Once this new system is online, numerous possibilities will open up.

Human Resource Implications and Lessons

The Thermo King story tells of successful transformational change. The story shows an instance of a company changing how it operates in a significant part of its business operations and displacing some people, while building a new, highly motivated organization. The company accomplished this change during a period of record demand for the company's product. A number of interesting lessons can be derived from this case.

This case demonstrates the value added when the senior management and Human Resources work collaboratively during periods of strategically driven change. This collaboration was enhanced by the third partner in this relationship, the outside consultants. The senior executive leading the change process, Human Resources, and the external consultants worked as a team to identify and implement those practices that would enable the strategy to succeed.

Management recognized that the change it wanted to make in the organization had a transformational nature and would impact the entire organization. This was not a case in which implementation of a vision was delegated to middle-level managers or staff. Senior leadership remained visible and actively engaged throughout the entire process, including Watson's tireless explanation of the strategy. The direct, personal involvement of a senior executive—McNulty—was important to the change process. The fact that Watson had a clearly articulated vision and strategy coupled with the personal involvement of McNulty provided both concrete evidence of management's commitment to change and a power base that ensured the change effort would not become sidetracked by more parochial interests of various functional departments.

However, McNulty realized that for the strategy to prove effective he had to build commitment in the larger organization and put in place the proper mix of people within the supply management organization. He relied on the expertise of Sager and Krefft for methods to meet these needs. McNulty himself was a learner, adopting such methods as the behavioral interviewing process and the transition workshops.

For their part, the internal human resource people and the external consultants worked collaboratively, using their respective areas of expertise to support the change effort. In an interview with the author, Sager commented, "The changes were viewed as top-management driven. The champions were within Thermo King. The consultants were suppliers of tools, not the owners of the effort. The Marshall consultants understood that well and were seamless partners with us." Human Resources and the consultants did not drive or initiate the change but became business partners with senior management in the implementation of the strategic vision.

In this instance, Human Resources made an imperative contribution to the successful implementation of corporate strategy. Failure to consider the human resource implications of the change would have left the strategy vulnerable at several points. This experience highlights the importance of asking the question "In what way is the success of our strategy dependent on Human Resources?" In this case the answers to that question were as follows:

☐ The new procurement function had to be able to work collaboratively with functions traditionally influential in the larger organization

☐ Working collaboratively with other influential functions required that these functions respect the expertise of the procurement staff

☐ The new staff had to have key competencies relevant to a strategic focus toward procurement

☐ The rest of the organization had to understand the new strategy and not become distracted by unfounded rumors of future company downsizing

☐ The larger organization needed to perceive the staffing process as fair to all concerned, including incumbents who might not find a place in the new organization

☐ The new procurement organization had to establish an effective working relationship with its senior manager.

The human resource practices described in this case focused on managing these dependencies. All involved in the effort tailored these practices to the needs of the strategy. Human Resources did not simply offer "canned" programs or approaches, tell management what it could not do, or defend the past.

This often required Sager to influence her own human resource organization. For example, not everyone in Human Resources felt enthused about the changes in the compensation program. McNulty had to sell the idea hard.

The change effort was driven by a model provided by The Marshall Group, which explicated the relationships between strategy, structure, staffing, and subsequent organizational synergies.[1] This model rests on the premise that organizations should identify their competitive strategy and then organize and staff themselves to effectively execute their strategy, not simply pursue head-count reduction. Organizational restructuring should focus on taking out costs, not necessarily people, through the definition of tasks that most add value to the business. The model drove the practices described in this chapter. First, the company must design an organizational structure consistent with the strategic vision, with the

---

[1] This model has subsequently been reframed into a more comprehensive one involving purpose, process, people, positioning, and performance. This extended model incorporates the principles of the model used at Thermo King and also draws on additional learning from work, such as the above. It provides the basis for the organizational interventions provided by Marshall-Qualtec, the firm created by the merger of Qualtec Quality Services with The Marshall Group Inc. in October 1995.

active involvement of much of the organization, along with an aggressive communication plan. Next, the company should identify key competencies and conduct behavioral interviews against these competencies as part of the staffing process. Then, the company should establish a new compensation structure to make the staffing process viable through the recruitment of people who have these competencies. Finally, transition workshops will help jump-start the organization. The model emphasizes the effective management of the change process in a holistic and integrative way, as opposed to a reductionistic and piecemeal process.

Conclusions

This case shares certain characteristics with other successful transformational change efforts studied by the author. The following principles summarize these lessons, although the author recognizes that exceptions to them can, and do, exist. First, the success of transformational change often depends on the effective application of appropriate human resource management practices. Second, the transformational change process requires the active involvement of the senior leadership of the organization. Third, transformational change involves a collective perspective transformation on the part of a significant number of organizational members, and Human Resources needs to provide interventions that facilitate the collective learning process that this entails. Fourth, the Human Resource Department needs to participate in the change process, partnering with senior managers leading the change and in some cases, such as the present one, with external consultants. Finally, transformational change requires a holistic and integrated approach to the change process. Failing to pay attention to these principles or giving them only partial attention can derail even the most thoroughly thought-out strategic change.

References

1. Galbraith, J. R. *Designing Complex Organizations.* Reading, Mass.: Addison-Wesley, 1973.

2. Marshall, R. B., et al. "Using Ego Energy in an Electric Utility," in *Managing Ego Energy.* R. H. Kilmann, I. Kilmann, and Associates (Eds.), San Francisco: Jossey-Bass, 1994, pp. 255–283.

3. Marshall, R. B. and Yorks, L. "Planning for a Restructured, Revitalized Organization." *Sloan Management Review,* Vol. 35, No. 4, 1994, pp. 81–91.

4. Katzenbach, J. R. and Smith, D. *The Wisdom of Teams: Creating the High Performance Organization.* New York: Harper Business, 1993.

3

Surveys and Survey Feedback: Essential Ingredients in Organizational Change

Dennis J. Adsit, Ph.D.

Introduction

This chapter tells about organizational change. Like solar panels adjusting to the movement of the sun or sails to the wind, organizations constantly change to align themselves with economic and market forces. Change is now a given. The remaining questions have to do with whether, how, and how easily organizations will adapt. This chapter also tells how human resource professionals can help their organizations continuously align and realign themselves. In particular, the chapter focuses on how one organization used surveys and survey feedback to support the change process.

We will begin with a discussion of why surveys play such an important role in effective organizational change. Answering this question will take us into the problem-solving literature and into a discussion about change management. From there, we will consider the introduction and use of surveys to effect behavioral and cultural change as part of a changing business strategy in the U.S. operations of a European-based high-tech company. After presenting the theory behind why surveys are so important for successful change and presenting one company's experience, the chapter concludes with a discussion of the critical success factors involved in leveraging surveys for organizational change.

General Problem Solving, Change Management, and the Role of Surveys

Before moving into the case, it may be useful to review the importance of surveys from a theoretical perspective. In the literature on problem solving, two broad classes of problem-solving approaches exist: domain specific and domain independent. An example of a domain-specific approach would be a set of step-by-step instructions about how to diagnose and fix an appliance or television. In a well-defined problem-solving situation, appropriate, domain-specific approaches are strong methods of problem-solving because, properly followed, they reliably lead to problem resolution. But as their name implies, the downside is that domain-specific approaches, while powerful, do not generalize well: knowing how to fix a television will not help you develop a political strategy or resolve a group conflict.

The other class of problem-solving tools is referred to as domain independent. Not specific to the characteristics of a given domain, this class can apply to a broad range of problem-solving situations. Perhaps the best example of a domain-independent problem solving tool is the general problem-solving model [1, 2], depicted in Figure 3-1.

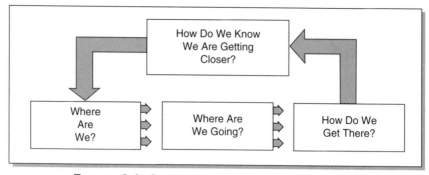

FIGURE 3-1. GENERAL PROBLEM-SOLVING MODEL.

The general problem-solving model applies productively to almost any ill-defined problem. The downside here is that the general problem-solving model has a weak approach: it won't help much in solving well-defined problems, and it also won't get you far without some domain-specific knowledge. So while it won't help much in fixing your television, it can prove very useful in solving ill-defined problems in the area of, for example, organizational change. In fact, the consulting firm I work for uses the general problem-solving model as the foundation of its change management practice.

The general problem-solving model, applied to change management, says that managing change requires, at a minimum, describing a vision of a preferred future, having some means for making adjustments and for moving the organization toward the destination, and finally, having feedback mechanisms for determining whether or not the organization is on course and getting closer. Though a solid change management approach should consist of a host of tools and techniques to help with each element of the change management process, surveys and survey feedback are the big dogs. Let's examine how surveys aid each step of the change process.

The first step, the assessment of current reality, requires you to answer the question, "Where are we?" Administering the survey and then reviewing the subsequent report will tell you about the state of the organization at a particular point in time. The key here is to get a picture of current reality, which predisposes people to change.

The second step is answering the question "Where are we going?" The answer is a statement of a preferred future. This most important step helps determine what the organization is striving for and creates the backdrop against which progress is assessed. Questions or items included in surveys would ideally be based on (1) research that shows particular items to be keys to effectiveness or (2) consensus by key stakeholders that certain items reflect organization goals.

Third, surveys define "How do we get there?" in two ways. First, if a component of your change process involves new behaviors, the survey questions themselves communicate what needs to be done. In other cases, the survey flags an issue but does not provide enough information about how to change it. In these cases, follow-up steps, such as additional surveys or focus groups, may be necessary.

Answering the last question, "How do we know we are getting closer?," involves aligning the feedback mechanisms around the key performance measures to track progress in a timely fashion over time. That is, you need to track key measures at a frequency that provides early warning of problems and also in such a way that trend information is available as an indicator of progress. In terms of surveys, this involves determining the right frequency for repeating the survey.

This brief overview of an approach to change management and the role of surveys in abetting that process was intended to provide the philosophical underpinnings behind the actions taken by an HR department to help an organization align itself. Let's turn to the case study now.

EG Inc.: Culture Change in a High-Tech Environment

People normally do not think of high-tech firms as needing to undergo culture change. The image people usually have of the high-tech environment is one that attracts smart, eccentric, entrepreneurial types of employees. As this case will show, the origins of a company greatly influence its culture, no matter what industry the company happens to be in. However, no matter what the company's starting point, the rate of change and fierce competitiveness of the high-tech market acts as a great leveler, and competing successfully necessitates establishing a culture that is highly adaptable and empowered to make decisions with the customer in mind.

Bandolier Systems (pseudonym), a high-tech company owned by a U.S. conglomerate, purchased another high-tech company that had a complementary product line in the 1970s and became, for a brief period, No. 2 in the high-tech arena. But the combined companies quickly began losing ground because the market was changing rapidly while the culture of the parent company was patriarchal and more adapted to slower-moving technologies and government contracting. With each successive innovation and new product introduction, Bandolier Systems fell further behind. The 1980s showed no mercy, and each year from 1980 through 1986, Bandolier Systems downsized. What kept it afloat was maintenance of and sales to a huge base of customers with such significant investments in Bandolier that they were slow to move business to a competitor.

In 1986, a government-owned company in Europe (EG Inc.) and longtime partner agreed to buy Bandolier Systems from the parent company to help EG Inc. expand into the North American market. Despite Bandolier Systems' long history, it took the name of its new parent, and Bandolier's 18,000 employees became employees of EG Inc. On paper, this looked like a good move because EG Inc. focused on this high-tech market. However, some of the same cultural issues that had surfaced with Bandolier Systems' old parent company applied to the government-owned parent in Europe: EG Inc. was slow, bureaucratic, risk averse, and paternalistic.

In 1992, a new CEO came on board and introduced sweeping change. The service side of the business, though highly profitable in its own right, heavily depended on product sales for its growth. The CEO encouraged the service side to pursue a new strategy to take more control of its own destiny by entering the highly competitive multivendor services (MVS) arena by providing networking and maintenance for competitors' products in addition to those sold by EG Inc.

MVS was and still is a growing market because it creates an outlet for companies to essentially outsource their service work; a company could provide field service for its product without carrying a field service work force. In this fiercely competitive, low-margin business, change is constant. As an example, field technicians have barely completed training on one product line when the next product line is developed and a new round of training begins.

In addition to massive changes in how the organization went to market, the company needed changes on the inside as well. The changes most relevant to this chapter were the efforts to improve the quality of management, give more voice to the employees, and create a new culture in the organization. The CEO's goal was to break the hierarchical, paternalistic, top-down management style that was hamstringing the organization. In place of this top-down orientation, the CEO's aim was to move toward a flatter, more participative operation.

The accomplishment of this goal would require many levers, but we in the HR Department decided to begin with an organization-wide survey that included an upward appraisal component (subordinates rating supervisors). Upward appraisal would not only allow us to see where we stood, but it would also allow us to find out which environments were most counterproductive. This also fit in with another aspect of the new CEO's style. He used to say that if he could get daily readouts on how each part of the business was doing financially, how the customers felt about the business, and how employees felt about the quality of management, he could run the business from home. Though this statement was obvious hyperbole, the survey would help us move toward his ideal kind of organizational dashboard.

Conveying the magnitude of what we undertook here is difficult. Long-service employees, especially those in the managerial ranks, populated EG Inc.'s U.S. service business. Some had worked for the company that Bandolier Systems had acquired in the 1970s. The average employee was forty-eight years old with twenty years of experience. These folks had seen new ownership and new administrations come and go, and a real this-too-shall-pass attitude prevailed. These managers had forged their work styles in the golden age of service—the 1960s, 1970s, and 1980s, when companies focused on proprietary equipment and had fat margins. Pulling off this kind of change in behavior and focus would be no mean feat. Many doubted we could achieve it, and some questioned whether we should even try.

Round I: Establishing a Baseline

In November 1991, top management announced that a survey would be done by HR in the first quarter of 1992, which would include an upward appraisal component for managers. Both employees and managers were informed that the quality of the environment and the quality of EG Inc. management were important to the future success of the business and that the company would, over time, hold managers more accountable for both.

With the company's history and current environment, many managers and employees felt threatened by the idea of upward appraisal. Given that, we had to use care in introducing it. To ease the transition for managers while underlining the earnestness of our effort to improve the climate and quality of management, we informed managers that the initial round of the survey would be "free"—that is, only the corporate HR survey team would have access to an individual manager's report. We encouraged managers to share their data with their employees and supervisors but did not require them to do so. However, we also told them that at the end of 1992, the survey would be readministered, and at that time, the senior line management as well as Human Resources would see the results of their surveys.

Employee trepidation about surveys stems from fear of retribution for giving negative responses to the survey. The employees who remained after several successive years of downsizing did not feel comfortable complaining about the person who decides whether they will remain through the next downsizing, a situation exacerbated by an economy in recession in the early 1990s.

To ease concerns, we told employees and managers that the surveys were anonymous and that no manager would receive a report if he or she had less than four responses to the survey. Response rate provides some indication as to whether employees feel safe responding, but we don't know the degree of bias that fear of job loss introduces into responses.

Between November 1991 and February 1992, the time period when the survey was developed, a steering team of people from Human Resources led the survey design process. The team included the organization development manager and HR directors reporting to each of the business segments. Using a review of the organizational behavior literature, input from an outside consulting firm on the items associated with high-performing environments, and the articulated values of the management team, the steering team drafted the first version of the survey. The team reviewed this survey with the CEO, the vice president of human resources, and the management teams of each of the strategic business units (SBUs). Based on feedback and suggestions, the steering team modified the survey. After two iterations, a final survey was approved. This method of compiling the survey gave the steering team members confidence they were asking the right questions and that buy-in to the process existed.

The items used in the survey created a portion of the answer to "Where are we going?" and were fairly typical of the type used in employee attitude surveys, with a few exceptions. The typical elements included joint goal setting, appropriate amounts of decision-making authority, consistent performance feedback, managers' openness to ideas and suggestions, investment in training, managers' ability to resolve conflicts, managers' ability to express opinions without fear of retribution, and managers' effectiveness as leaders. Each SBU within the company could also add up to ten questions of particular importance to that SBU's goals.

The somewhat atypical survey items involved assessment of the degree of understanding of the company's strategy and also perceptions of each manager's manager. The move into the multivendor services arena constituted a big change. No longer would the technicians work only on the high-end mainframe equipment. They would be working on other companies' PCs, printers, and workstations. The survey asked questions about the company's strategy to make sure everyone understood the importance of moving into the multivendor services environment for the success of the business.

The CEO believed that all levels of management required effective leadership, so the survey asked questions about each manager's manager to gain perspective on the current leadership at each level. We wanted to make sure the district office employees felt the regional manager's leadership. So the survey asked questions about awareness of district office issues, degree of empowerment, ability to obtain resources, and visibility in the offices.

Running parallel to the survey development process was an effort to speed the turnaround process to produce quick results. Since we knew we were going to administer the survey twice in a calendar year, we knew we could not take the typical two to three months to get the survey results to the managers and fed back to employees. To shorten the latency from response to results, we set up a phone response system using the same hardware and process used for the annual benefits open-enrollment process. This system was essentially a voice mail system with prompts for each question to guide employees through responses to the survey. Each employee received a hard copy of the survey, a list of manager codes, and a phone number to call to register their responses. After dialing the number, employees heard a recorded voice read each question, which they could answer by pressing the corresponding telephone buttons at any time. As a result of using this approach, survey reports were being generated twenty-four hours after the deadline for responses. Managers received reports within two weeks.

This phone response system presented our steering team with an interesting dilemma. If we allowed employees to call in without an access code, someone might give more than one response for a manager or even enter responses for a manager he or she did not work for. If we did use access codes, it would raise the employees' suspicion that we would trace their responses. After several rounds of debate, our team decided not to use an access code. The intent of the survey was to help the managers, the work groups, and the organization, and we trusted our employees to treat the survey seriously and to help us improve all three fronts.

Even without the access code, employees still felt concerned that we could trace their calls in some way. As a rule, the best way to ease this type of employee concern is to run a few rounds of the survey to demonstrate that neither the company nor the managers have access to an individual's responses. However, since this was the first round of the survey, we could not do much other than repeatedly assure employees that we would keep their responses confidential. Now we had to deal with the managers' concern that, without the access code, they would not get accurate feedback. We asked them to make the leap of faith with us, with the assurance that we would check the number of responses against the number they were supposed to have. If we found a discrepancy, we told them we would resurvey their employees using the traditional paper-and-pencil approach.

The convenient response format, speed of reporting, assurance of anonymity for employees and managers, and our willingness to redo results for managers gave the Round I survey process a lot of credibility. Employees saw us treating the survey seriously and investing a lot in this process, and they seemed to treat it seriously as well. We had a high response rate (78 percent) and very few problems with too many responses for a manager. We followed up the survey administration with training sessions for managers about how to interpret their results and how to hold a feedback session, should they wish to do so.

The survey revealed negative perceptions about the corporate organization in Europe, as anticipated. However, perceptions about the new CEO and his top management team were very positive. Further, employees answered our probes about understanding and supporting the strategy with resoundingly positive responses. Feedback about each manager's manager and the managers themselves was also positive (most mean scores were less than 3.0 on a 5-point scale, where Agree equaled 1 and Disagree equaled 5). The managers scored lowest in the areas of facilitating employee career development and permitting employees to influence what goes on outside the department, both of which would be expected in a field organization. Considering everything, the results from the first administration of the survey were more positive overall than we anticipated.

We found the real story, however, in the individual managers' results. An examination of individual managers' scores revealed that twenty-one of approximately one hundred managers had scores on the thirteen-item management practices section that averaged to be greater than 3.0 on a 5-point scale (the lower the score, the more positive it was). Several managers' scores averaged greater than 4.0. Though we did nothing with this information in Round I, a key goal of subsequent rounds of the survey was to improve the performance of this group of twenty-one managers.

Our concerns about using the phone to gather survey responses with the concomitant potential for contaminated results appeared largely unfounded. When it came time to survey again, neither the employees nor the managers raised any concerns about a telephone survey.

Round II: Raising the Stakes

The second round of the survey, ten months later, had three key differences from Round I, all three of which we designed to add impetus to the change effort. The first difference had actually been introduced even before we administered the first round of the survey. The head of the service organization had tied a portion of the Customer Service senior management team's year-end bonus to how much the team members improved the climate and management practices items (from the survey) within their divisions between the February 1992 and December 1992 administrations of the survey. The head of the service organization was as committed as the CEO to improving management practices throughout the organization, and this was his way of adding some incentive to the changes he wanted to make.

The second change was that when the Round II results came in, we required the managers to hold a feedback session with their direct reports. We provided them with guidelines and told them that someone from HR would help them if they desired. The rationale underlying this requirement was as follows: because several of the survey items focused on creating a more open, participative environment, we wanted the way the managers handled their survey results to reflect that environment.

Finally, we told managers in the service organization that their survey results would also be seen by managers in the levels above them. We told employees and managers that the reason for doing this was both to recognize managers who were doing outstanding jobs and to identify weaker managers and help them improve.

Having the same people complete the ratings at Time 1 and Time 2 required a certain amount of organizational stability, something in short supply in an organization with declining market share. And, in fact, during the summer another reorganization occurred. The company eliminated some managerial positions, and other managers inherited more people. This shift threatened to render comparisons between Round I and Round II for many field managers virtually meaningless.

We knew that many of the managers were taking their survey results seriously and had worked between Round I and Round II to improve their results. The management team of the service business was also trying to raise the overall level of managerial performance in its respective organizations. The steering team and the service organization's Human Resources Department had committed to giving managers the clearest view of the progress they had made. To this end, in the Round II survey, we created two codes for every manager who was managing a significantly different group of people than had responded to the Round I survey. Employees who had worked for the manager in question all year used one code to indicate this on the survey, and employees who had recently started working for that manager used the other code. So, managers who had inherited new people received two reports: a Round I/Round II comparison of survey responses given by the group they had all year and a Round II report showing their new employees' responses.

Once again, the work we did behind the scenes gave the survey process more legitimacy. The managers saw us working hard to support them and give them the best view we could of their progress. This led them to see the survey more as a developmental process and less as a "Gotcha!"

Results improved in a statistically significant way in Round II. Only a handful of items got significantly worse from Round I to Round II, and most of these negative impressions again pertained to questions about corporate leadership in Europe. As had been true with Round I, we observed more telling results when we examined individual managers' scores. At the managerial level, the number of managers whose average scores on the thirteen items in the management practices section exceeded 3.0 fell from twenty-one to fourteen (note: part of the reduction in the number of managers with poor survey scores was due to the fact that some had been laid off in the mid-year downsizing). The company recognized some of the top-scoring managers in its newspaper and reported about their approaches to managing. A senior vice president contacted each of the fourteen managers whose scores remained above 3.0 to discuss the situation and exchange ideas on what needed to improve. The fourteen managers were also asked to send a one-page letter to the general manager of the service business to describe the situation and what they were doing to fix it.

In terms of bonuses for the management team, four of six saw increases in both the climate items and the management practices items and received the full bonus. One saw increases in climate but not in management practices and received a portion of the bonus, and one had scores that went down in both categories and did not receive that portion of his bonus.

Round III

We repeated the survey in the fourth quarter of 1993. For the third round, we extended bonus eligibility to the two other levels of management in the field. Any regional manager or district service manager who increased his or her scores from the end of 1992 Round II survey to the end of 1993 would receive a $1,000 bonus.

The criterion for the bonus at the district manager level provided the subject of much debate among managers. On one hand, the rationale for paying managers for improvement alone has many problems. Consider this example. Which manager more deserves a reward: the one whose score goes from 2.1 to 2.4 (worsening performance, but still quite good) or the one who improves from a 4.5 to a 4.2 (better, but still showing significant problems)? We considered some complex criteria, but in the end, the simplicity of using improvement as the criterion prevailed.

We anticipated a very positive response on the part of the managers to the bonus scheme and the chance to earn an extra

$1,000. To our surprise, many expressed concern about it and were not sure it was fair to them. With the challenging business environment, the continued downsizings, and redistricting, many managers felt the company should not expect them to improve their scores on climate and management practices questions. They felt it was too much to ask. Their reaction did not alter the bonus plans; however, it provided a good reminder that a company cannot determine a "benefit" by its face value alone.

Halfway through the year, we combined the reports of each manager who had received two reports at the end of 1992 into a new report (showing responses from both the employees they had for all of 1992 and the new employees they inherited during the reorganization in mid-1992). We told the managers their Round III scores would be compared to these combined reports for bonus purposes. Though this created a fair amount of extra work for the Human Resources staff, it aided our effort in two ways. First, the mid-year distribution of the combined reports created a platform for communicating the importance of climate, culture, and certain management practices to managers. Second, it again demonstrated to the managers how diligently we were working to ensure the most valid and fair comparisons possible.

The survey had garnered managers' attention, and some started asking for more help. We realized as well that we had to do more than just hold them accountable; we had to do a better job of showing them how to improve. In September of that year, we augmented our survey effort with a training program for district managers designed to lead the transition toward more effective self-directed work teams (SDWTs), teams that manage themselves with little supervision. District managers' territories often covered a lot of geography, and the service reps could go a few weeks without seeing their managers. The training complemented the questions asked in the survey and gave the managers concrete suggestions and practice on how to manage their local and remote teams. During the training, we brought in managers and employees from Xerox who had gone through the transition toward

SDWTs, and this had a huge impact on the managers. They really started to believe they could achieve this transition.

We readministered the survey in early December 1993, (still Round III) and the overall results again showed improvement. At the managerial level, two thirds of the managers received the bonus check, and only nine managers scored poorly, with averages above 3.0 (note: part of the reduction was again due to removing poorly performing managers in the downsizing). Managers scoring above 3.0 were again expected to send a letter to the general manager describing the situation and telling about their plan of action. Not surprisingly, overall the managers' view of connecting bonus money to the survey results improved markedly when so many of them received bonus checks!

Demonstrating Bottom-Line Payback

As we entered the third year, the survey had gained quite a bit of acceptance and started to become part of how the company did business. Nevertheless, grousing still existed on the part of the managers, usually in the form of statements such as "I don't have time to worry about these climate and management practices issues. I have a business to run."

To counter these challenges to the relevance of the survey, we researched the relationship between business results and the climate and management practices data [3]. We used the data about customer satisfaction, productivity, and administrative effectiveness that had long been tracked by the field and related these data to scores on the survey. What we found was dramatic. Using discriminant analysis, two functions emerged: team orientation and performance orientation. The units with more positive attitudes about the degree of team orientation performed higher on the three dependent measures (customer satisfaction, productivity, and administrative effectiveness). The relationship between attitudes about the degree of team orientation and performance held true over time; that is, managers who encouraged participation and pushed the importance of teamwork maintained higher performance on all three dependent variables when assessed ten months later.

We communicated these findings to the managers to demonstrate the importance of how they were managing attending to climate. Given the relationship we observed between the survey results and the performance dimensions coupled with the fact that the managers also had bonus money tied to their performance results (customer satisfaction, productivity, and administrative effectiveness), increasing the degree of participation and focusing on climate had the potential for significant financial payback for the managers.

The situation after three rounds of surveying had both good and bad points. On one hand, momentum for change was really building. The research showed managers the change was important and that it had positive outcomes for them and the organization; the SDWT training showed them how to accomplish the change; the regular survey rhythm gave the managers a way to keep score and track progress; the bonus and follow-up letter to the general manager demonstrated management was in earnest. On the other hand, the overall business results were slipping. The installed base continued to erode, and the MVS sales were not ramping upward as quickly as we had hoped. Though we knew we had far to go, we believed this story would end with "and they lived happily ever after." However, today, "happily ever after" lasts about a week, and giants, in the form of other companies, have the same pernicious impact as the giants in the fairy tales.

Over the summer, just as we were getting ready to again release the combined reports for the reorganized districts and communicate about the year-end survey, the announcement came that Fast-Back Enterprises would purchase EG Inc.'s North American service operations. We halted plans for the fourth round of the survey, the SDWT effort was abandoned, and the organization turned its focus to the pending acquisition.

Surveys in the Trenches: Lessons Learned

Attempting to change the culture/climate and management practices of an organization is a long-term proposition. We tried for 2½ years before a merger derailed our effort. A discussion follows of several lessons from this effort that guide my work as a consultant with organizations that are trying to change.

Having the wrong model is better than not having one at all. In this case, we had two models and both proved valuable. The first modeled what we wanted to create. This came from the CEO's vision and values. This model drove the items we included in our survey and the content of the training we conducted. The second was the consulting firm's change model (Figure 3-1)—the general problem-solving model described at the beginning of this chapter. This model helped us keep our focus on what we strove to create. Also, because we knew the importance of the feedback loop, we knew the survey had to be more than a one-shot event—we knew we needed to continue to breathe life into it.

The statement "Having the wrong model is better than not having one at all" might seem like a bold statement, but having a model gives you something to communicate. By hanging your assumptions out there, it increases the likelihood that people will debate the right issues and that, if you do have the wrong model, the debate will lead to finding the right model.

Organizations don't change; people change. This may seem obvious, but it implies something important: the manager or work group is the most important unit of analysis, not the organization. When a company does an organization-wide survey and only reports results averaged across departments, the responsibility for changing the organization falls into the hands of the senior management and HR, two of the least likely candidates to affect what happens at the work group level. The feedback created by a survey has to get into the hands of those who can make the changes:

work groups and individual managers. If the feedback reaches this lower level, accompanied by the top manager's expectations for what will happen with the feedback results, people will start to change in the desired direction.

For this reason, we always encourage our clients to use manager codes when they do organization surveys and to look at individual managers' results. To not include a manager code diffuses accountability, protects the managers, and delays the change process. Who can afford that, given the competition and the current rate of change?

Accommodate, but don't compromise. To help get buy-in to the survey and the change effort, you need to communicate clearly and frequently with employees and be willing to make some accommodations, but don't lose sight of what you want to change. For example, when introducing the survey for the first time, if too much fear exists in the system—such that employees and managers are not ready to give and receive feedback—make the first survey "free," meaning only each manager sees his or her own results. If any managers complain that the survey is invalid because they have different employees working for them during the second survey round than they had during the first round, make some work for yourself and use multiple manager codes for those managers.

The point here is that, although we were willing to make adjustments, we never lost sight of our goal to make managers more accountable for their results and the way they were managing.

Doing a survey is not the goal; helping people change is the goal. To this end, how you survey is as important as what you survey. Survey steering teams often spend weeks debating the items that will go in the survey but hardly any time discussing the *hows* of the survey: How will we communicate? How can we turn the results around faster than we did last time? How do we build trust? How do we encourage and support behavior change? How often should we do the survey? How do we convince people that the survey is relevant and therefore worth completing and worth putting time into? The answers to all these questions speak volumes to everyone involved about the importance of the survey. If you take two months to get the data back to managers, it undermines any sense of urgency that may have been communicated about the issues covered by the survey. If behavior change does not occur on the part of the managers and HR does not push hard to achieve it, employees will begin to question whether their participation means anything.

All the work we did behind the scenes—the bonuses, the recognition, the letters to the general manager, the training support, the research to demonstrate relevance, the regular rhythm of the survey—fueled the change effort. Despite the fact that the acquisition halted the effort, changes were occurring as a result of this array of supporting mechanisms.

Change is not impossible; let's begin right away! Organizations often avoid making the changes they need to make for a host of reasons: the timing isn't right, it will take too long, it's too expensive, and they don't believe people can change. And organizations that feel that way are mostly correct: the timing never is right, it will take too long, and it will be expensive. It is all true.

But we must be cautious about the last reason listed above—not believing people can change—as to why we should not take on large-scale organizational change and, instead, guard against losing faith in people's ability to change. People rarely give up on themselves; they always believe they could change if they really wanted or had to. They remain optimistic that they can change. But how quickly those same people will give up on someone else and assume that person can't change. My work on this project proved to me unequivocally that given the right environment, the right pressure, the right incentive, and the right support, individual and organizational change is possible.

References

1. Newell, A. H. and Simon, H. *Human Problem Solving.* Englewood Cliffs, N.J.: Prentice Hall, 1972.

2. Anderson, J. "Problem Solving and Learning." *American Psychologist,* Vol. 48, No. 1, 1993, pp. 35–44.

3. Adsit, D., et al. "Relationships Between Employee Attitudes, Customer Satisfaction, and Departmental Performance in a Customer Service Organization." *British Journal of Managerial Psychology,* Vol. 15, 1996, pp. 62–75.

4

A Close Look at Organizational Transformation: What Works and What Doesn't

THOMAS DIAMANTE, PH.D.

Introduction

As the year 2000 approaches, organizational change has become a notorious business dynamic affecting both business strategy and the quality of work life. Literature about organizational change blankets the walls of everyone's nearby bookstore. As a topic of theoretical, practical, and continuing research interest, the profession of industrial and organizational psychology has elaborated on the dynamics of change [1].

Change, as many readers already realize, is complicated. Even changing the behavior of one person is an extremely complex issue. How then can an organization possibly change its entire work force?

The case study in this chapter describes a planned change initiative from the perspective of the targeted work force, which essentially refers to middle management and the employee base. The author attained this perspective by consulting with an organization regarding its people problems, which seemed to be getting in the way of a desired transformation.

This case will likely be of great interest to human resource (HR) practitioners who have played helpful but not necessarily decision-making roles in moving their companies forward. Unfortunately HR professionals often perform supportive roles in organization change efforts rather than strategic, decision-making roles.

This must change. Employing knowledge of human behavior in the context of organizational behavior is what makes change genuine; here is where HR contributes by partnering with business leaders to align people practices with business practices. This case will crystallize issues and obstacles that develop during a change process. An inspection of these crystals can help HR professionals learn to deal with organizational resistance and enhance the fidelity of the HR professional as a catalyst in the change process.

This chapter will also look at behavioral and attitudinal responses to change. The extent to which management and employees buy in to a change effort often varies by level in the organization, which is often a function of a political strategy taken by the individual for the sake of career development (or perhaps career security). Consequently, top management and middle management often view the same planned change action very differently [2].

Leaders of organizations should find the following case study illuminating. It will demonstrate how good intentions can go astray. The case presents an opportunity to realize that people who are the targets of change initiatives think, interpret, and respond to the actions of leadership. These responses are not always what management wanted or intended to yield. In short, the case will visit what works and what does not.

Planned interventions often overcome resistance to change. Oddly enough, although many change efforts include a humanistic quality, the use of power and politics often eliminates resistance [3]. In the case to be presented, readers will see that power was often applied as a means of stifling antichange sentiments. Readers will discover the consequences of such a strategy. It does not take long for a manager or employee to learn the "proper" responses to questions about future business direction. In fact, just in case the manager or employee does not know, organizations usually supply the words, sometimes supply the music (typically on video), and always make known the consequences of nonconformity to a new vision.

One can find many organizations repeating a message about the benefits of a new operating strategy or reaffirming commitment to a new set of values in an almost meditative, mantralike style. Some organizations have even gone to great lengths to include attitudinal change strategies that capitalize on linking physiological changes with organizational experiences (for example, adrenaline-producing outdoor activities) as a means of linking "feeling states" with the new visions of leaders. Quite literally, such a methodology can easily cost millions of dollars.

The result of establishing the new culture is that critical thinking is put on hold, should anyone question the new order. Everyone, in a ritualistic sense, pays homage to the rationale and vision bestowed upon the organization by the leaders. In case employees haven't learned the correct response, brochures, vision statements, and other "training" materials are available. Such a forced change process can result in organizational delusions as leadership begins to believe that everyone has bought in to the new vision since people say and do the right things.

In reality, planned, forced-change strategies that minimize nonconformance through power are a means of avoiding the pain or complexity of developing genuine leadership in an organization.

People change is a difficult and personal topic and, if taken seriously, requires considerable human intervention and strategic involvement from HR professionals.

Consequently, the mantra of wonder lulls the corporate giant to sleep—anesthetizing it from realizing that true metamorphosis will not take place. The giant refuses to feel the pain, the conflict, and the angst that goes along with transformation. The spinal connection with the body of the work force is disconnected, avoiding the need to obtain consent and avoiding the very essence of energy that makes transformation genuine.

The Business Situation

The word *turmoil* best describes the changes that took place in this organization that employs nearly 10,000 people nationwide to manufacture and sell a product. After more than fifty years of predictable, stable growth, this company found itself in the midst of unprecedented turbulence. Specifically, competitors launched attacks that had the potential to affect profitable volume. The company's products that enjoyed a solid market share seemed to be slipping away. Brand equity, the backbone of the company, gave way to signs of decay.

To make matters worse, standards that affected the sales and distribution of the product were under inspection by federal and even local governmental agencies. Whereas the company usually managed these issues in a strategic fashion (through lobbying), a tension grew within the company that regulatory changes would be made that would significantly affect the business.

As if governmental and severe competitive activity (both in pricing and new product lines) wasn't enough, consumer behavior also began to change its predictable path. In particular, sales volume decreased for specified market segments, and social values shifted, which made the products themselves worth less.

In sum, after many years of stability, this organization faced unprecedented challenges from consumers, governmental agencies, and competitors. The early years of stability enabled the growth of a large, bureaucratic organization that, in the past, thrived on a work force that executed business strategy by following rules and well-planned business procedures. Management traditionally valued people who did what they were told, thereby not getting in the way of an effective, established way of doing business.

Up to this point, problems that arose had been fairly easy to solve. Rules, policies, and functional specializations enabled the company to handle such stable problems routinely. This routinization fueled the effectiveness of having predetermined ways of solving problems, encouraging the growth of an organization that thrived on execution of established business strategy.

This structural, operational, and human asset became a major liability.

Career Management and Life in a Stable Environment

This organization managed careers in a planned, simple, and completely internal manner. Moving up the ladder required a person to produce stable business results or to meet specified numerical objectives. Solid performance, interspersed with an occasional relocation to vacancies that required the uprooting of oneself (and perhaps one's family), was the way to move up in this organization. The company would target employees as "loyal" if they were willing to do what they were told and, better yet, even willing to make personal sacrifices for the good of the company.

The business scenario, however, shifted for this company. Competitive pricing strategies surprised the industry, especially when they hit the premium product lines. In addition, competitors introduced lower-priced goods, and consumers apparently abandoned brand loyalty to save a few dollars at the supermarket.

To make matters worse, consumer buying behavior changed, not only in regard to the purchase of cheaper alternatives but also in regard to the purchase of products consumers perceived to be healthy. The company, therefore, not only faced a marketing challenge but also addressed a major change in consumer behavior or perhaps even social values.

The successful monolith found itself decaying, piece by piece. It simply had not been built to adapt to such a dynamic business environment [4]. Fortunately, a strength of this company had always been its heavy investment in attracting and retaining high-quality people. In this time of turmoil, the company's first move was a smart move: to go with the company's strength, to focus on the people.

Human Resource Management in the Wake of Change

Human Resources in this organization played a supportive role in transforming the organization from highly bureaucratic to a more organic, or flexible, culture. In particular, while top management in business units directed changes, the company gave HR the responsibility for handling people problems that would inevitably erupt. The strategic alignment of human resource practices with the new business direction would prove pivotal in making the new, more adaptive organization.

Specifically, as top management developed new business goals and strategies, it held HR accountable for:

☐ Identifying competency deficiencies throughout the organization

☐ Attracting and selecting high-potential people for the organization

☐ Communicating new operating strategies company-wide

☐ Overcoming weaknesses in management skills

☐ Building a performance management process that guided behavior toward adaptive, successful strategies rather than compliance with bureaucratic structure

☐ Redefining leadership from the standpoint of accomplishment at all levels of the organization

☐ Overcoming a culture of complacency by building systems that nurture achievement.

The people of this organization were the ones who had to respond to the changing business (and social) environment. Were they prepared for such a challenge? Could they manage with current internal resources, or had the game changed so much that a need existed for the organization to relearn the rules and the models of success? Traditionally, the work force had been a "turnkey" operation, efficient and effective. Had this operational excellence now become a liability?

In summary, a traditional, large bureaucracy faced the challenge of becoming more flexible and responsive to adapt to shifts in consumer and business demands. Internally, a clearly defined chain of command existed, communication flowed by hierarchy, promotion came from within the company, and getting ahead meant staying clear of trouble, which translated into, "Do what you're told. Don't think on your own." Jobs were well defined, as were career paths and job security. The business had been stable, solid, and secure, and so were the people. This had to change.

The rigid, automatic, reflexive nature of solving problems based upon predetermined strategies (once a strength) had become an Achilles' heel. The organization needed to move security-oriented people into a high-need-for-achievement environment. Could this be done?

HR's role was to align internal behavior with given business strategy. As is often the case, HR played an advisory role in the process of change, but not necessarily an executive role. HR added value by designing methods to achieve stated objectives that would otherwise negatively affect employee relations. With an eye toward the transformational model of change [1], this chapter describes organization change activities from the perspective of one (of several) external change agents as well as from the perspective of employees.

A Strategically Haphazard Methodology: An Honest Look at Transformation

HR took part in the change process to facilitate the achievement of specific internal objectives. As stated earlier, these objectives centered on improving everyone's capacity to handle the dynamic business situation in which they now found themselves.

As a result of relying on a variety of experts, both internal and external, to guide the change effort, the organization stumbled as it moved forward. Some changes worked, some didn't, and some eventually took root after much fine-tuning. Consequently, although this chapter will read in a logical, straightforward fashion, this change effort description should properly read as one would peruse the *New York Times:* a reader might start with the major heading, dabble a little in the columns beneath it, switch to another major heading, and eventually finish the first story the reader started by venturing into another section of the paper to find the story's continuation. Eventually, the reader hopes to have all the stories straight and a good sense of the news of the day, but the process of transforming individual stories into a big picture of the day follows anything but a logical sequence.

Organizations that embark on change and involve HR have the added advantage that HR is trying to keep the overall story (or big picture) straight. That is, as organizations alter business strategies, downsize, build new performance evaluation systems, and bring in new leadership, the affected work force can become upset. People feel uncertain about their own futures. They question the credibility of business initiatives, and the stress and strain of work can seem overwhelming.

HR as a transformational agent can bring distinct value by integrating, clarifying, and implementing business and HR imperatives so that some sense of stability or certainty (an internal manager might choose the word *sanity*) exists as the transformation occurs. This helps everyone develop a sense of the future state with a degree of credibility. HR keeps everyone's eyes on the ball.

Be that as it may, it is important to understand that the process of transformation is not always a clean, logical flow. No one knows all. People get hurt. People lose jobs; others gain wonderful experiences. Some are promoted; some demoted. Some practices produce the desired outcomes, and others don't.

By disentangling myriad elements of a change intervention undertaken by this company, the author hopes the reader has an opportunity to view organizational transformation from a close, practical perspective. This chapter attempts to give the reader a feel for what it is like to be involved in a change scenario. The author refers to this organizational process as "strategically haphazard" because sometimes that's the way it gets done. If readers would imagine someone deciding to move forward by falling down a flight of stairs, they'd have a sense of one way to move forward that is haphazard yet strategic.

Actions for the Sake of Change

Leadership and Business Strategy

To handle the complexities of the business, this organization broke stride with the past and hired from outside the organization for very senior levels. With little explanation, this traditional bureaucracy behaved in a peculiar manner. Not only was the new vice president of business strategy an outsider, but a new CEO came on board as well. These new people had impressive achievements, and while such placement looked strategic from top management's eyes, it appeared invasive and perhaps even sacrilegious in the eyes of the loyal, middle-level manager and the work force.

Concern throughout the organization was high. "Who are these people? What do they want? They're not one of us!" The corporate clamor began, and the word on the street was, "Don't worry.

They'll only last two years, and then we can go back to normal." Then, more outside hires came in at upper-middle levels, and the chatter turned to silence.

Telling Why

Top management conducted its first national meeting to share a new vision for the company and to set forth new business operating strategies soon after the organization announcement about newcomers weighed down everyone's desks. These strategies incorporated not only business specific objectives but human values as well. Top management spoke from a stage in a large ballroom and bestowed its wisdom onto the masses. No, it was not well-received.

First, the sales managers in attendance already had a business strategy; they believed they already knew how to succeed. Second, people felt their human values were just fine and wondered how this CEO dared to suggest that they embrace his values. And finally, rumors spread about possible downsizing. The meeting, one might say, lost its focus.

Top management provided little or no rationale to support a change in operating strategy, which immediately fueled people's resistance. Unfortunately, a meeting that was conducted to clarify and motivate employees generated confusion and conflict.

Comments afterward included, "These people have some audacity to come here and question my values," "My business results are good. Why should I change?" and "There's something wrong when someone says he values participation but acts like an emperor. I don't trust him, but don't look at me to tell him he's got no clothes."

Consequently, the relationship established between the new senior management and the managerial work force responsible for business execution got off to a rocky start.

Send Them Away

Transformation was going to be more difficult than simply running a work force through a set of overheads that stated a new mission and a new set of values. Top management had produced something less than a highly motivated work force after the national meeting.

In response to growing negativity, top management sent the lot of the work force away. The company had planned a series of team-building excursions for the work force, to occur off-site. Utilizing the adventure training approach to building human relations, the company decided to engage in outdoor, somewhat physically challenging activities to facilitate interaction among the managerial ranks.

Nearly all of management "voluntarily" attended a weeklong set of outdoor activities with team-building sessions interspersed. (Of course, peer pressure to participate was enormous, and not attending, unless for bona fide physical reasons, was perceived as an act of treason.) Generally, the goals of the sessions were to develop an understanding of the business situation through conversation and to improve internal working relationships (see Table 4-1).

These team-builing sessions marked an important attempt by the company to get middle management to accept the senior team's leadership. The use of dialogue, small group interaction, external facilitation, and a strong business focus enabled middle managers to discover for themselves the need to consider becoming something new.

Collectively, senior management and selected middle managers implemented a variety of strategic initiatives as outcomes of these team-building sessions:

☐ Start a massive communication campaign to build strength for the vision and values

☐ Launch projects necessary to improve the caliber of the organization's work force

TABLE 4-1.
STRATEGIC PLANNING OVERVIEW: INITIAL FOCUS OF
CROSS-FUNCTIONAL MANAGEMENT TEAMS.

Customers	What drives market share?
	How do we measure satisfaction?
Consumers	Do our consumers value the product?
	Is there loyalty to our brands?
Competitors	What are the weaknesses of our competition?
	How can we take advantage of our strengths?
	What has eroded profitable volume?
Team Strategy	How do we utilize cross-functional expertise?
	Is our work force trained to take on a challenge?
Human Resources	Do we hire the best qualified people?
	Do we develop people strategically?
	Can we help adapt to change?
Motivation	Are the rewards contingent upon performance?
	Do we support the efforts we need?
	Do we eliminate nonperformers?
Business Execution	Does everyone understand the new operating strategies?
	Can we all live by the value set provided?
	What bureaucratic obstacles stand in the way of our success?

☐ Translate new business strategy into a practical competency model that can be used to design a performance evaluation system that will drive the business

☐ Build market share, and focus on profitable volume

☐ Bolster developmental programs to prepare the work force to perform in the new, achievement-oriented culture.

During the team-building sessions, someone suggested that the work force had grown complacent. The culture of the organization was security-minded, and not surprisingly, over the years the company attracted and selected security-oriented, low-risk individuals, some of whom even excelled in the business [5]. In addition, little exchange of information occurred among sales professionals, and when communication did occur, the bureaucracy destroyed the message and the timing.

Human Resources initiated a variety of workshops, seminars, and change management programs and developed specific HR practices, all of which had a singular goal—to align internal behavior with external demands on the organization. The following sections highlight these initiatives in terms of content, rationale, and perceived impact on people.

HR left communication regarding these initiatives to the discretion of key decision makers within respective business units. Consequently, less than desirable integration occurred, and in fact, often because of the lack of communication (or concern for possible miscommunication), HR had to include a communication phase prior to implementation of these initiatives. This was done on a case by case basis depending on what had been accomplished (or not accomplished) by key business leaders in regard to the change initiative.

Change Management Workshops

Concerned for the strain placed on the work force as increases in performance expectations and restructuring loomed, HR implemented a workshop that combined issues of change management with issues of personal growth. The workshop occurred off-site with people divided into small groups. Confidential career and stress counseling sessions were part of the program [6].

This workshop sent the message that life and work always place people in demanding situations and that learning skills that enable them to adapt not only will make them more effective in the changing company but also will improve their overall well-being. The workshop took a realistic yet positive approach to preparing management and employees for the new culture they were all responsible for growing.

TABLE 4-2.
ADAPTING TO CHANGE: MANAGING SELF TO
MANAGE OTHERS.

List of Key Ingredients

☐ Establish a climate of safety and trust
☐ Frame an understanding of change within the context of organization development
☐ Link stress management with job performance
☐ Frame anxiety as fuel for achievement
☐ Capitalize on past personal experiences of participants who have faced change in their lives and survived
☐ Experience stress reduction modalities
☐ Personalize an action plan for each individual participant to expand his or her confidence level
☐ Rejuvenate energy and perhaps interest in stepping up to new business demands and performance expectations

---

The key ingredients of the change management workshop referenced by Table 4-2 positioned individuals to face the challenges confronting them in a realistic, practical way. The workshop combined organizational development issues with individual development as a means of helping everyone see the big picture—which would lead to more effective behavior both personally and professionally.

Employing a small-group approach, the workshop, facilitated by the author, was an experience that dealt with organizational change and positively equipped the work force to change behavior (if necessary) or to make other difficult professional choices.

The workshop context included an agreement of confidentiality between the facilitator and the contracting organization; in other words, the facilitator promised not to tell the company what its work force said at the workshop. This agreement, no doubt, contributed handsomely to enabling the facilitator to develop an honest relationship with participants. Conversations focused on specific behavior and targeted change that was needed on an individual level to improve performance and personal well-being.

The content and context of the workshop contrasted with heavy-handed approaches to change that the work force had experienced at other times in the organization. For many, the workshop was an important step toward embracing personal and professional deficiencies that required development if one was to contribute to results in the new culture.

Employee Assistance Program (EAP)

Not typically discussed as part of a change program, an EAP was used by HR as a means of introducing a concern for people in the new culture [7]. Surprisingly, the company had no genuine EAP for its organization. As a means of providing support and guidance, HR selected an EAP provider capable of delivering family counseling, legal guidance, and other supportive services for the entire organization. HR implemented this service while phasing in (less attractive) changes in healthcare benefits, hoping the two would balance the new organization's perspective on healthcare benefits.

While the EAP in itself had value, HR used it to highlight the company's commitment to excellence by use of support. HR was attempting to demonstrate the company's concern for people since its apparent focus on profit (at the expense of people) had fallen under harsh criticism by middle management.

Competency Development

Performance in the new, dynamic, achievement-oriented company was foreign to most of the work force. This did not yield good positioning because the company, historically, had been very successful. Things had simply changed. Old strategies just didn't work anymore.

By comparison with existing performance standards, the new performance benchmarks were indeed different. The proverbial bar had been raised, and with the help of HR, the company introduced the new performance evaluation system as a springboard for the development of innovative business activity. The role of HR in this process was to design a system that identified competency deficiencies, rewarded exceptional behavior, and set a developmental course for high-potential employees.

The parameters of the process included the following:

☐ The performance model must be linked to the established organizational values

☐ Acceptable performance in the organization is to be benchmarked at a new, higher level of attainment (using market data to measure business results and subjective data to assess effort)

☐ A probationary period will be used for low performers

☐ An implicit norm will be followed whereby everyone complies with the expectation from top management that, at best, the organization may have some adequate performers but for the most part performance evaluation ratings should be skewed toward lower ratings

☐ All individuals in a business unit will be compared against each other's performance, not against job requirements alone.

Despite anticipated employee relations problems resulting from the move toward a peer comparisons method of appraisal (that is, evaluating performance relative to others rather than on job requirements), management steadfastly sent a message that the best workers will receive rewards and that the company no longer tolerates mediocrity. Obviously, the process was drenched in power and political realities surrounding the change initiative. The grapevine viewed this process as a formal way of building documentation for and against key players. This view produced the perception of an "in" group and an "out" group, which would lead to divisiveness and unhealthy conflict [8].

HR built a competency model that incorporated both external and internal relations (for example, utilizing cross-functional teams, capitalizing on internal resources, monitoring the behavior of competitors). Smartly, the competencies specifically addressed bureaucracy-breaking behavior, such as overcoming administrative obstacles, finding faster ways to get work done, and doing more with less. Rule breaking would be fashionable if it led to improved performance.

The purpose of the new performance measurement system was to redefine acceptable performance. Essentially, performance once judged as very good the company now rated as barely acceptable. As one can imagine, this once familial, warm, and secure company had found a new persona. The word on the street about the "new and improved" performance management system was that it was a tool to eliminate those workers not fitting in with the new zeitgeist.

Managerial Skill Weaknesses

As a means of helping lower- and middle-level managers understand what they needed to do to improve the organization, qualitative interviews with senior levels of HR and business unit managers were conducted by the HR Department. The results suggested:

☐ Technical knowledge of the business was deficient

☐ Business units were competing with each other in an unhealthy fashion (poor communication, no communication, misleading communication)

☐ Employees perceived managers as untouchable.

With HR as the leader, a communication blitz began. That is, all managers went through a 360° evaluation, the company conducted team-building sessions when collaboration was required to solve presented problems, and importantly the company addressed the knowledge deficiency by building an in-house management center. This center offered workshops about contemporary technical and managerial topics on a strategic basis for each level of management.

Consistent with the culture of performance, workshop facilitators evaluated individuals attending the management center and provided verbal and written feedback to each participant's boss. This feedback essentially consisted of judgments made by workshop facilitators regarding participation and level of competency. In theory, the company used the feedback developmentally only, but needless to say, fear regarding the feedback existed in the workplace, and jokes went around about the possibility of sniper activity whenever a gathering of people took place.

This process fueled panic and created unnecessarily high states of anxiety. In the context of establishing a learning environment, such a state did not breed trust and creativity. Instead, it locked in a state of fear and perhaps even paranoia since workers even perceived the developmental aspects of the job as hazardous to their career health.

Attraction and Selection

Traditionally, much hiring occurred through unstructured interviews, and employee referrals were not unusual in this company. Entry-level positions were relatively low-skilled and labor-intensive; the company basically expected entry-level employees to simply do what they were told.

In the new age, the company redesigned these entry-level positions. People with computer skills had an advantage since entry-level workers were now to use laptop computers to communicate with peers, supervisors, and information systems that monitored market activity. In addition, expectations for new hires changed drastically. It was no longer acceptable to remain in an entry-level position—workers either moved up or out. Consequently, the company significantly upgraded the cognitive demands and decision-making responsibilities of these jobs. In short, entry-level positions were a track to management. If people had no management potential, they had no jobs.

HR provided the selection tests, methods, and strategies necessary (including validation) to hire individuals who would qualify for management after only six months in an entry-level position. Using task-oriented approaches to job analysis, HR established a thorough examination of the knowledge, skills, and abilities requisite for success (that is, competencies) and built a management potential assessment process. HR was hunting for new blood.

A college relations program was designed and launched to attract bright, talented students to the company [9]. A strategy was developed to visit select college placement offices and develop a relationship with the deans and administrators on the campus.

The company used new technologies to position itself well against competitors (laptop computer presentations, menu-driven interactive programs, and futuristic marketing brochures), and HR positioned the new, achievement-oriented company onto college campuses.

In addition, all hiring done on campuses (and off-campus) was coordinated through HR. Human Resources therefore became a key player not so much in final decision making but in making certain that business decision makers benefited from the available selection devices. Using customized tests, simulations, and panel interviews, the new sales organization began to experience the benefits of hiring high-skilled, computer-literate, achievement-oriented business professionals.

Organization Structure

Top management continued to make strategic operational moves while HR addressed the people issues. To facilitate more flexibility and strategy setting at lower levels of the organization, the company made symbolic personnel changes. Managers whose styles contradicted the newer, livelier thrust were removed, and people with distinctly different managerial styles replaced them. Typically, the replacements had experience from other industries, had advanced degrees, or otherwise embodied a company trying to do things differently rather than resting on its laurels.

The company expected management and employees to make more decisions that affect business. They were also accountable for significant mistakes in this regard. Managers who did not accept additional responsibility or questioned strategy were, at times, dealt with strongly. Eventually, lower management understood that they must comply, do more, and yes, agree 100 percent with the new strategies. No one openly discussed the paradox of forcing people to establish an empowered culture.

The structure was trimmed through attrition and through the competency-based performance management process. The ranking procedures and the higher bar to jump over began to identify a percentage of employees as unsatisfactory performers. Anyone could see the strain on employee relations as the company informed long-service employees of their levels of inadequacy while welcoming fast-trackers from college campuses with open arms.

How the Target Would Explain the Game: Perceived Outcomes of Change Actions

Like many organization change interventions, outcomes are not easily measured. It is also difficult to determine whether a given outcome is positive or negative since it represents but one point in time. For example, the company is experiencing much stress. Given the increased job responsibilities, the changes in the performance evaluation system, and the nature of the work force being more security-oriented than achievement-oriented, it is not surprising to find employee relations issues surfacing. People feel confused, perhaps fear is high, and many interpretations exist of every new method the company implements to improve business.

The performance management process that includes rank ordering along with increased standards for acceptable performance has yielded obligatory compliance but is perceived by many workers as just a means to reduce head count. The silent majority might suggest that simply downsizing once (and getting it over with) would be a more effective strategy—if indeed that is the true goal of the performance system.

The perception that the performance system does not facilitate change presents a problem. If workers truly perceive the system as a pretext for a slow, painful downsizing, then obviously a critical element of the change process is failing [10].

Many issues surround performance and its measurement. First, the company has made performance a critical issue; people feel afraid to have a bad month. Performance is also measured by group assessment. That is, supervisors must "present" the ratings they give their employees to the supervisor's own peers for approval. Logically, this helps standardize ratings and makes for more comparable benchmarks. However, a sales professional would say that this only lets people know who works for the best manager, since managers must "sell" the ratings to others.

Workers do not universally embrace the process used to change job performance by the rank-ordering system. While employees understand the performance bar has risen, the methodology of use is bringing a tide of resentment and perhaps even hostility.

Bring in the Coach: Transformation Is Personal

Individuals not equipped for the company's transformation from large, hierarchical, and bureaucratic to smaller, autonomous, and more flexible were holding the organization back. Table 4-3 lists reasons for resistance to change at senior levels. It is apparent that organizational transformation is a rather personal issue. It is also apparent that the nature of the resistance varies with the unique history and perception of each person coached. Table 4-3 gives a sense of different perceptions of change on the same topic.

Coaching is a process gaining usage in corporate America to facilitate change in an organization by working with the percep-

TABLE 4-3.
KEY POINTS OF RESISTANCE UNCOVERED THROUGH
COACHING SERVICES.

People Issues	"The current work force is fine—new management is attacking our skill level as a pretext for taking control for the sake of gaining power."
	"New management is too slow to act—we must act forcefully and directly and get people moving now."
Technology	"The desire to become high-tech is a waste of time and money—we should have spent the millions on people, not on machines."
	"It is advanced use of technology that will enable us to work smarter. We're already behind—anyone not capable of dealing with this skill can seek alternate employment."
Structure	"The supposed autonomous organizational design will wreak havoc on management—top management is trying to ensure that field managers fail so it can play its next hand."
	"It's not job titles that make money; it's people. We change job titles around here like we change our socks. When will we learn that so-called re-engineering is a cover-up for downsizing?"
Process	"Anyone believing that we should be more open with all levels of management is either gullible or stupid—this new doctrine of disclosure is an obvious ploy to find and keep followers while eliminating anyone with half a brain."
	"This organization is blocked by structure—I want to eliminate all administrative obstacles tomorrow and let my people loose to get the job done."

tions and consequent behavioral styles of organizational leaders [11, 12, 13]. Typically, companies provide such a service for those executives who have difficulty with a transformational process.

As Table 4-3 indicates, defining the main source of resistance is an individual matter. The important note here is to realize that large-scale cultural or organizational transformation, which often reads as an impersonal, strategic mission, comes across very much as a personal issue.

Topics not mentioned in Table 4-3 that also become apparent when coaching services are under way during organizational transformation include power and political strategies [14], retaliation for past experiences, decision making based upon protective needs ("nothing will happen to my people"), and overcoming the emotional aspects of dealing with loss, an underlying theme of the process of change that becomes apparent to anyone providing coaching services in this context.

Change Actions and Reactions: A Practical Overview

Table 4-4 presents a synopsis of change activities and consequent responses over approximately a three-year period of time. Organized as a chronological sequence, the table allows readers to grasp a framework for understanding change at organization, group, and individual levels of analysis.

Lessons Learned: Viewing Transformation from the Inside Out

HR As a Business Partnership

Business executives initiate change with or without the help of Human Resources. The neglect of HR involvement in planning a change strategy can prove tragic at worst and ineffective at best.

HR professionals must, if necessary, fight to become key players in deciding how their companies will implement operating strategies. Too often HR is given the role of executing policy, not creating policy. Underutilization of the knowledge and skills of HR professionals likely relates to the amount of litigation and employee relations disturbance experienced in the course of change. Where organizations focus on litigation, HR does too.

Executives managing human resource functions, who also happen to be caught in the wake of change, need the composure to be

TABLE 4-4.
ORGANIZATIONAL TRANSFORMATION PROCESS UNCOVERED:
READY, FIRE, AIM.

History of Business Stability

☐ Large, bureaucratic organization
☐ Job design is clear, functional territory
☐ Communication by chain of command
☐ Attracts, selects, and retains security-oriented people

Sudden Outbreak of Business Instability

☐ Organization structure impedes response to marketplace
☐ Job design is myopic; focus is on minutia; company is losing sight of big picture
☐ Communication by authority does not allow the company to benefit from those close to the marketplace and "in the know"
☐ Competency of work force is questioned

Leadership and Business Strategy Transformation

☐ Injects foreign bodies into organization; new top management hired from outside the industry
☐ Top management tells organization of new vision and values
☐ Complexity of change management handled by internal authority and external "experts" imposes emotional, personal disclosure sessions and questionable approaches to people change (such as adventure training)

For Every Action, an Equal and Opposite Reaction

☐ Organizational system rejects foreign elements
☐ Work force resents being told to embrace new values/takes offense to implication that current values are not good enough
☐ Personal disclosure and a codified principle of openness become a wildfire as people verbally attack each other
☐ Work force pushed by new performance standards raises antennae for employees' legal avenues to retaliate; conflict runs high, suggesting the possibility that retaliation to the company occurs in the form of legal battles and conflict

Change Actions in the Midst

☐ Coaching services initiated to control/retain key decision makers
☐ Experimentation with autonomous job designs
☐ HR struggles to get hold of the change process
☐ Small group seminars dealing with individual and organizational change come into demand
☐ Employee relations issues monopolize time and energy of HR professionals

a business partner in making decisions that affect people. This is often difficult because top management in HR does not always get invited to the right parties. If HR is to be a formidable element in organizational transformation, the profession must position itself to be viewed as part of key business strategies. This speaks to the extent to which the department has been involved with understanding customers, learning core business strategies, and generally getting close to the business.

Needless to say, it's much easier to earn credibility as a business-building professional during good times than bad. HR professionals should link themselves with non-HR activities as often as possible. This will enable them to stay in touch with the business and to be called upon when human issues are on the planning table.

Finally, anyone involved with change has two general concerns that must be acknowledged if this chapter is to speak genuinely about the topic. Unfortunately, these concerns ring truer for HR folks than other functions although the concerns are certainly pervasive. First, how does a person become influential to key decision makers (outside HR) to impact the making of strategic change actions? Second, what are the political ramifications of potential disagreement with the planned change actions of the business units?

So, there is the professional concern about the transformation process, and there is the personal concern about immediate career safety (as opposed to career development). Again, these factors are affected by the extent to which the HR Department truly and significantly involves itself in the profit-producing aspects of the business. Altering the direction of a change intervention can be a monumental and career-threatening task.

Educate the Consumer

Business executives moving forward to change an organization often have a misunderstanding of Human Resources. Typically, the essentials of HR are limited to compensation and benefits.

While these two items certainly play a key part in the profession, the developmental aspects of our business are much less known— so much so that executives are often surprised to learn of the research available to experienced experts who deal with organizational change.

Many consultants offer services, especially on hot items such as change, diversity, and competencies. Fox [15] provides a review of this issue as it touches the profession of psychology, which is often called upon to assist organization development. HR professionals benefit their organizations and their profession by educating key decision makers on the issue of competency in the area of organizational consultants.

For instance, in this chapter's case study the company initiated many change actions with little regard for outcome measurement or, worse, strategies and principles that neglected human responses in the context of a working organization. Unfortunately, the company implemented some silly (and perhaps even conflict-providing) initiatives.

For example, the company encouraged workers to attend an organization-wide seminar on disclosure at which participants openly criticized each other, often with disregard for the impact of remarks on recipients. In the absence of a performance-based context or any structure at all, conflict heightened, and working relationships often suffered. Oddly, the company intended this workshop to strengthen relationships under the "safety" of a company change principle that touted the virtues of honesty. Left ill-defined, unstructured, and negligent of the need for a skilled process facilitator, disclosure and emotion doesn't always lead to bonding.

Paradoxical Transformation

Beware of Pseudo-Change Strategies

HR professionals understand that management change actions are not equivalent to rhetoric. When management uses fashionable words to energize people (also known as empowerment), it must prepare itself to give people real power. When words and realities do not agree, management credibility is destroyed.

Neither management nor HR should tell people they have power when they don't. It won't fool anyone. It is much more effective to be forthright and explanatory than try to get workers to ignore the person behind the curtain.

A case in point is the performance management program mentioned in the case study. While positioned as a positive, motivational program that would drive the business forward, the program also served as a means of identifying the bottom rung of workers, to eliminate nonperformers. Validity aside regarding performance appraisal design, the work force quickly ascertained the negative or consequential aspects of the program and inferred that management's neglect for mentioning these consequences must mean that the true goal of the program was to reduce head count.

By providing a complete rationale and describing overall ramifications of moving to a competency-based appraisal system, the work force may accept (albeit reluctantly) rather than reject the new standards.

Don't Let Outside "Experts" Run Everything

Internal HR professionals live and work within their distinct cultures. Knowledge of that culture coupled with education on human behavior in the context of change is a leverage that few others have in the organization. HR professionals should use that leverage!

Often this author has worked with HR professionals on strategic initiatives, and they've sadly reflected on past actions taken against their better sense. The reason they listened to others rather than themselves often hinged on the political clout of the external change agent suggesting the action (in other words, a senior executive brought him or her in). HR professionals should work with consultants to plan and implement programs and not assume that their input is less valuable than the perspective of an external. Often, best practices result from a collaborative approach in which diverse perspectives come together to generate novel solutions.

Don't Try to Delude Others

Changing an organization causes stress, perhaps even emotional pain. People involved in these efforts should never try to fool anyone—because it can't be done. When moving forward with a re-engineering project that may (or is designed to) affect the size of the work force, videos, brochures, and other communication programs should not be created to mischaracterize what will soon take place. No one wins when actions and words are inconsistent. This is especially true for HR professionals whose integrity and credibility are vital to effectiveness.

The company in the case study struggled with providing guidance for group behavior to reduce conflict. Group dynamics in the organization had experienced three phases. The first phase was as a family. This didn't work out because it was too supportive and implied that the organization would take care of everyone. Phase 2 focused on teamwork. This didn't work out because the employees had no real need to work as a team; everyday tasks simply didn't call for a team effort. Finally, the company used a community orientation to guide behavior. This, too, developed problems because employees realized that the butchers in town could fiercely compete with them to provide needed services to the community—and the town was not big enough for both of them.

Teams are not simple creations, and much literature exists for readers to draw upon for guidance [16]. Unfortunately, organizations often want simple, popular solutions to complex problems. HR should not shy away from the literature. Teams should be designed by taking into consideration the nature of the task, the complexity of the problem, and the skills and abilities that will bring value.

Also, companies shouldn't use a team to hammer a nail. In today's team-obsessed climates, people are too often reluctant to assign a task to a person rather than to a task force. HR must not fall victim to this faulty paradigm. Teams should be used as strategic tools.

View Your Consultant As a Power Base

Sometimes the power and political circumstances facing HR affects the degree of force it can leverage to impact change actions. A consultant can and should be used as an additional power base for HR concerns to be heard. *Power* is no longer a dirty word in the world of change management because people have learned that without it, little occurs [3].

Choosing a legitimate power base and political strategy to influence organizational direction, however, is an important issue. HR should benefit from the experience of its consultant not only in planning the content of HR practices but also in overcoming any context issues that need to be addressed. Consultants can ease the pain at times, when HR professionals are struggling with the tug-of-war between personal career issues and fighting the practices of key business units or internal client groups.

A Final Note

Organizational transformation is here to stay. The nature of corporate America is evolving. Like any evolving system, some variations will work, and some won't.

HR professionals offer catalytic elements to the change process. These elements, however, must be included in the operational and human resource planning aspects of change. The HR professional must become a key player in the profit-making aspects of the business to survive. The position of the HR/business professional will grow in the years to follow where responsibilities for both building business and managing human resources blend.

Finally, changing organizations includes changing people. As a practitioner, the author notes that executives should include the personal or human aspects of organizational transformation into their plans. This, of course, is not easy since everyone is unique. However, through change actions that are considerate of individual histories and through communication strategies that are realistic, not idealistic, the reactions of the work force will be better managed. This can facilitate transformation as people come to learn and plan for the realities before them.

References

1. Porras, J. and Robertson, P. "Organization Development: Theory, Practice, and Research," in *Handbook of Industrial and Organizational Psychology,* 2nd ed. M. D. Dunnette and L. M. Hough (Eds.), Palo Alto, Calif.: Consulting Psychologoists Press, 1992, pp. 719–822.

2. Argyris, C. *Integrating the Individual and the Organization.* New York: John Wiley and Sons, 1964.

3. Greiner, L. and Schein, V. E. *Power and Organization Development.* Reading, Mass.: Addison-Wesley, 1988.

4. Beer, M. *Organizational Change and Development: A Systems View.* Glenview, Ill.: Scott, Foresman, 1980.

5. Schneider, B. "The People Make the Place." *Personnel Psychology,* Vol. 40, 1987, pp. 437–453.

6. Kahn, R. L. and Byosiere, P. "Stress in Organizations," in *Handbook of Industrial and Organizational Psychology, Vol. 3,* 2nd ed. M. D. Dunnette and L. M. Hough (Eds.), Palo Alto, Calif.: Consulting Psychologists Press, 1992, pp. 571–650.

7. Philips, S. B. and Mushinski, M. H. "Configuring an Employee Assistance Program to Fit the Corporation's Structure: One Company's Design," in *Stress and Well Being at Work.* J. C.

Quick, L. R. Murphy, and J. J. Hurrell, Jr. (Eds.), Washington, D.C.: American Psychological Association, 1992.

8. Thomas, K. W. "Conflict and Negotiation Processes in Organizations," in *Handbook of Industrial and Organizational Psychology, Vol. 3*, 2nd ed. M. D. Dunnette and L. M. Hough (Eds.), Palo Alto, Calif.: Consulting Psychologists Press, 1992.

9. Schein, V. E. and Diamante, T. "Organizational Attraction and the Person-Environment Fit." *Psychological Reports,* Vol. 62, 1998, pp. 167–173.

10. London, M. and Mone, E. M. "Managing Marginal Performance in an Organization Striving for Excellence," in *Human Dilemmas in Work Organizations: Strategies for Resolution.* A. H. Korman (Ed.), New York: Guilford Press, 1994.

11. Diamante, T. and Giglio, L. "The Durability Factor: A Systems Approach to Managerial Endurance." *Leadership and Organization Development Journal,*Vol. 13, 1992, pp. 14–19.

12. Waldrop, J. and Butler, T. "The Executive as Coach." *Harvard Business Review,* Nov.–Dec. 1996, pp. 111–117.

13. Diamante, T., Giglio, L., and Urban, J. "Leadership Coaching: Leveraging Change at the Top." *Journal of Management Development,* 1998 (in press).

14. Offerman, L. R. "Power and Leadership in Organizations." *American Psychologist,* Vol. 45, 1990, pp. 179–189.

15. Fox, R. "Charlatanism, Scientism and Psychology's Social Contract." *American Psychologist,* Vol. 51, 1996, pp. 777–784.

16. Dyer, W. *Team Building*. Reading, Mass.: Addison-Wesley, 1987.

5

Developing the Next Generation of Leaders: A New Strategy for Leadership Development at Colgate-Palmolive

JILL CONNER AND COLEEN A. SMITH

Somehow, the cream always rises to the top.

This common-sense notion has been the key driver of succession planning at Colgate-Palmolive for nearly two centuries. And the approach has worked well, steadily replenishing the ranks of Colgate's top-tier executives who, in turn, power the company's remarkable growth.

Colgate-Palmolive has grown over time from a modest starch, soap, and candle business into a corporate giant that now brings dozens of products to the global market. One of the best-known consumer goods companies in the world, Colgate's portfolio of popular products includes Colgate toothpaste, Palmolive soap, Mennen deodorant, and Ajax cleanser. In 1995, the company's revenues topped $8 billion. The core businesses—personal and household care products—have not changed over the decades. But beyond that, the Colgate of today bears little semblance to the small enterprise William Colgate launched on Dutch Street in New York City in 1806. Today, Colgate has its headquarters in midtown Manhattan. And *Fortune* magazine ranks Colgate as No. 158 in the *Fortune 500*.

The company opened its first overseas operation in the early 1900s, thereby becoming a trailblazer in international business and anticipating today's global economy. One dramatic result of the company's early overseas ventures is that more than 5.6 billion people in 212 countries and territories now consume Colgate products.

Throughout Colgate's long history, the management cream did rise to the senior executive levels. The company selected the right people at the right times; and a steady stream of talented executives drove the business to its strong industry position.

A Problem with the Pipeline: More Jobs, Fewer Candidates

For some time, Colgate's vision of becoming "the best truly global consumer products company" has powered the company's business strategy of aggressive geographic expansion. In the 1990s alone, Colgate opened subsidiaries in twenty-five countries, including Bolivia, Nigeria, Senegal, Romania, Vietnam, and China. This pace of expansion shows no signs of slowing. Indeed, the company predicts it will need to fill as many as thirty-five new general manager[1] (GM) positions by the year 2000.

---

[1] A key operating position, the general manager is responsible for all aspects of a geographic unit. Each GM, together with a team of other functional executives, is responsible for a specific business unit.

In the early 1990s, Colgate's senior leadership team began to question whether the management pipeline that had always delivered the company's new executives would have the breadth to support the planned global expansion. Some concern existed that the company might face a shortage of managers who had the requisite skills and abilities and who were willing to accept key operating positions around the world. If this shortage took place, it could put the company at a disadvantage in the global marketplace [1, 2].

The senior team recommended that the company take proactive measures to ensure that the executive pipeline continues to have a good flow of high-potential candidates. This recommendation was critical, given both the projected growth in future overseas assignments and the projected number of job vacancies over the next decade caused by retirements, attrition, and promotions.

External Pressures on Internal Planning

A cluster of external trends also concerned Colgate's leadership, trends that were—and still are—impacting executive development strategies in corporations across industry. Here are three examples:

☐ *Tougher requirements for the next generation of senior executives.* One result of accelerating globalization, constantly emerging advanced technologies, and ever-sharpening industry competition is that leaders must have a set of skills and a body of knowledge that allows them to adapt readily to rapid change in the marketplace. Furthermore, with the pace of innovation only speeding up, such capabilities will be in even greater demand in the future.

☐ *Stepped-up recruitment of Colgate managers by industry competitors.* Professionals with international experience in consumer products have become much-sought-after candidates for positions in competing global companies. This trend makes clear the need to develop a strategy at Colgate that will give the company a stronger hand to play in retaining high-potential people.

□ *More managers in dual-earner families.* Increasingly, managers aren't greeting the prospect of overseas assignments—positions that customarily have been the springboard to Colgate's executive career ladder—with much enthusiasm. More and more, a manager's reluctance to relocate overseas is related to the needs of dual-income families. Before the dual-income family became commonplace, few managers ever declined the offer of an overseas assignment.

By the early 1990s, issues like these had turned the company's executive succession strategy into a front-burner issue for Colgate's top team. Clearly, the time had arrived for designing a strategy for discovering and readying the next generation of executives—decision makers who would lead the company's global expansion in the new century.

Getting Ready to Design a Strategy

These internal and external pressures persuaded Colgate's senior leadership team to rethink how Colgate would continue growing its pool of global managers. In early 1995, Colgate's CEO and chairman of the board, Reuben Mark, challenged the vice president of global human resources, Bob Joy, to address the company's future leadership development needs. Even though Joy had an in-depth knowledge of Colgate, he decided to develop a comprehensive view of the issues by personally consulting with key decision makers across the company. This would give him the opportunity both to explore the full range of leadership development issues Colgate managers were dealing with and to identify priorities from a more informed perspective.

Traveling extensively through the Colgate world, Joy affirmed his initial sense that many executives considered the expansion of the general manager pool the most important human resource issue the company could undertake in the coming years. Through his series of meetings worldwide, Joy gave key people the opportunity to define the issue from their particular perspectives and to contribute to the formation of a leadership development strategy. Joy gained an additional advantage from this round of meetings by getting influential people within the company to support the leadership development initiative as a top priority.

Early on, Joy became convinced that to implement a leadership development strategy effectively, the company needed to integrate the activities of succession planning, executive staffing, and training and development. This judgment led to the creation in early 1996 of a new HR unit called People Development. Jill Conner, an HR professional who had recently joined Colgate and who had expertise in leadership development, was selected to head the People Development team.

First Steps: Learning the Lay of the Land

Preliminary groundwork had to be done before the leadership development team (the authors) could prepare a strategy to identify and develop the next generation of business leaders. Specifically, we needed to deepen our understanding of the leadership development issues that might potentially enhance or inhibit Colgate's future growth.

We determined that face-to-face interviews with high-level decision makers would be the best and quickest way to get to the heart of these issues and challenges. So, early on, we conducted in-depth interviews with twenty senior managers. The interviewees included the presidents of the divisions and the heads of the corporate functions—the executives who report directly to the CEO—and key general managers.

We expected these conversations to enhance our understanding of the strategic issues and give us insights into aspects of the culture that might accelerate or hinder our progress as we moved forward in the work.

The initial interviews were purposefully structured to gather information and data efficiently yet gain the understanding and perspective we needed. We built the interviews around three core questions (listed below with the key findings). After these interviews, we engaged in the process of reviewing, analyzing, and understanding the responses. A revealing picture of top-management opinion quickly emerged. For example, the interviewees broadly agreed that, as the process of developing talented people had become increasingly complex, the company needed a more structured approach to this task.

Below are the core questions we asked every executive, followed by some highlights of their responses.

1. *What experiences will best prepare people for senior management positions?*

☐ Executives agreed that significant responsibilities early in a manager's career as well as a variety of assignments in different geographic locations provide the best preparation for executive jobs. It was noted that Colgate had to develop a systematic way of providing this experiential background to its high-potential people. Speaking candidly, one executive said, "New general managers tell me they would benefit from having even broader, more cross-functional experiences before receiving their promotions."

☐ Interviewees told us corporate assignments can provide important career-building experiences too. For example, gaining first-hand knowledge of how things really work in an organization is a key advantage linked to corporate jobs. Other payoffs include the numerous opportunities corporate jobs give young managers to build a broad-based network of superiors, colleagues, and subordinates and to learn how they can exercise personal influence to get things done.

☐ A number of executives acknowledged that one or two of their bosses had coached or mentored them at early stages of their careers. One manager said, "Along the way, I had several mentors who spent time teaching, nurturing, and helping me. They weren't sheepish about giving me honest, sometimes painful criticism."

2. *What internal and external factors could produce a talent shortfall at Colgate?* Executives noted several trends that could inhibit the development of a talent pool at Colgate and possibly hamper the company's growth.

☐ In this context interviewees frequently mentioned the growing number of general manager positions. Said one executive, "We used to have several excellent candidates for each management vacancy. With the growing number of these positions today, it's more difficult to find as many candidates to choose from."

☐ The people we interviewed also noted that one of the most serious external threats comes from the increasing global competition for talent. Colgate people are now being targeted in many countries. This is most common among competitors in high-growth areas and in new industries that are looking for managers with particular skills and experience in certain regions.

☐ Colgate is also aggressively entering new markets. Interviewees mentioned the fact that this growth is complicated by the reality that many of these new subsidiaries will be located in areas that are not among the most desirable places to live.

☐ Advanced technologies, corporate re-engineering, outsourcing, and other business tools will continue to transform the way people work, respondents said. Only a steady stream of managers equipped with the skills and capabilities needed tomorrow will permit the company to stay ahead of its competitors.

☐ And while not strictly a business condition, executives pointed to the changing personal values regarding the balance of work and personal life as a new bias in the business environment that has to be taken into account.

3. *Is the current practice of executive development working well, and how can it be changed to make it more effective?*

☐ Most managers agreed that the traditional way of identifying people for key positions will not serve the company as well in the future.

☐ A common view was that decision makers must be more willing to take risks when selecting people for management positions. This means identifying talented people earlier in their careers and planning challenging assignments for them. One executive said, "We shouldn't wait for exact fits anymore. We'll waste time and talent searching for managers with the perfect functional background, the right experiences, and a total knowledge of the markets and products. We should make the most of today's talent pool by giving them developmental assignments as soon as they are ready for such challenges."

☐ Respondents also emphasized the need to broaden the company's internal and external sources for hiring. These executives noted, too, that the company relied too heavily on its marketing department as a source of future leaders. They said other functional areas, such as finance, manufacturing, and sales, should not be overlooked as valuable reservoirs of high-potential people too. In addition, for key positions outside the United States, respondents said the company should consider recruiting local high-potential people and developing them for regional assignments.

Preparing a Profile of Colgate Leadership

The one-on-one interviews with senior management not only gave us practical information and insights on leadership development practice and philosophy at Colgate but also gave the interviewees the opportunity to describe the traits and skills they believe distinguished high-performing executives at the company.

Thus, from the interviews, we developed a composite of leadership qualities observed in the company's best-performing executives. Here are the salient attributes:

☐ *Leaders have business savvy.*

High-performing Colgate managers have an exhaustive knowledge of the business, including sales, marketing, finance, manufacturing, and other areas. This knowledge supports their decision making.

☐ *Leaders know how to use their personal influence.*

They know how to tap into and leverage corporate resources, including formal and informal networks. Their communication skills are excellent, extending upward, downward, and laterally. Similarly, their negotiating skills are well-honed.

☐ *Leaders bring a global perspective.*

Their knowledge and view of the world is broad. They demonstrate a high degree of cultural sensitivity. For instance, when they live in foreign countries, they are eager to learn the language.

☐ *Leaders have strong character.*

They talk about vision, purpose, and values with clarity. They can be counted on to do what is right. Should they be pushed to do something they oppose, they aren't reluctant to resist.

☐ *Leaders know how to manage people effectively.*

They provide the glue that holds a team together. Because they can effectively engage people, they consistently get the best performances from their team members. In addition, they are equally skilled at working with people on the outside.

☐ *Leaders act like entrepreneurs.*

This means they take risks. Because they seek results, they have become skilled at overcoming obstacles. They also have a sense of urgency that inspires them to do things fast. Most important perhaps, they are self-starters committed to their work.

Other qualities respondents mentioned less frequently should also be noted: Outstanding executives combine a big-picture perspective with analytical thinking; they know how to leverage technology; they can manage change; and they are creative individuals who inspire others to be innovators.

The Next Phase: A Top-Tier Commitment to Change

After we synthesized and analyzed the findings of these companywide interviews, it became apparent that senior management wanted a more proactive approach to leadership development because interviewees expressed skepticism toward the time-honored waiting-for-the-cream-to-rise approach.

In fact, we found consensus around a cluster of related points: Colgate must be more deliberate in identifying employees who show the potential to advance to key positions; the company must plan more systematically the career moves of high-potential people so each assignment will develop leadership capabilities; and one way to accomplish these goals would be to move high-potential people through a variety of functions and businesses in diverse geographic sites. In addition, executives agreed that the company must start identifying and planning for talented people earlier in their career paths, taking prudent risks to drive those with obvious potential onto the general management track much earlier than has been Colgate's custom.

One executive summed it up succinctly: "Let's identify people, get them out early, and really move them. And let's stick to it."

As the leaders of People Development, we knew we had to take action now. Our job was to design a leadership development strategy that would resolve the concerns raised by top managers. And it had to be a strategy that could thrive in the company's culture.

Even as we reviewed the professional literature and surveyed the best practices of other companies, we realized the only feasible way to introduce and integrate a new initiative in the Colgate culture would require the engagement of senior management [3, 4]. This was confirmed by other HR professionals at Colgate who had developed executive succession programs in the finance and manufacturing areas. The commitment we needed would directly involve all the corporate function heads and division presidents. After thinking carefully about what would be practical—and fair—to request of these executives, we decided to challenge them to make the following commitments:

☐ *To support the company's strategy of continual global growth by aggressively looking for talented employees*

For all executives, identifying high-potential people in their areas should be a top priority. In addition, executives have a responsibility to bring high-potential people to the attention of senior management.

☐ *To practice new behaviors consistently and uniformly*

A strategy to nurture future leaders can be effective only when top managers invest time and energy in the effort—and personally and collectively accept responsibility for making the process work. For example, all executives must take part in selecting high-potential people to fill the pipeline; equally important, they must spend time getting to know the high-potentials, no matter what function or business the high-potentials are in. And responsibility doesn't end there. All executives have to cooperate in assigning high-potentials to cross-divisional and cross-functional positions, even though this may seem a risky undertaking. There are ways to manage such risk. A newly assigned high-potential, for instance, could report to a seasoned manager; or a more-experienced professional could be appointed to work under the high-potential employee.

☐ *To consider the traits of high-performing executives when identifying, selecting, and evaluating high-potential people*

High-potential people should have the capacity to demonstrate the qualities captured in our initial interviews. To repeat, these include traits such as business savvy, entrepreneurial behavior, good people-management skills, and a global perspective.

☐ *To discover talented people early their careers*

High-potential people must be found early in their company tenure. This will give the organization a head start in providing them the broad-based business experiences that can serve as a foundation for their management careers. Similarly, executives must take the risk of moving untested high-potential people into positions that cross geographic and functional boundaries.

☐ *To use multiple approaches for developing high-potential people*

This can be done by shepherding high-potentials into diverse assignments, moving them into different functions, appointing them to a variety of task forces, and assigning them to special projects. High-potentials should also be encouraged to attend workshops, training courses, and executive development programs. Working in different countries will broaden their business experience and perspective, while sensitizing them to cultural diversity. Corporate positions can teach high-potentials about company resources and the most effective ways to use them. Multifaceted experiences such as these help people expand their formal and informal networks, another key advantage. Research findings support this multi-experiential approach and corroborate the conventional wisdom that people strengthen their leadership skills by being exposed to diverse bosses with different managerial and business styles [5]. One practical example Colgate used after the People Development team was instigated was to have twelve high-potential individuals from around the world facilitate and lead work sessions at Colgate's Worldwide General Management Meeting.

☐ *To look at varied sources of talent when filling vacancies*

Executives should broaden the search for general management positions by considering high-potential people in functional areas other than marketing—the traditional source for most general manager positions at Colgate. In this way, the company can balance the immediate needs of the marketplace with the long-term development of the company's next generation of leaders.

☐ *To accept increased accountability for preparing future executives*

To make a leadership development strategy a part of the culture, it is essential that division presidents and function heads share accountability with the human resource organization. Executives and the high-potentials who work with them should regularly talk about career aspirations and possible next moves for the future managers. In addition, executives should monitor the progress of each high-potential, intervening when necessary to keep a developmental plan on course or to help alter it if the individual's aspirations or personal circumstances change. If a high-potential's assignment involves risk, the executive should be prepared to help handle and minimize that risk. At appropriate intervals, executives should provide insightful feedback. And if the view of someone's potential changes, it is the executive's responsibility to recommend removing that individual from the talent pool.

Putting a Priority on Work Experience

We made one more request of the senior executives we had interviewed. We asked them to expand their monthly meetings by adding a leadership development segment focused solely on the developmental needs of the company's high-potential people. During this session, executives would discuss high-potential individuals case by case, exploring the work experience and professional training each person needed to move ahead in his or her career. The discussion of each high-potential would end with a committee decision on the next two work assignments determined to be the most beneficial for the candidate.

Because we understood the company's culture, we decided it was best to focus initially on developing the high-potentials through work experience. Many companies, we knew, shape their leadership development strategy around a strong education component, teaching people new concepts, skills, and behaviors in formal and informal classes, programs, and seminars [5, 6, 7]. But we knew this approach didn't match the Colgate mind-set. Executives across the company share a tacit assumption that to be successful at Colgate, you need to understand how the company really operates. This translates into actually learning how to do marketing, finance, and other functions the way Colgate does business.

Another reason for taking the experiential approach was our knowledge of research, which shows that 50 percent of learning takes place through work experience, 30 percent happens through interpersonal relationships with bosses, peers, subordinates, and professional contacts, and 20 percent occurs through formal education and training [8]. Even Steve Kerr, director of General Electric's Crotonville School, notes that the majority of significant learning experiences occur on the job and not from formal training [9].

A New Role for Human Resources

From the start, the People Development team understood that this course of change couldn't be limited to the participation of Colgate's top executives. To get a leadership development program up and running, the roles and responsibilities of the Global Human Resource Department and the human resource executives in the divisions and functions had to be clarified, even expanded. Following are the recommendations we presented to these units.

At the corporate level, Global Human Resources would have the job of ensuring that high-potentials get superior developmental opportunities by encouraging every executive to design assignments that provide broad-based business experiences and build leadership skills. Global HR would be responsible for tracking such assignments and for recommending a process to move people in and out of the jobs. Global HR would also advocate the movement of high-potentials into positions across the business and functional areas of the company. In addition, Global HR would design tools and techniques for executives to use in identifying and tracking high-potentials, thus ensuring uniform standards and a consistent approach across the company.

To be most effective at moving talented people into critical openings, Global HR had some homework to do. It required getting to know the high-potential people and understanding their individual preferences and career aspirations. Moreover, Global HR would now track the progress of each global high-potential.

The responsibilities of HR executives in the divisions and functions were equally important. Getting to know the high-potentials—their experiences, plans, and aspirations—would be top priority in the divisions and functions. This would support the relationship-building process essential to the HR function of advising people on career options and would make it more feasible to keep track of a high-potential's progress. HR executives across the company would also be valuable sources of feedback on the high-potential people.

Revisiting Top Management, Finding Consensus, Getting Buy-in

Once we had formulated the commitments we would seek from senior managers, the next step was to revisit the top twenty senior managers—the division presidents, function heads, and the chief operating officer—who had participated in our initial interviews. This return engagement would serve a host of objectives:

☐ Assure executives that their leadership development concerns were being addressed in a thoughtful, timely manner

☐ Review the major findings of the interviews

☐ Allow the opportunity to assess the validity of key conclusions and to decide on the feasibility of implementing changes called for by a new leadership development strategy

☐ Provide a forum to reach consensus in potentially sensitive areas, such as the validity of the leadership profile generated from the interviews, the possibility of becoming more flexible in sourcing future leaders, the imperative for more risk taking, and the ideal size of the talent pool

☐ Start the process of identifying the first pool of global high-potential people

☐ Win the buy-in of our top executive team as early as possible in the process.

This follow-up presentation was a success, with only minor revisions made to our set of recommendations. These revisions were incorporated into a second presentation made to CEO Reuben Mark, who was deeply involved in developing the company's next generation of leaders. Mark offered his personal support to play a visible role in accelerating the leadership development initiative.

Now the initiative had the endorsement of the very top leaders—support essential for making the program work in Colgate's culture.

Filling the Talent Pool

The stage was now set for the People Development team to launch the company's first formal leadership development program for general managers. We began by breaking the initiative into parts that could be rolled out smoothly and quickly across the company. The first task was a critical one—picking the individuals to fill the first company-wide pool of high-potential people.

The most direct way to create this first pool was to ask the top executives to identify a number of high-potential people from their own organizations. Each senior manager was asked to name those people who had the potential to become a general manager in the next five years. As part of this process, senior managers were also asked to identify at least five people who were in an early stage of their career—people with two to four years of work experience—who might eventually become general managers.

Our priorities at this time were helping the senior team become comfortable with the idea of developing a global talent pool and having that team accept the discipline of identifying high-potential people early in their careers. So, aside from showing the potential to take on a general manager position in the next five years, the qualifications we recommended for high-potential candidates were broad. We asked that candidates consistently demonstrate exceptional performance, that candidates give strong evidence that they could learn from experience, and that candidates express a willingness to relocate wherever the company needs them worldwide.

Because we believed discussions about specific competencies could seriously sidetrack the entire leadership development initiative, we did not present the senior managers with a set of competencies to focus on in their selection process. Nor did we give them the leadership profile developed from our initial interviews. (This profile comprised the leadership qualities the managers had cited as the best indicators of high performance.) In short, the qualifications for high-potential people were intentionally ambiguous, leaving open the possibility that the senior team would use very different standards in the selection process.

Once candidates for the first high-potential pool were named, we began the process of reviewing their credentials, aspirations, and developmental needs during the new leadership development segment at the senior managers' monthly meetings. As mentioned before, the purpose of this session was to decide on two successive work assignments for each high-potential that would maximize his or her professional growth. Our goal was to assess eight to twelve high-potentials a month. Follow-up would come from the managers themselves, as they were responsible for tracking the individual to make sure the recommended actions were carried out.

A Tool Kit for Individual Development Planning

The success of the new leadership development strategy will depend largely on how well the senior management team can make assignment decisions that match the professional and personal aspirations of each candidate. Fortunately, the team is helped in this decision-making process by the results of an independent development-planning initiative launched in the fall of 1996 by the People Development team.

We believe development planning is a powerful process that can empower people with the knowledge, skills, and behaviors they need to excel in the global business environment. Careful development planning can help people improve job performance, achieve professional growth, and increase personal satisfaction. It is, in short, a practical tool that people can use to support their career and development goals.

People involved in development planning first evaluate their own competencies, weighing their relative strengths and pinpointing their developmental needs. They use this evaluation to decide which specific actions to take to reach their professional career goals. This analysis is intense and demands objectivity and realism. But the exploration pays off by giving people a better understanding of their professional expectations and a more focused direction to their career. Following through on the action plan will bring benefits too, including an increase in the high-potential's effectiveness on the job.

Because development planning is new to many people and can be difficult to do on one's own, People Development designed a self-paced, three-piece tool kit to guide high-potential individuals through the process—from learning what development planning is to completing an individual development plan. The first piece of the tool kit, *Managing Your Professional Development: Your Guide to Individual Development Planning (IDP),* is a step-by-step manual that states the responsibilities of people for their own professional planning and clarifies the roles of both the individual and the manager in the development process.

The manual breaks the development planning process into six sequential steps:

☐ Assessing individual competencies and values

☐ Defining personal strengths, developmental needs, and options for career growth

☐ Identifying developmental actions

☐ Crafting an individual development plan

☐ Meeting with one's manager to discuss findings and to decide together on a course of action for the Individual Development Plan

☐ Accepting the challenge of managing professional development by implementing the Individual Development Plan.

The next piece of the tool kit is a set of five worksheets that high-potentials work with to further define and clarify their personal attributes:

1. They start with a confidential **Competency Assessment** to determine how effectively they demonstrate leadership and management skills and how well they accomplish the tasks demanded in their current position. It also prompts people on how to set priorities for their own developmental needs. To help the user with this worksheet, a completed sample is provided in the tool kit.

2. The **Personal Values Survey** helps people gain a better understanding of their deepest values. For purposes of the survey, values are divided into five broad categories. In the first group are work environment needs, such as the need for challenge, visibility, or a predictable workday. Second are work relationship needs, like the preference for working autonomously, the need for camaraderie on the job, or the attraction to assignments that offer variety. The third category looks at work task needs, such as one's disposition toward work that offers opportunities for being creative, for making decisions, or for attending to detail. The fourth category examines lifestyle needs, and the fifth, personal needs. These cover such things as geographic preferences, how people feel about taking on demanding work,

and how important it is to have ample time to spend with family and friends. The values survey is also confidential.

3. The **Development Activities Chart** breaks out on-the-job learning and development opportunities that derive from particular activities. This exhaustive list is designed to inspire professionals to take charge of their own development by exploiting routinely available opportunities, such as teamwork.

4. A companion piece, the **Global Training Curriculum Grids,** links the company's courses and seminars to the competencies they are designed to strengthen. Presented in easy-to-read charts, the guides are organized by business function—finance, marketing, sales, manufacturing and engineering, and research and development. Completing this guide is a chart that shows how each of the leadership and management programs supports specific competencies.

5. With the fifth worksheet, the **Individual Development Plan,** the high-potentials transform the awareness they've gained so far into a course of action. A sample IDP is included in the tool kit to help guide users through this work. High-potentials' completed IDPs will serve as their blueprints for reaching their short- and long-term career objectives.

The third component of the tool kit, *Defining and Understanding Global Competencies,* is a concise reference guide designed to encourage and ensure that people across the company speak a universal language when talking about the skills required for business success. The guide is dictionary-like, defining the range of management and leadership skills as well as the functional competencies that the company values. It also describes some behaviors associated with each competency to illustrate either strength or weakness. For example, the management competency of *team building* is defined as "creating a commitment to common goals." An individual who "provides clear direction and defines priorities" demonstrates strength in team building. On the other hand, somebody who doesn't readily share information with colleagues gives evidence of a developmental need in this area.

Once the set of worksheets is completed and participants have drafted their IDP(s), the next step for the high-potentials is to discuss the results of this personal review with their managers. While each development planning session will take its unique course, the goal here is for the manager and the high-potential to talk openly and realistically about objectives, to reach agreement about future development actions, and to set a time frame for completing the plan. At this point, it is up to the high-potential to set the plan in motion and plunge into the process of professional development.

Finding Favor Company-Wide

As we write this chapter, we are still in the early stages of rolling out the leadership development strategy. Yet companywide, favorable signals already indicate that the initiative is gaining acceptance. For example, the senior executives clearly took some risks in selecting the more than one hundred high-potential people who are in the first pool of global talent. Many of these are people are being placed in extremely challenging assignments that wouldn't have been available to them before the leadership development strategy got under way.

Another positive sign is that the senior managers no longer give top priority to just filling job vacancies. Instead, they think ahead about the developmental needs of each high-potential, asking what assignment will deliver the most benefit to which individual. And they aren't doing this in a vacuum. They are asking for the high-potentials' IDPs so they can feel confident that the planned moves will align well with the individuals' needs and aspirations.

In fact, signs are so strong that the new leadership development strategy is a good fit for Colgate that we are now planning to expand the initiative to positions beyond general manager. The first expansion will focus on identifying people who show the potential to become marketing directors within the next five years.

Once this is in place, we will again expand the program to include people identified as good prospects for sales director positions in the next five years. With one exception, the selection and development process for both groups will be identical to that designed for general management. Because the demands on the senior managers would become overwhelming, this team will not be involved in managing the development of the high-potential people in these two groups. This work will fall to the senior marketing team and to senior sales executives.

As mentioned earlier, Colgate's finance and manufacturing groups have had leadership development strategies in place for several years. So, once our planned expansions in leadership development in marketing and sales take place, a high-potential pool will exist for each critical function.

Looking Ahead: Some Resistance to Change

Because the People Development team must continue adding value to this initiative, we are looking ahead and trying to anticipate possible stumbling blocks to its progress. So, even as the work moves forward, we are figuring out solutions to potential problems.

For example, we know the company still has some managers who will be reluctant to tinker with the tradition of just letting the management cream rise. After all, this is the way they and their peers rose to the top-management ranks—and it sure seems to have worked. One of their legitimate questions: Why take the risk of shifting to a proactive process that identifies and prepares high-potential people so early in their careers? To offset this anxiety over change, the People Development team focused part of its strategy on getting the full commitment of Colgate's senior-most management *before* introducing the program to managers company-wide.

Here are other problems we may face down the road, followed by some steps we're taking now to avert, or at least minimize, such obstacles:

☐ *Managers may be reluctant to assign high-potential people to responsible positions "too early" in their careers.* A number of Colgate businesses around the world have been identified as starting points for the first-time general manager. Most of these businesses typically generate $5 million to $50 million in revenue. So, People Development pinpointed Colgate's smaller subsidiaries—generating revenues roughly between $5 million and $25 million—as good stretch opportunities for high-potentials. These businesses may also be located in countries with less-heated competitive environments. Or the business may not have manufacturing or may carry fewer product lines and therefore be a less complex operation to manage.

☐ *Managers may resist moving high-potential people or may favor a candidate who isn't from the high-potential population.* Colgate's second-in-command, Chief Operating Officer Bill Shanahan, and the head of HR, Bob Joy, are both taking a very active—and visible—role in promoting the candidacies of high-potentials. In fact, they are very directive in ensuring challenging growth positions for the global pool of high-potential people. Both executives are, in effect, asking managers to exchange their "local hats" for "global hats" by taking a chance on the high-potentials. By exerting their influence in this way, top decision makers are demonstrating Colgate's commitment to nurture the company's global high-potential population.

☐ *Managers may fear the loss of high-potential people if job assignments are made that don't match their individual professional or personal goals.* To avoid working in a vacuum and making independent decisions about people's careers, we are taking steps to increase the flow of information between high-potential people and the senior team. Most important, we want to make sure that executives review the completed Individual Development Plans of high-potentials *before* decisions are made about their next two assignments. In addition, we now provide a summary of key operating jobs open worldwide to all general managers so they are aware of these opportunities when decisions on new work assignments are being made.

These examples epitomize the work we're doing now to overcome current and future management obstacles, recognizing of course that resistance is inherent in any change process. Before moving away from this point, it should be noted that we are now working on ways to encourage and support the focus on People Development. One idea being considered is the creation of a recognition program that singles out managers who effectively manage people.

Keeping Talented People on Board

When looking ahead, the People Development team also anticipates difficulties that the high-potentials themselves will pose. Again, we've already begun work to counteract certain conditions as much as possible. Here are the likely key issues and some steps we're taking to deal with them.

☐ *High-potential people are reluctant to accept assignments in less attractive locations.* Creative compensation packages are being offered to high-potentials who take assignments in less-developed areas. Additional incentives in these packages can include the typical post allowance (an amount of money that accrues in a special account for the employee while on assignment) plus a mobility premium and a special retention bonus that is paid out after a specified period of time in the assignment location.

We make an international move easier for family members too by offering them cross-cultural orientation programs and language training. We also provide the spouse $7,500 to use for things like buying computer equipment, maintaining contact with a current employer, or starting a new business. The spouse can also participate in the tuition reimbursement program. Rest and recreation breaks, as well as special shopping trips, are other incentives for people working in less-developed areas.

☐ *High-potential people will be recruitment targets for other companies.* We are trying to avoid these circumstances by encouraging managers to meet regularly with high-potentials to discuss the careers they can expect at Colgate. The local and divisional human resource staffs are responsible for supporting managers in this effort. Obviously it will take a dedicated team effort to retain today's most talented people.

In addition, Colgate has designed a financial incentive specifically for managers in developing countries where competing firms are more aggressive in their efforts to recruit Colgate's experienced local managers.

Clearly, as the leadership development program takes root, other snags are bound to occur. But the strong acceptance of the initiative to date gives us confidence that whatever problems arise will be managed by Human Resources and the company's executive team.

Some Lessons Learned

Remembering that we are still relatively early in this leadership development journey, we present some of the key lessons we've already learned.

1. *Colgate will realize the full value of the leadership development strategy when the general managers take ownership of the program.* When we launched this initiative, we zeroed in on gaining the support of the top executives. But the program's long-term effectiveness will hinge on the support and active participation of the general managers. In an effort to educate and involve this important group, we will soon distribute a handbook that explains the strategic importance of the program and defines the general manager's role in the process. We will reinforce this information by having members of the People Development team meet one-on-one with selected general man-

agers worldwide to explore the challenges and the impact of the leadership development initiative.

2. *The leadership development strategy is most effective when it is aligned with other HR practices.* As we continue to focus on leadership development, we will look for new opportunities to link our efforts with other HR initiatives. Compensation, training, and sourcing are among the first areas where we will work to create an alignment that reinforces the various activities. We will also partner with HR colleagues to discover new ways to strengthen how we manage our high-potentials around the world.

3. *The criteria for identifying high-potential people must be uniform across the company.* Managers find it hard to distinguish between employees who are high-potentials and high-performers. The distinction we want managers to make is that high-potential people demonstrate the capability to function in a senior role. The process of developing consensus around more precise criteria will take time.

4. *The organization must figure out ways to motivate high-performing employees who are not included in the high-potential pool.* Only about 5 percent of Colgate's people are designated as high-potential employees (these people generally are told that they are extremely valuable to the company but are not specifically told they have been designated as high-potential). So we must find ways to challenge the rest of the work force to continue reaching for high-performance standards. In addition, we must find ways to reward high-performers throughout their careers.

5. *The leadership profile is most useful as a blueprint for the specific qualities and competencies we want to develop in high-potential people.* Once we compiled the leadership development profile—a summary of the skills and competencies valued by Colgate's senior managers—there was a temptation to use this as the criteria for selecting the first pool of high-potential people. But research and discussion persuaded us that the most crit-

ical qualification is the ability to learn from work experiences. If we give efficient learners the right experiences, they will develop the skills valued by the company's senior managers.

6. *Mechanisms must be designed for following up on development plans.* We are scrupulously tracking development decisions to be sure intentions translate into actions. If, for example, the senior management team decides that a certain high-potential needs to be moved into a more challenging position in five months, that individual is added to the agenda of the managers' monthly meeting five months forward. More mechanisms like this must be created to track decisions, career moves, and other developmental activities.

7. *Finally, we are dedicated to building synergy by looking at apparently non-related company events, decisions, and changes as opportunities to promote the leadership development initiative.* For example, when we learn of an upcoming meeting of general managers or other senior managers, we attempt to expand the meeting by adding a presentation on leadership development. With the visible support of the company's top executives, we have been successful in most of these efforts. We're confident that by taking advantage of the right opportunities at the right time, we will enjoy some big payoffs.

A Means for Measuring Success

Once the leadership development program is fully in place, we will be responsible for both continuing the development of high-potentials in the first pool and overseeing the discovery of new management candidates. The increasing depth of the candidate pool will be a clear sign of People Development's effectiveness in building the high-potential population.

In line with our focus on the high-potentials, we will continue to work with managers at all levels and with the HR professionals who partner with them. Our role here is to support their local efforts to develop the high-potentials. As top executives and managers create new opportunities for grooming potential managers, we will score this as a success for the new leadership development strategy.

People Development will also continue generating candidate lists of high-potentials to fill the vacancies worldwide for general managers and other key operating jobs. Today, some 1,000 jobs fall under this umbrella. If the leadership development program is succeeding, Colgate will have plenty of managers to support its continued global expansion. In the next year or so, for instance, we expect to handle several hundred job openings annually. One indicator of our success will be how fast and how accurately People Development can identify high-potentials who are the right matches for these positions. Another sign of success will be when managers take the risk of selecting recommended high-potentials instead of hiring people who are more familiar to them.

Most important, we will measure the progress of this strategy by monitoring the careers of the high-potentials, zeroing in on whether or not—and how quickly—they move up the career ladder at Colgate. Another key metric will be the feedback from the high-potentials themselves. If they tell us they are satisfied with their careers at Colgate, and if their retention rates remain high, we will know we have reached our goals and that the leadership development strategy is making a difference.

The real-world measure of success, of course, will be the magnitude of Colgate's performance in the global marketplace. If the company can keep expanding, can keep satisfying its customers, and can keep leading its competitors, we will confidently assert that the leadership development and executive succession strategy has helped secure the future of Colgate's profitability and growth.

References

1. Towers Perrin. "Priorities for Competitive Advantage," Research report, New York: Towers Perrin, 1992.

2. Ulrich, D. and Eichinger, R. "State of the Art '96," Paper presented at the annual meeting of the Human Resource Planning Society, Palm Springs, Calif.: Apr. 1996.

3. Burke, W. W. and Litwin, G. H. "A Causal Model of Organizational Performance and Change." *Journal of Management,* Vol. 18, No. 3, 1992, pp. 523–545.

4. Beer, M. "Critical Path to Corporate Renewal: Developing Human Resources While Focusing on the Business." *Proceedings of the 1991 Corporate Sponsor Forum of the Human Resource Planning Society,* 1991, pp. 13–66.

5. McCall, M. W., Lombardo, M. M., and Morrison, A. M. *The Lessons of Experience.* Lexington, Mass.: Lexington Books, 1988.

6. Baird, L., et al. "World Class Executive Development." *Human Resource Planning,* Vol. 17, No. 1, 1991, pp. 1–13.

7. McCall, M. W. "Executive Development As a Business Strategy." *Journal of Business Strategy,* Jan.–Feb. 1992, pp. 25–31.

8. Dodge, B. "Empowerment and the Evolution of Learning." *Education and Training,* Vol. 35, No. 5, 1993, pp. 3–10.

9. Sherman, S. "How Tomorrow's Best Leaders Are Learning Their Stuff." *Fortune,* Nov. 27, 1995, pp. 90–106.

6

Creating a Global World-Class Investment Bank Through Transformational Human Resource Development

STEPHEN JOHN, ED.D.

Introduction

I knocked gingerly at the door of a small office cluttered with computer equipment, cell phones, fax machines, and so forth. The young managing director I was about to interview concerning our human resource initiatives was screaming at a colleague in Europe through the speaker phone about the sad state of affairs in the newly merged organization. He didn't know how he could go on doing global investment banking deals with organizational conditions as they currently existed. He closed the call with an epithet to senior leadership about how well the integration was going: "Bull!" He said the only thing senior leadership had integrated was office space, and it had done a poor job at that. Where were the global teams to serve global clients, where were the right people for the right teams, and where were the new prospects for deals to come from?

As he said good-bye to his colleague, he spun around to face me. He sighed wearily. He had forgotten he promised to give me an hour of his time early in the day, and his day was already not going well. His eyes were dark, and he started the interview by clearing his throat and sniffling. He never stopped sniffling for the entire interview. Airplane air plus incredible levels of stress can do that to the youngest and healthiest. He had returned to New York from London the night before and had gotten very little sleep. Sleep was a rare commodity for him lately, for he had to go to London almost every Sunday now that the integration had occurred. He didn't look very happy for a twenty-nine-year old executive who had just planned and executed one of the most exotic and profitable deals in the investment banking world.

"These deals are the future for us. I know it," he blurted out before I had a chance to tell him my specific purpose for the interview. The old-fashioned, plain-vanilla deals, which involve bonds and common and preferred stock, were no longer profitable or fun to do. Exotic deals, on the other hand, which used derivatives, hedge contracts, and swaps, required enormous energy to create and execute and could be extremely profitable, although they were very risky to all parties—the business seeking the deal, the investment bank structuring the deal, and the public investors whose money financed the deal. Here was a wide-open area in which to compete against the Top 5 investment banks. These exotic deals were new to everyone. No one had a competitive advantage *yet*.

He spoke rapidly, without stopping, about the kind of people and organization it would take to make SBC Warburg (SBCW), the investment banking division of Swiss Bank Corporation, one of the Top 5 in the investment banking world. He rattled off the criteria: "Number One—it's client focus, pure and simple. The client wants and needs teams of specialists from all regions of the world and all technical specialties. Number Two—the clients want the best and brightest thinking on their deals, which means we've got to know who out there [in SBCW] knows what about what. And Number Three—the client expects complex deals to be flawlessly executed, which requires the right technology in the hands of the right people at the right time. I need all three to deliver value to my clients and one other thing—sweepers. You know, they're the the people who scour the world looking for deals to feed to the team. Sweepers can make or break my career and the bank's chance at the Top 5. That's why I'm in London every Sunday to Wednesday, lighting a fire under the sweepers to sweep. I used to know all the sweepers on a first-name basis before the integration. There's so much noise in the organization here, so many new people, so many people leaving. What's senior management doing? I can't do it all."

It's an all-too-familiar story in today's business environment. An industry changes the way it does business in a fundamental way, but senior management in some organizations insists on maintaining the status quo. To compound the problem, competition from previously unheard of places comes out and "eats the lunch" of industry incumbents.

It happened to auto and electronic manufacturers more than a decade ago. Insurance brokers and underwriters, as well as accounting and tax firms, have also felt the pain of major changes in the way they do business. Revolutionary industry changes have now hit Wall Street-type firms, especially investment banks, and most don't seem to like it one bit. Major pockets of resistance in these firms have surfaced, hoping that the good old days will be back before long.

Swiss Bank Corporation is an exception. While still reeling from three major acquisitions in as many years, senior leadership identified the changes necessary to make SBC Warburg one of the Top 5 investment banks and began the journey to make these changes a reality. Along the way, senior leadership would have to find answers to a number of critical questions. What was the role of senior leadership in the new organization? How could global teams be formed quickly and efficiently across regions (continents), functions (product and service lines), and organizational boundaries? Which individuals had which skills and competencies now to serve on a team? What competencies could junior people start developing to be team leaders in the future? Where were the technology platforms to support global product and service delivery teams?

The answers to these questions would require focused direction-setting from senior leadership, a transformed HR function, and cross-regional/functional cooperation that has never been seen on the Wall Street landscape. Marcel Ospel (CEO), Roland Wodjewodski (CEO–Switzerland, Latin America), and Robert Zeltner (global head of HR) were three board members, however, who were ready to catapult SBC Warburg toward its vision.

Background—The Investment Banking Industry

The investment banking industry, responsible for routing trillions of dollars around the world, has undergone tremendous change in the 1990s. For decades the Top 5 investment banks have dominated this industry. They have thrived in a business environment where clients selected investment banks primarily based on reputation and rank. All five of these banks originated in the United States and have spent considerable sums of money to develop sophisticated products and services, technology systems, and reward and development processes for their employees. These banks now face competition from both the United States and Europe. The Solomon professor of finance at New York University, Professor Ingo Walter, suggested that in addition to these five, at least twenty-five organizations have publicly stated that they intend to be one of the Top 5 investment banks by the year 2000.

Just what do investment banks do? Investment banks design and develop financial products and services for existing businesses to expand current operations or to create new lines of business. In addition, they provide financial products and services for start-up businesses. Finally, these banks provide expert advice on how to restructure business operations, including mergers and acquisitions. These products and services, such as the creation and sale of stocks and bonds, options, and derivative products, are considered complex financial instruments. Huge sums of money flow from investors into these products and then to the business organizations that need capital for their operations. The investment bank makes its profits from the creation and sale of these financial products, as well as from professional advice to client organizations.

The services required by investment banking clients have changed in a fundamental way over the last few years. Global teams of highly specialized technical talent using sophisticated technology are now needed to service global clients. For example, a start-up business in Malaysia may seek its capital in Germany, with investment bankers from London served by technology systems built and operated in Japan.

Providing these services has implications for the kind of talent and skills sought by investment banks. Formerly, the major criteria for employment at these banks were client relationship ability, technical skills, and a deep desire to accumulate substantial personal wealth early in one's career. Today's emphasis on global service teams now requires competencies for building cross-cultural and cross-product-line teams, as well as for leadership and management.

Taken together, all these factors require that investment banks critically examine the roles of senior leadership and the banks' human resources—in particular, how they recruit and develop their talent. Where appropriate, these banks must make incremental or transformational change to these roles, functions, or processes. This case focuses on how SBC Warburg utilized HR development to start the transformational changes required to attain its goal of being ranked as one of the Top 5 investment banks.

Overview of SBC

Swiss Bank Corporation (SBC) is more than one hundred years old. SBC was basically a commercial bank (which handles loans to businesses and individuals, checking account services, lines of credit, and so forth), not an investment bank (which creates equity [stock] and debt [bond] instruments for sale to investors to finance new and existing businesses). SBC did engage in some small investment bank deals, mostly in the United States. To do so, it had to utilize other licensed investment banks as the primary deal makers through a series of acquisitions because investment banks are heavily regulated and because each country has its own laws and regulations governing which banks can engage in investment banking.

In the 1980s, however, SBC decided to enter the investment banking industry as a major player. To do so, senior management decided to gain the investment banking expertise it needed.

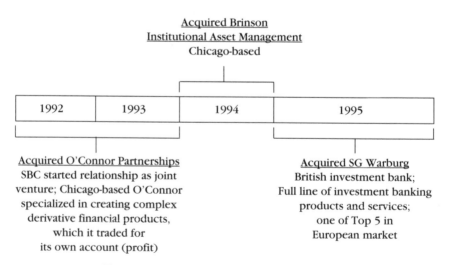

FIGURE 6-1. SBC ACQUISITION TIMELINE.

This decision proved successful until the bank made its third acquisition in 1995. The difficulty of maintaining profitability through the integration process (that is, absorbing a British investment bank) caused senior management to re-examine its approach. The amount of capital required to keep SBC growing into one of the Top 5 global banks would be staggering; but, of more importance, senior leadership understood that integrating the cultures of these vastly different organizations was its real leadership challenge. The senior leadership urgently recognized that its focus had to be on leading and managing the bank into the Top 5, not on acquiring its way in, because the latter would not enable the bank to sustain its position over the long term. In August 1995, senior leadership came to Human Resources for advice and assistance in creating a large-scale culture integration effort.

The Problem

Typically, Wall Street-type firms have not modeled world-class HR practices, especially leadership and management practices. Nor are they known for teamwork and cooperation across regions or technical specialties. Recent books, articles, and Hollywood movies portray Wall Street as placing little value on respecting employees in general or valuing employees who can lead and manage. These popular characterizations show people who are better at manipulating and outwitting fellow employees, along with the competition. They show that individuals are rewarded for revenue generation capabilities and contribution to the bottom line, not for leading teams.

Wall Street does have its exceptions. JP Morgan's culture is described as professional, collegial, and team-focused. JP Morgan has made substantial investments in leadership and management development, as well as in performance management, having established a process that focuses on teams as well as individuals. Like SBC, JP Morgan was also a successful commercial bank; however, the latter had been continually building its investment bank operations for the last fifteen years. SBC was not content to wait fifteen years to build a performance-based culture.

One other salient, people-related issue concerns the industry practice of selecting the very best and brightest (and perhaps greediest) recent university graduates. The Generation X population is now the primary demographic group recruited. Major shifts in Generation Xers' values from those of prior generations regarding work and what they expect from employers, as well as what they will give to employers, have caused turmoil in retaining the best and brightest for SBC. Generation Xers want to work on the biggest and most challenging deals, use the latest technology, be well paid (now), and be promoted to senior advisory positions quickly—some say in nanosecond time periods. They are also intensely interested in working on teams with people from other cultures. Only the top investment banks will be able to satisfy this generation's needs and wants. The term used in the industry for such banks is *the gorillas* (that is, the strongest of jungle creatures). Only the gorillas will have the deals that provide the "juice" (profits) to fund the people and technology systems to create and execute more deals. As noted above, it also appears that the "juice" is found in exotic deals, which require global teams and sophisticated technology. These business requirements match nicely with the Generation Xer wish list.

To summarize the problem, the individual contributor working against everyone in and outside the organization for personal gain is no longer a viable business model. Global investment banking must be done by cross-cultural and specialty teams, which in turn must be led and managed professionally to ensure profitable results over the long term. This requires highly specialized technical employees to be team players and to take on leadership roles when needed. These employees must clearly understand what contributions and competencies are needed for success. Each team must learn as a team and then transfer that learning across the organization to leverage the high cost of recruiting and developing technical talent [1]. Finally, the role of senior leadership must become one of fostering an environment that supports team as well as individual accomplishment.

Taming the Gorilla

As mentioned above, senior leadership came to HR in August 1995 seeking advice and counsel. It asked for two major items: (1) a performance and leadership competency framework and implementation plan for moving SBC to a professionally led and managed bank and (2) a performance framework that emphasized contribution measures in addition to revenue or profits. Senior leadership understood it was, in fact, asking for a transformational culture change—from the current culture to a culture that recognized and rewarded what people contributed, as well as how they contributed it.

The Impact of the O'Connor Acquisition

SBC, as a commercial bank, always had a well-regarded management development process, which included both group training programs and key developmental work assignments. Commercial bankers had the opportunity to develop client relationship skills, as well as management, leadership, and team-building skills. In fact, some mid-1980s internal publications referenced learning-organization concepts (that is, the ability of all employees, managers in particular, to create and share learning across the organization) as critical to the bank's global success. In addition, Fitz-Enz [2] cites SBC as an example of an organization that had in place a well-defined performance management process that required managers to coach, mentor, and develop their direct reports. This process emphasized contribution measures in addition to economic ones or profit. Jim Minogue, a senior human resource executive, had moved these initiatives toward world-class status prior to the O'Connor acquisition. Then something happened.

The O'Connor acquisition apparently resulted in major changes to all of these processes. The O'Connor Partnerships, formed in 1982, specialized in creating complex financial instruments called derivatives (which it traded for its own account, meaning it did not have external clients). This partnership became successful and attracted highly technical individuals who wanted to acquire significant wealth: the traditional Wall Street individual. There was a total of 600 employees in O'Connor, 25 of whom were partners, when SBC acquired the company in 1992.

The O'Connor organization believed almost entirely in strong technical education, leading-edge technology, and rewarding individual achievement for economic contribution. As a result, formal management-development activity outside of Switzerland slowed or stopped completely. O'Connor's culture and values about developing and leading people clashed with the bank's but, in most respects, became the dominant culture and set of beliefs, even though the Warburg investment bank acquisition was considerably larger in dollar size and employee population. Some people in the new organization referred to the partners as the Wolfpack or the Boyz in the Hood. One wag in the new organization who had spent several years in one of the rough-and-tumble Top 5 investment banks wrote his interpretation of how people were treated during this time (see Table 6-1). Secretly many employees hoped the conservative and professionally led Warburg organization would reign. However, Warburg's financial performance had faltered in recent years, and its people were not in a position to secure high-level and influential positions in the new organization. Many Warburg people left as a result of this situation.

Although the situation looked bleak from a leadership and human relations perspective, there were bright spots on the horizon. Several executives had been recruited from outside SBC or its acquired companies. Roland Wodjewodski had been recruited from JP Morgan and would play a pivotal role in what happened next.

TABLE 6-1.
PROGRESSIVE DISCIPLINE MODEL.

Level 1—Reprimand	1–2 minutes corrective discipline for a small performance gap
Level 2—Slapping	5–15 minutes for a serious performance gap; meant to teach a lesson; degrees are mild (in passing), intense (normal level), and vicious (he had it coming)
Level 3—Flogging	30 minutes or more for major performance gap that a slapping won't cure; given in private or public depending on impact and repetitive nature of gap
Level 4—Face Ripping	1 hour or more, used when employee is not getting the message on major performance gap after repeated floggings; sometimes in severe situations, first three levels are bypassed, and manager goes directly to a face ripping
Level 5—Execution	Self-explanatory

Preparing for Transformational Change—Reorganizing HR

Prior to the July 1995 Warburg acquisition, SBC had created a Human Resources Planning and Development (HRPD) function within each regional HR department. Three such departments existed: one in Zurich, one in New York, and one in Singapore. I was responsible for HRPD–New York. HRPD used an organizational development process as its operating framework. The business strategy was analyzed, and current human resource processes, such as recruiting, development, rewards, and succession planning, were evaluated for their impact and effectiveness on business imperatives. Weekly conference calls between the three regions, as well as face-to-face meetings in Zurich approximately every six to eight weeks, enabled the HRPD heads to coordinate regional efforts with global requirements. There were also a substantial number of people and business operations in London. However, HR management in London chose not to have an HRPD function but rather had a senior HR executive represent its views at the weekly conference calls.

Senior management, in January 1995, was convinced that the HR function needed to be globalized, meaning each HR professional would be responsible for all HR processes for all regions of the bank. As a result, HRPD became a globalized function similar to the business units. This meant that all HR processes would be developed with global requirements first, and needed regional modifications would follow.

In the late summer of 1995, a global HRPD team was formed, with Otto Jaggy as the new head. He had been recruited from an industrial company headquartered in Switzerland. HRPD was renamed Sourcing and Development (see Figure 6-2). The business strategy was to focus first on building a strong presence in Europe, followed by the United States and Asia as the year 2000 approached. In the fall of 1995, I relocated from the United States to Zurich to define and implement organizational learning and development processes.

Two initiatives became the foundation work for the newly formed Sourcing and Development Department as a result of the September 1995 board of directors meeting. These two major initiatives were: (1) a world-class performance management process based on contribution *and* competency and (2) a formal develop-

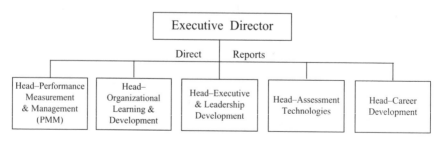

FIGURE 6-2. SOURCING AND DEVELOPMENT TEAM STRUCTURE.

ment process for potential executive and leadership talent. The board was silent on developing a process for cross-regional/functional teams. Everyone, however, wasn't on board with these two initiatives. I overheard a powerful managing director (from the O'Connor Partnerships) saying, "There's no time for 'kumbayah' in this bank," in reference to measuring more than profit and loss performance and to developing leaders to run the business. In contrast, Wodjewodski, as well as Marcel Ospel and Bob Zeltner, fully supported these two initiatives. They were also on the investment bank's board of directors, which added substantially to their global influence.

Two major points were now surfacing in the organization: (1) only hard data were acceptable for measuring economic contribution, (profit and loss) and (2) increases in technical expertise and technology skills were more important than increases in leadership skills and, therefore, should be rewarded more. Underlying these points was a major difference in how senior leaders thought about the investment banking industry. Some viewed the industry as composed of businesses to be managed, while others saw it as composed of deal makers in a game of chance that required street smarts and shrewdness, not business and leadership skills. This dichotomy of opinion was found not only at the work-unit level but on the board as well. This duel between opposing mind-sets would ultimately slow down—but not stop—the transformation process that started with the board's request for a performance measurement and management process, and a leadership development processes.

What We Did

Sourcing and Development (S&D) went right to work. The two major initiatives would require a multidisciplinary team that did not yet exist. Recruiting efforts were under way for an assessment technologist, a management trainer, and a career-development specialist, as well as for administrative support in Zurich and London. External consultants would be utilized where appropriate internal skills were missing.

First Things First—October

The board, as part of its mandate, insisted that the performance management process that would be recommended by S&D be in place by year-end of 1995. The leadership development process would also have to be designed and implemented in the first quarter of 1996. That left less than ninety days to design, develop, and trial a new performance management process for the board and the 125 managing directors. (The officer title structure in SBCW was, from highest to lowest, managing director, executive director, director, and associate director.) A task force was formed of the S&D team and HR generalists representing the functional areas of the business (for example, rates, foreign exchange, equities, and technology). This task force was ably led by Lynne Fisher, the S&D team's London representative, who had been an accomplished HR consultant for a Big 6 firm before joining SBC. She immediately collected all performance management processes and competency data being utilized throughout the bank. In all, thirty-nine competencies in thirteen different processes were being utilized. Parallel to this data collection, a task force meeting was planned to reduce the number of competencies and to design a performance management process that minimized the executive time required to engage in the process while maximizing the results to the individual and the bank. As a result of this meeting, the thirteen processes were replaced by one performance management process, and the thirty-nine competencies were reduced to nineteen in six clusters.

Task force members then went to the line managing director for feedback. As a result, four contribution areas were identified, with the profit area last on the list. The nineteen competencies were reworked and revised into four clusters, with a new total of twelve competencies. The overall performance management process of measuring competency and contribution stayed intact. After lengthy discussions, the task force named the new process the Performance Measurement and Management process (PMM). The PMM was to be based on multirater feedback. Wording for the user guide and forms was changed to eliminate the HR feel and reflect the language of line management. The clock was ticking. It was now early November—less than sixty days to roll everything out.

The competency clusters and contribution areas started to take shape in October. The four competency clusters defined the important knowledge bases, skill sets, and behaviors for the transformed organization. These competency clusters focused on: displaying integrity and technical knowledge; leading client service processes; initiating entrepreneurial business ventures; and utilizing resources effectively, especially through global teams, to deliver results. Contribution was to be measured using a balanced scorecard approach, that is, by measures of client service, people leadership, contributions to the larger organization versus the work unit, and profit and loss. Although I was a member of the PMM team, I also took lead responsibility for creating the leadership learning experiences for executives and high-potential employees. These leadership experiences would utilize learning organization concepts. Self-assessment and multirater feedback would be used to enable individuals to identify their baseline competence, with coaches and mentors providing guidance on the developmental experiences needed to advance. Later, lessons learned by individuals and teams would be transferred to a data base for all in the bank to access. Development experiences would include:

1. Global, regional, or local work-unit group training programs
2. Action learning teams working on developing new products, services, or internal processes

3. Distance learning methods utilizing Lotus Notes groupware and multimedia formats, which were designed to support busy professionals who can't get away to attend group training events.

It was planned to utilize all three techniques together or separately, as individual and business needs dictated. For example, high-potential associate directors (ADs) would attend a group training session that focused on the four competency clusters and the leadership skills required to produce superior results from their work teams. These associate directors from around the world would meet for 2 to 2½ weeks at a central location in Europe. As prework, they would have their leadership capabilities assessed using multirater feedback. (The Benchmark instrument from the Center for Creative Leadership was utilized until an internal instrument was developed.) They would also bring with them business problems they were facing at home. Action learning teams would be formed to work on selected business problems, utilizing technology (groupware and multimedia) as a distance learning tool. The lessons learned about the associate directors' business problems, including solutions, would be presented to the board for implementation. These associate directors would then use internally developed business cases to teach SBCW employees at the next global training program. A similar type of experience would be designed for directors and executive directors. Managing directors and board members would work on action learning teams and have briefing sessions for their ongoing development in place of formal group training events.

Two additional initiatives were being planned for developing executive talent. The PMM process would result in rankings for each employee and provide feedback on the competencies they would need to develop for reward and/or promotion in the near future. Accelerated competency development programs would be designed for each of the twelve competencies and offered within the region. SBCW would partner with INSEAD, IMD (Lausanne), and leading U.S. universities such as Harvard, Wharton, and the

Massachusetts Institute of Technology to develop and deliver these programs. Introductory-level leadership and management skills training for nonofficers would be designed by another SBCW department with feedback from S&D. These skills programs would be assessment-based and would cover traditional topics such as team building, delegation, and coaching.

November–December

The PMM process started to take shape. Flowcharts of the processes were prepared with critical milestones and due dates. A pilot test, which would be useful in working out the bugs, was scheduled with ten managing directors for the first week in December. An outside vendor was selected to process the paper forms and to provide individual and work-unit-level reports on contribution and competency.

The first global leadership development program for associate directors was designed and developed for implementation in February. Discussions were started with university professors for the accelerated competency development programs. I then began researching best practices techniques for developing distance learning applications.

January–February

The PMM user guide and forms were sent out to board members, the CEO, and all managing directors (total population of 125) in December. This population then selected who it would ask for feedback and forwarded appropriate forms to these evaluators. Each line of business would set up an evaluating committee, which would review completed PMM packages for the managing directors in that line unit. This committee would make compensation decisions based on contribution *and* competency ratings and would endorse development goals set by a managing director for the next year. Top-tier performers (approximately thirty managing directors total) would be discussed by the SBC Warburg board as possible candidates for senior management positions. Throughout the time period, managers would be meeting with their direct reports and discussing business and development goals for the following year.

The global leadership development program was coming together. All instructors had been contacted and their session material customized for the first group session in Switzerland, scheduled for the last week of February. All leadership training would be by invitation only. Until now, only a small group of managing directors had been notified about these programs, and nominees were usually drawn from a select group of employees. In some respects, who you knew had mattered more than what you knew or contributed when it came to securing a place in the program. I prepared an announcement letter and brochure to be used as a mailing to managing directors. I left for a New Year's vacation in Italy, and one of those ubiquitous miscommunications happened. The package was sent to every managing director, executive director, and director in the bank around the world. The response was heartwarming. More than 250 people out of a population of 1,200 were nominated for the February session. A breakthrough in the bank's culture for providing soft skill (kumbayah-type) training had occurred. Since the February session was a pilot, we limited the class to twenty-five participants. A follow-up letter to line managers indicated we would conduct other sessions as needed throughout 1996.

In mid-January, I received a call from my boss, who was attending a senior-level meeting that had a purpose of restructuring senior management in both divisions of the bank. The meeting determined that the CEO of the investment bank would now be responsible for both the investment and commercial bank divisions. We had lost a visible and vocal champion of the PMM and executive development process. It was decided at this meeting that an overall strategic framework was needed to give coherence to all the initiatives that were starting to evolve in HRD. This framework would come to be known as Shaping a Performance-Based Culture. Now, if we could get senior leaders to act on their thinking, the HRD initiatives would take off in the bank.

I immediately started an outline of the key elements of a performance-based culture, as found in the literature. Kotter and Heskett [3] were influential in our thinking. In addition, as a client of McKinsey [4], we had access to its library of articles and briefings. Throughout February, Otto Jaggy (my boss) and I hammered away until we had an executive report that focused on the:

☐ Key characteristics of a performance-based culture in comparison with our major competitors

☐ Role of senior management in a performance-based culture, that is, as direction setters and cross-functional and cross-regional team builders

☐ Role of employees in self-directing their careers using the PMM contribution and competency model.

The key to successfully launching a performance-based culture initiative was the transitional role of the new CEO. A March meeting was scheduled in Paris for all managing and executive directors in the bank. Would he endorse the performance-based culture concept and make it the centerpiece of his transition strategy? S&D prepared a detailed presentation for the managing and executive directors at the Paris conference based on building a performance-based culture. We hoped for a vote of confidence by senior leaders of the bank that the performance-based culture was putting the bank on the right path to achieving its vision.

Every indication had pointed to the new CEO and the Paris attendees' mandating the implementation of this performance-based culture concept, which included the PMM, an executive education process, and formation of global cross-regional/functional teams. We had rolled the dice that a 1½-day meeting would set the strategic and cultural strategy of the bank. As Jaggy said:

"We have chosen the risky strategy and have rejected the *kinder* strategy" (*kinder* means "child" in German).

March–April

The PMM process was completed by all managing directors. The results of individual PMM reports were summarized by business unit heads, and top-tier performers were identified. These top-tier individuals were discussed by the board at its March meeting as possible succession candidates for key positions in the bank.

The connection of the PMM to compensation was much less clear and direct than the succession plan connection. Bonus payments were made March 13; however, many managing directors had pre-Warburg acquisition contracts that stipulated specific sums be paid regardless of performance. There was also little evidence found that development plans were prepared and goals set for 1996 as a result of the PMM.

The PMM team needed implementation process feedback from the managing directors. As a result, we interviewed and surveyed them for specific process and content improvements. We also started planning for a technology solution to the PMM process. Our most difficult discussions took place over the issue of minimizing executive time in the process. Just how much complexity should be added to the pilot process? This question kept haunting our team, with major disagreements surfacing between the PMM team leader and the executive director of S&D.

The pilot session for the global leadership development program ended in mid-March. The participants represented every continent and business line in the bank. Board members were instructors and facilitated sessions versus doing presentations to the group, as they had done in previous leadership programs. Specific changes were suggested, such as keeping the program to 2 weeks versus 2½ weeks. Content changes were also recommended and were being acted on. The board approved a summer session with forty participants. SBC Warburg–specific cases would form the backbone of the revised program. The board also approved the accelerated competency development program. Content and process discussions for these programs were started in S&D and then expanded to include line managers.

The Paris meeting (performance-based culture workshop) of the managing and executive directors did take place in March, but it didn't produce a mandate for radical culture change. Cross-regional and cross-functional teamwork became the Paris post-meeting slogan, but no one mentioned specific ways to get these processes into place.

May–June

Work continued on revising the PMM process and the executive development process. The senior leadership changes took hold at the CEO and COO levels. Major differences of opinion surfaced about the best way to recruit, develop, and retain the "best and brightest." S&D attended meeting after meeting, making its case for the PMM, the executive development process, and the performance-based culture framework. The O'Connor power base started to emerge and dominate key positions in the bank. S&D retained the PMM process and the ancillary skills training needed to implement the PMM. The executive development process became fragmented, with S&D overseeing part of it while a former O'Connor partner (managing director—head of graduate recruiting, technical and technology training) gained responsibility for management development. His area overlapped the S&D function. Turf battles ensued within the HR function. HR reorganized, and S&D started partnering with other specialists in HR because it was losing its lead position on the initiatives it was developing. For example, PMM partnered with the director of compensation, and executive development partnered with the head of technical training. Both of these non-S&D heads were former O'Connor partners. The HR generalists took primary responsibility for providing service to employees in the business units. S&D started to find itself isolated in the organization, within both the HR Department as well as the line units. Its power base supporting transformational change was eroding.

July

I left SBC Warburg. The S&D team regrouped and moved the PMM and executive development process improvements forward. The performance-based culture framework was no longer a deliverable for the S&D team and, as a result, was no longer discussed. In six months (October 1995 to March 1996), S&D did the impossible. The team formed and then designed, developed, and implemented two major people-based initiatives: (1) the PMM process and (2) the executive development process. These processes were major mind-set changes for the bank's senior leaders and employees. In addition, these processes were intended to make clear what it would take to succeed in the new organization from a contribution and competency perspective. Both processes would give an employee the knowledge and tools to be a "player" in the bank. The performance-based culture was a casualty, however, and has never been reinstituted. Why is still a mystery. In the end, SBC Warburg would never be the same again. A growing number of employees had tasted world-class HR development processes, and they wanted more. S&D was committed, as were some key business leaders, to providing what these employees wanted.

What Happened

As the old saying goes, there is good news, and there is bad news—which do you want to hear first? The good news is that 124 of 125 managing directors participated in the pilot of the PMM. More than 50 percent participated in a follow-up survey or interview on how to improve the process. Their overall evaluation of the process was positive. They recommended several changes be made before introducing the PMM to the larger employee population:

1. The process instructions were "too bare bones," that is, more direction (the user guide provided thirteen pages of information) was needed about how to select multiple evaluators, complete the performance review package, and have a feedback meeting between the line manager and the employee. It was suggested that the HR generalists take the role of assisting managers and employees in facilitating the use of PMM. A facilitator's guide, with much greater detail than the user guide, had been developed for use by HR generalists and line personnel in December 1995 but was not implemented.

2. A more defined follow-up development process needed to be designed so employees could prepare development plans, discuss them with their managers, and identify development resources required to build desired competencies.

3. Technology (internal versus external vendor) should be utilized for the entire process of completing forms, processing them, and producing development plans. Also, management reports should be provided that identify who has what competencies, at what level of competence they are, and where they are stationed.

Plans are being formulated to address the above points. By May 1996, the board had approved moving the implementation down at least one level to executive director, which includes approximately 750 employees worldwide. Some board members wanted the PMM to be rolled out to all 12,000-plus employees in 1996. However, S&D advised that such a rollout would require astounding amounts of resources to do well. Discussions continued taking place at senior levels in the bank about this issue.

On a less positive note, some powerful senior executives believed that the PMM process took too much of senior people's time for little or no payback to the individual or the organization. These executives openly stated that, perhaps, every two years is sufficient for senior-level personnel to participate in the PMM. Unfortunately, Marcel Ospel, the CEO of SBC Warburg and primary champion of the PMM, was promoted to head the entire bank (investment and commercial) and as a result had much less time to devote to specific initiatives like the PMM. However, he still remained a staunch supporter of the process and is working with his successor to ensure the PMM's place in the bank's culture.

The S&D team members continued to take a leadership role in moving the PMM process throughout the bank. They actively worked on validating the competencies for the tiers of employees below managing director, developed a technology solution for the paperwork, and began designing and implementing training programs for the 1996–1997 rollout.

The executive/leadership development process and programs were also moving forward. The first global leadership development program for associate directors was a resounding success. It was designed around the PMM competency model, with individuals receiving multirater leadership assessments and then preparing development plans. I initially designed the group training event (sixteen days in Switzerland) to be followed up by action learning teams. These teams would be composed of global leadership development program participants, and they would focus on the business issues that surfaced at the training program. Solutions would be developed and presented to the board for approval and implementation. These teams would utilize groupware technology to collaborate across regions. This design was never operationalized. The participants formed teams but never followed through after they left the group session. My successor didn't consider use of these teams a viable concept in the bank and, as a result, didn't pursue the issue.

The board, however, did recognize the need for continuous global leadership development and is actively working with all constituencies (traders, investment bankers, and technologists) to design a process that fits the company's culture and business environment. The S&D team also started designing a framework that provides on-the-job and group training experiences to meet these leadership development needs. The focus is on providing employees with a variety of experiences to develop their business and leadership capabilities. There is still some deep-seated resistance to these efforts from some high-level managing directors, who refer to these efforts as "kumbayah." The implication is that leadership development is too soft for the culture.

There was also good news for the young managing director that I interviewed. His message about the need for cross-regional and cross-functional teams was heard loud and clear by senior management. Several initiatives were identified and started to be discussed and resourced:

1. The bank's senior technology executive has been charged with developing a process to integrate the business plans across products, services, and regions

2. The use of action learning teams as a follow-up to group training events is again being explored to gain direct business results from group training investments and to more rapidly develop business leaders

3. A new internal organizational development (OD) consultant has replaced me and is actively working on: (1) building the HR Department into a high-performing team by placing HR generalists and specialists on HR process improvement teams, where each team has a specific HR process to focus its attention on, such as, recruiting, development, reward and recognition, and succession planning; and (2) developing basic team-building skills starting with the technology group. He describes his work as OD 101, meaning the organization is still in its infancy regarding the role of teams, competencies in the teams, and how teams go about their day-to-day business activities.

Finally, the Corporate Center (responsible for both the investment and commercial bank) has been charged with designing and implementing HR policy, in other words, a consistent and well-communicated HR strategy. The strategy's thrust is twofold. First, efforts will be directed toward the identification and development of the contribution and competency needed to gain and sustain world-class bank status. This is a critical priority for the entire bank. This work includes identifying appropriate metrics for each contribution and competency. Second, efforts will be made to ensure that line management, not the HR Department, owns the HR development process. The two executives driving HR policy are committed to bringing the best practices of professional service firms to Wall Street—not a task for the faint of heart. Their commitment to developing high-performing talent and treating people with respect is critical for SBC overall and specifically for SBC Warburg in meeting its goals. Nothing less will do for a Top 5 investment bank.

Lessons Learned

Transforming an organization through human resource development is both exhilarating and frightening. I have experienced tremendous highs as well as lows throughout the process. At the time I am writing this chapter, almost six months have passed since I left SBCW, and I am still haunted by the face of that young managing director. In his mind, the organizational support and infrastructure he needed to be able to reach world-class status were straightforward and should have been easily crafted, if not already present, in the company.

The literature about organizational change, as well as practitioners and HR generalists, notes that once you have a clearly identified business model and strategy, you can then design and implement a change strategy. This is for me the most powerful lesson learned. Getting everyone to articulate and agree on this business model is difficult in global organizations. In a complex business, like global investment banking, the business model gets fragmented and lost in the discussion and arguments that take place on a day-to-day basis. Senior people, like my young managing director friend, often feel powerless to make the changes necessary. Survival takes precedence. Why else would such a professional make a weekly trip to London?

I am not convinced that raising the credibility of the HR professional will make the change process easier. The changes required of people today are philosophically profound and will impact their day-to-day roles and tasks. I liken the magnitude of these changes to the discovery of quantum mechanics almost one hundred years ago, a discovery that everyone predicted would rapidly replace Newtonian physics in explaining the physical world. Today, Newtonian physics is still the core curriculum in many universities around the world, and we are still only scratching the surface of the meaning quantum mechanics has in our lives. Likewise, we are truly at the beginning phase of understanding transformational change, its nature, and its impact on people, processes, and systems. The diversity of opinion that exists in organizations about how the business is changing and how HR can partner with business professionals is enormously complex and needs constant attention. This is often not done in the rush of the day-to-day work environment.

I was and still am dumbfounded that line employees did not embrace action learning teams. They simply weren't interested in working on business problems with people they met at the course in Switzerland once they returned to their jobs. Even the carrot of presenting their solutions to business problems to the board was not enough to get them excited about the process. When asked about it, they just shrugged and remained silent. Perhaps they are too busy or, worse yet, too unmotivated to participate.

Finally, the role that technology plays in facilitating the implementation of transformational change cannot be overstated. SBC Warburg was a patchwork of several differing technology systems. The chief technologist, who was also a board member, conceived a brilliant strategy for the future. He had difficulty convincing business leaders of the efficacy of his plan, and HR as a function was often not at the table when important discussions were occurring. A senior HR generalist was finally able to establish HR's place at the table; however, development efforts were focused on technical competencies. This narrow focus (thanks to the "kumbayah" principle) was a major impediment to rolling out the PMM process, as well as the use of distance learning technology. Technology within HR was not robust enough to provide management reports that would facilitate deploying talent on global teams, needed to better serve clients. From my view, it didn't look like the bank was getting its arms around the technology issue.

At a personal level, the S&D team was a global team that required traveling extensively, living in Europe without my family for months at a clip, and working through cultural issues among the team members. Miscommunication, or at least misunderstanding each other, was frequent. For example, I use the words *system* and *process* interchangeably, at least in conversation, while the S&D team leader understood these words as having separate and different meanings. It took us months of closely working together to discover this miscommunication was the cause of our issues with each other. For both of us and the rest of the S&D team, it was a painful process.

Conclusion

SBC Warburg identified several transformational changes needed to achieve its vision of being one of the Top 5 investment banks by the year 2000. Fundamental changes in the industry, including the entrance of new competitors, were driving this transformation. The business strategy had to shift from acquiring companies to building internal capability. Senior leadership had to focus its attention on creating cross-regional and cross-functional synergies with line management, thereby creating global service teams for meeting clients' business needs. Multiple criteria for contribution to the bank had to be identified to create the desired organizational synergies. Line management had to be engaged in identifying which employees had the competencies needed to serve on these teams. Employees had to have a clear understanding of the competencies required for success and be self-directed in preparing development plans for their futures. Line management had to develop its people through coaching, mentoring, and the PMM process, as well as provide an environment that is change friendly. HR professionals had to have business and industry savvy, as well as be change agents. The tool kit of the organizational development practitioner had to become the tool kit for every employee in the organization. This was a monumental undertaking, to say the least.

Many diverse factors affected S&D's day-to-day work, as well as the overall impact of our work on the organization when viewed on a long-term basis. The short time windows the bank's senior leadership set for the transformational change created a sense of urgency for everyone in the bank. Technology played a key factor in the day-to-day business and the change process as well. Understanding and working with different cultures in complex areas like performance, leadership, and team building added to the chaos. Luckily, HR was at the table at the beginning of the acquisition and transformational change process discussions. The global business model added significantly to the complexity of the change process, as did the time pressure that HR was under to deliver products and services for the new organization. Finally, out of many possible initiatives, HR selected competency development and performance management as keys to starting a successful transformational change.

In reflecting on my experience at SBC Warburg, I feel proud to have been a part of this initiative—to get it started and structured and to see it starting to gain a life of its own, that is, to be self-sustaining. I found it exhilirating to see concrete examples of the power of ideas played out on a day-to-day basis, by individuals and teams. In many respects, the challenges ahead are more formidable. The pressure of day-to-day operations takes the edge off the focus on these ideas. People revert back to tried and true behaviors and business models, even in the face of overwhelming evidence that tells them otherwise.

All employees in today's organizations need to constantly reexamine the assumptions on which their business models are based. Fundamental questions need to be continuously asked about how the business is changing and the assumptions that underlie the new model. The SBCW story should be further developed to communicate the transformational changes needed for an organization to flourish in today's business environment. This story should utilize the words and anecdotes of SBCW's business leaders, both formal and informal.

All employees are responsible for structuring the change process and implementing it. To accomplish this, they need to be well versed in systems dynamics and thinking. Understanding both the systemswide and component changes required may facilitate the change needed by individuals, teams, and the organization. Finally, courage and the will to create the changes needed are required. Global organizations require every bit of energy you have every waking moment. The personal sacrifice required to have the change take hold and flourish cannot be underestimated. It took its toll on me and my family, but I wouldn't have traded my two years at SBC Warburg for anything. I hope I get an invitation to the celebration in the year 2000, as SBC Warburg lives its dream.

References

1. John, S. G. "A Study of Team Learning in a Professional Services Firm," Unpublished doctoral dissertation, New York: Columbia University, 1995.

2. Fitz-Enz, J. *Human Value Management.* San Francisco: Jossey-Bass, 1990.

3. Kotter, John P. and Heskett, James L. *Corporate Culture and Performance.* New York: The Free Press, 1992.

4. McKinsey & Co. Articles/briefings to senior management, Selected material focused on the role of the CEO, creating cultural change, and characteristics of high-performance organizations, Various dates 1994–1996.

7

Transforming Human Resources to Create a Global World-Class Investment Bank

STEPHEN JOHN, ED.D., AND CAROL GORELICK

(Note: This case is described from two points of view, the first by Steve John and the second by Carol Gorelick. Lessons learned and conclusions are presented jointly.)

Steve John's Perspective

Introduction

Swiss Bank Corporation (SBC), in the late 1980s, decided to change its business strategy from a commercial bank to a global investment bank. Senior management operationalized its strategy by first joint-venturing with the O'Connor Partnerships in Chicago and then acquiring O'Connor. Several other acquisitions quickly followed, including Brinson and SG Warburg. A more detailed discussion of these acquisitions is provided in Chapter 6. Each acquisition expanded the expertise of SBC—newly named SBC Warburg—in the investment banking world.

Investment banking, as SBC Warburg was building its capability, was also changing dramatically. Most investment banking deals were still being awarded to firms that had long-term reputations in the field. These firms usually had a history of working with the corporation that needed investment banking services. It wasn't uncommon for a large corporation to refer to its investment banker in the singular, meaning that no matter what type of deal the corporation needed, only that firm would be called in to advise on the deal. However, in the 1990s, deals were becoming increasingly more complex. Businesses were facing global competitors and worldwide sources for capital. Technology was faster and smarter. Products and services could be designed anywhere, funded, and then delivered anywhere in the world. The speed, complexity, and size of the deals were also growing at a frightening pace. These changes, taken together, would require transformational changes in an investment bank's business strategy and work processes. These changes, in turn, would fuel similar changes in the human resource processes of recruiting, developing, retaining, and rewarding technical talent. Business and human resource professionals would have to communicate, coordinate, and collaborate with each other in new ways. They would frequently be working on global teams with team members that represented many different specialties and cultures. Team members would need to perform much of their work without face-to-face meetings. The team's resulting work would have to be flawlessly delivered to clients to remain competitive. Finally, the lessons learned by these teams would have to be shared for other teams to utilize the teams' work. The cost of creating specialized knowledge and leaving it in the file folders of an individual or team was too great to not transfer the lessons learned to the larger organization.

During these turbulent times, SBC Warburg (SBCW) publicly stated its intention of being one of the Top 5 global investment banks by the year 2000. At the time of this case study, SBCW was arguably No. 11 on the global league charts. Chapter 6 described in detail the challenges such a goal presented to the organization and how Sourcing and Development (S&D) designed two initiatives to support the bank in its aspirations. (S&D, as described more fully in Chapter 6, was established in July of 1995 with Otto Jaggy as its head. It was composed of HR specialists whose mission was to design, develop, and implement HR processes for recruiting, development, rewards, and succession planning.) In general, these challenges included the following: (a) senior leadership would have to provide an environment that supported individuals as well as teams, (b) all employees would have to understand clearly the contributions and competencies needed for success in the present and future organization, and (c) highly specialized technical employees would have to work on diverse teams and assume leadership roles when needed.

There were significant barriers to meeting these challenges. Most investment banks, even the Top 5, were all only starting to design and deliver products and services across the world by teams that were "virtual" in their work processes. Team members often worked "on the road," and teams met face-to-face only when absolutely necessary. In addition, investment banks were often structured along product or service lines (equities, foreign exchange, and interest rates) and regionally (United States, Latin America, Europe, and Asia-Pacific). These structures often impeded the formation of global teams. Finally, technology systems, while getting "smarter" and more user friendly, were also somewhat country bound, meaning they were subject to the telecommunication practices and laws that existed where the systems were physically located. Seamless and accurate communication between these systems, while a goal, was rarely achieved at the level of accuracy needed in investment banking deals.

The Human Resource Department also encountered the organizational structures, work processes, and technology systems issues described above. Country customs and laws frequently made designing and delivering world-class HR products and services a nightmare. Yet high levels of service to employees, as well as accuracy, would be needed if SBC Warburg were to achieve its strategy. It became increasingly clear that initiatives specifically focused on the Human Resources Department would be needed to create a world-class investment bank.

Furthermore, as the business initiatives started to take shape, I (Steve John) realized that Human Resources itself must be transformed in order to successfully support senior and line management, as well as all the employees of the bank.

Background of the Human Resource Department

Robert Zeltner, who was located in Zurich, was the global head of Human Resources. As a member of the SBC Warburg board, he had considerable influence and impact on the bank's strategy and the role Human Resources would play in operationalizing that strategy. Zeltner was also HR's link to the Corporate Center, which was responsible for coordinating the bank's three divisions: the commercial bank, the investment bank, and the private bank.

SBC Warburg had four geographic regions: (1) Switzerland; (2) Europe (sans Switzerland); (3) the Americas, which included Canada, the United States, and Latin America; and (4) Asia-Pacific. Each region had a head of HR, who reported directly to Zeltner and the respective region CEO. The regional head of HR ensured that the centrally developed policies and procedures were properly modified for local conditions, customs, and laws, and then implemented.

Each business unit (foreign exchange, equities, and interest rates), as well as the operations processing and information technology units, had a senior HR generalist (client relationship manager, or CRM) that served its unit's human resource needs. Each CRM reported to his or her regional head of HR, as well as to the appropriate business unit head. The CRMs were supported by a number of intermediate- and junior-level generalists, depending on the business unit's employee population and geographic dispersion. SBC Warburg also had at the regional level a number of senior HR specialists who reported to the appropriate regional head of HR. There was a specialist for compensation and benefits, recruiting, education and training, and human resource information systems. The specialists served all CRMs as needed.

Prior to 1994, the bank determined that it wanted its HR professionals and line managers to think and act as change agents. To support this and other intentions, senior management approved the formation of an HR Planning and Development Department (HRP&D). The primary focus of HRP&D was to work with line and HR management to create a performance-based culture in the investment bank (as described in Chapter 6). In 1994, I was the first HRP&D specialist hired, with responsibility for the Americas region. The plan was to hire HRP&D specialists for all the remaining regions as the new department started to take shape in the bank.

All CRMs and specialists were trained HR professionals with significant experience in HR processes, usually within a variety of organizations and geographic locations. In contrast, the global head of HR and some regional heads of HR were line executives who now held direct HR responsibilities within the bank. They had substantial expertise in business processes, with little or no formal HR training. This mixture of specialties added diversity of thought but also added significant time to completing all projects. In contrast, line units were, for the most part, staffed with specialists in only one area of technical expertise. These specialists shared similar work processes and jargon. This gave the line the ability to move with lightning speed in designing and implementing its business initiatives. However, high levels of communication, coordination, and collaboration were more difficult to achieve in both HR and line units when specialists from other areas had to work with each other.

Transforming Human Resources

Employee satisfaction survey data indicated that HR professionals needed to act as strategic business partners and change agents and also be able to flawlessly execute HR transactions in areas such as compensation, benefits, employee relocation, and staffing. Survey data also indicated that the existing HR Department had a long way to go to reach world-class status in *any* one of these areas. Three initiatives were planned to address the HR function issues: (1) re-engineering of all HR processes, (2) developing an HR information system, and (3) globalizing the role of all CRM and HR specialists.

Fortunately, re-engineering was not a new concept to the bank. The chief operating officer of North America had established a Business Process Re-engineering Technologies Department (BPR) in New York during the early 1990s. The department's formation was inspired by Michael Hammer's work at the Massachusetts Institute of Technology (MIT), as described in his best-selling book [1]. BPR customized Hammer's techniques to work effectively in the business and culture of the bank. The BPR staff consisted of internal consultants and administrative personnel who assisted line and support units within the bank throughout the re-engineering process.

In the summer of 1994, the regional director of HR assigned the responsibility of re-engineering HR in the Americas to Jim Minogue and myself. Our strategy was to successfully re-engineer HR in the Americas and then offer our model to Global HR in Zurich for use in the other three regions. The head of BPR was excited about the prospect of HR re-engineering itself. In her work with MIT, she found that, as of 1994, no financial service organization had re-engineered its HR department. These organizations had done exactly what SBC Warburg had done. That is, they had started re-engineering their business processes but had not gotten around to HR. Speed was critical, as SBC was looking to acquire a major investment bank (SG Warburg) in Europe. HR, as a function, would now be expected to conduct itself at a world-class level both strategically and tactically.

The re-engineering plan included training HR professionals in re-engineering techniques and tools as well as providing roles for BPR's internal consultants. The plan was presented to the North American Management Committee for approval. Months went by with no response. Fall and winter of 1994 passed without a word from the committee. Minogue and I pressed for an answer. Still no response. Even inquiries about a potential global HR re-engineering plan out of Zurich were met with silence. In the early spring of 1995, the CEO of North America visited us to explain why no response had been forthcoming from the committee. The SG Warburg acquisition was about to be announced. Finally, in March 1995, the news broke: SBC would acquire SG Warburg. HR, both regionally and globally, would now become consumed with the enormous amount of legal and regulatory paperwork that needed to be done to have the merger take place by July 1995.

In addition to re-engineering HR processes, the second of the major initiatives to address the HR function issues was being organized: the development of a sophisticated HR information system (HRIS). A global team had been formed to investigate the existing HRIS platforms of all acquired companies and to make recommendations to senior management. The team's recommendations focused on providing a standardized workstation and software system to handle all employee-related information, including payroll, benefits, and demographic data. Enhanced future versions of the system would include data from recruiting, development, and succession planning. As this team moved from recommendation to project planning and delivery, I started developing a team-building process and training program designed to operationalize the team as quickly as possible. However, as the globalization of HR specialists took place, I was not able to implement the team training.

Finally, as July 1995 fast approached, senior management globalized the role of all CRMs as well as HR specialists, as discussed in Chapter 6. All senior HR professionals were assigned global responsibilities with regional focus as a secondary responsibility. All HR processes had to be designed from a global perspective and then implemented regionally based on local conditions.

Globalizing both the function of HR and the bank's business units at the same time presented HR with a problem of enormous proportions. The solution to such a problem would require nothing less than a transformation of HR.

The Problem

To support the global business strategy, HR had globalized the role of its senior personnel. However, during the critical first months of the new business entity (SBC Warburg), it became clear that the HR reorganization was merely a paper reorganization. Global HR processes and tools were not available, nor were they being actively developed. In addition, HR was considerably behind the business units in its use of technology. Many processes were paper-driven, requiring manual input into software systems. These software systems were internal to the HR Department; little or no access was available to line management or employees. As a result, phone and fax communication was required to start and complete many HR transactions. These transactions, such as employee relocation across continents, were often complicated and generated voluminous amounts of paper. While minimally tolerable in a regional structure, phone and fax communication quickly became an impossible process in a global structure. Sensitive employee and organizational information was in danger of being compromised. High-quality service required by employees would never be a reality in such a system.

Furthermore, individuals and teams within HR did not have work processes or tools that enabled them to collaborate and communicate with each other, or employees, from anywhere in the world at any time. Nor did they have a central data base and work space that would ensure the integrity and confidentiality of employee data. Based on my own earlier work [2], I concluded that groupware, properly designed and implemented, had the potential to facilitate the globalization of the HR function. It would enable HR to provide the levels of service needed by employees and senior management as they worked toward becoming a global world-class investment bank. I remembered meeting Carol Gorelick at a networking luncheon. She was an expert in groupware and was also completing a doctorate in human resource management. She co-founded a company called SOLUTIONS. I scheduled a meeting with her, and things were never the same again.

Making Sense of Chaos

Gorelick and I met several times during the summer of 1995 to discuss how groupware technology might be used to support the HR Department's transformation from a regionally focused to a globally based function. Our conversations focused on integrating the concepts of teamwork and a performance-based culture with an enabling technology. Gorelick had identified four key elements needed for an enabling technology: (1) coordination of business processes, (2) organization and sharing of information, (3) collaboration of teams, and (4) communication among colleagues and other organizations. Our success would require: (1) a well-designed and implemented infrastructure, both in technology as well as in work team processes, and (2) a culture that supported individuals and teams in their work.

If HR could create a collaborative team work process within its own function that was global in purpose and operation, a model could be transferred to the rest of the organization for use in building a global world-class investment bank. As we were to find out, this was a big *if*.

HR from 1990 to July 1995 had undergone tumultuous change. SBC prided itself on identifying in its existing organization and each newly acquired company the best talent, processes, policies, and systems to be part of the merged organization. As a result, the present HR function was a composite of SBC, O'Connor, Brinson, and SG Warburg. Integrating differences quickly was required to keep the organization on track to reach its goal by the year 2000. Jim Minogue referred to this integration process as "having to change the tires on a bus while the bus was moving." Our groupware initiative could be a catalyst for integrating SBC Warburg and turning chaos into order.

Gorelick would take the lead on this initiative from a technology and training design perspective, with me shaping the team process design and navigating the culture based on my understanding of the bank's business strategy, culture, and the new role the HR department would need to play if the bank was to realize its global strategy.

Carol Gorelick's Perspective

What We Did

SBC signed the SG Warburg acquisition agreement in early July 1995. SBC Warburg started to do business as an investment bank everywhere in the world except the United States. Federal regulatory requirements in the United States delayed licensing as an investment bank until early 1996. SG Warburg continued to operate as a business in the United States until these regulatory requirements were met, and then SG Warburg (United States) merged into SBC Warburg. Steve John spent the summer, fall, and early winter as a key player in forming the newly created Sourcing and Development Department (S&D). John moved to Zurich in the early fall and traveled extensively between Zurich, London, and New York. The S&D team had, during this time period, developed its mission, vision, values, and project responsibilities. In addition, individual team member roles and responsibilities were starting to be defined, with project leaders identified for the performance management and leadership development initiatives described in Chapter 6. There were team members in London and Zurich, with CRMs and other HR professionals outside the S&D

Department also assigned to specific initiatives. These CRMs and other HR professionals were located in Zurich, London, the United States, and Asia. Face-to-face meetings became difficult to schedule and execute due to the varied location of team members and the heavy work load all HR professionals carried due to the SG Warburg acquisition.

Communication, work coordination, and collaboration started to become strained. Extremely tight project deadlines created enormous stress levels in the project teams. John used this opportunity to build consensus for using groupware as a tool to produce high-quality project deliverables on time and on budget.

The S&D team routinely had to develop documents that were authored and reviewed by multiple people, and most required distribution to senior executives or to employees bankwide. Otto Jaggy, the head of S&D, had the job of reviewing the documents before they were finalized and distributed. As noted above, S&D team members were located in multiple offices and traveled extensively throughout the world, so this collaborative authoring and reviewing process was often difficult to coordinate. John envisioned a system that would have all documents in one electronic or virtual space. Authors would be able to create documents in software they were already familiar with: Word for text, Excel for financials and spreadsheets, PowerPoint for presentations, and Microsoft Project for project plans. The new system would be easy to use and would encourage team collaboration. Team members would be able to view each other's documents and make comments in one central electronic or virtual library. The system would include both documents in process and finalized documents, the latter for reference and possible reuse at a later date. The starting point for the system design would be a central library with discussion capabilities, particularly for the process of co-authoring documents.

Designing and implementing this system would not be easy. Infrastructure issues impacted the functional requirements of the system we envisioned, and the bank was also developing software standards, such as Lotus Notes, that were unfamiliar to members of the S&D team.

February 1996

Carter Crawford, who is my partner in SOLUTIONS, and I reviewed the requirements John had articulated and believed that two viable, technology-based alternatives existed. The first option was to implement a traditional document-management software application that would handle co-authoring, storage, and retrieval of documents. This alternative involved buying a software product that was not on the SBC Warburg standards list and therefore would not be supported. The second alternative was to develop a custom Notes application to provide the collaborative capability desired for the team to operate anywhere at any time. The advantage of this alternative was not having to purchase and learn a new software product that was not a bank standard. This alternative also provided the HR Department with a work process that could be utilized throughout HR on a global basis. This work process could in turn be utilized by the bank's team of investment bankers to deliver the team's products and services on a global basis. The capability for supporting robust collaboration would be available to SBC Warburg teams. We agreed with John that a custom application would be the way to proceed, and my partner and I developed the project plan.

March 1996

SOLUTIONS developed a flowchart as the starting point for programming specifications. The core of the new system would be a collaborative document management process. Meine Bruhin, an S&D team member in Zurich, was designated the project coordinator and liaison between the SBC Warburg technology group in London and SOLUTIONS. John remained the project leader and continued to shape the system as it evolved.

Crawford and I recommended reviewing the specifications with the entire S&D team to minimize programming changes after the initial software development work was completed. Otto Jaggy was reluctant to include the whole team in the specification discussion because he was anxious to get the system up and running. Based on experience, however, Crawford and I strongly recommended a walk-through of the proposed system with the team. Ultimately a global videoconference was scheduled, with the team in London and Zurich and with Gorelick, Crawford and John in New York. This meeting raised a number of significant issues, such as how the team would work together, if individual differences should be accommodated, and if only one core process should be designed and implemented.

There was also a heated discussion about how documents would be approved for distribution. Should all documents be approved by Jaggy or only certain documents, such as those going to the board of directors? The system flowchart was refined after the videoconference and follow-up conversations between John, Jaggy, and SOLUTIONS.

April 1996

SOLUTIONS presented a project timetable to Jaggy:

S&D personal computers (PCs) updated for the new application	April 22
Generic Notes training (computer-based)	Begin April 22
Notes application installed and tested	End of May
S&D team training on application	June

A decision was made to work with a vendor in New York who had experience in developing a similar type of document management application for investment banks. Building global and collaborative team work processes into the application was new territory for all of us.

May–July 1996

The vendor completed the application development in May, as scheduled. We agreed that the collaborative team systems training should be done in classroom format for the entire team because the training covered the mechanics of using the application as well as team work processes and procedures. We planned to do a case study, using actual S&D project documents, for the training. The training session was designed to produce a usable work product for the team.

On July 11, the vendor installed the application on SOLUTIONS' PC equipment. We could simulate the computer environment that traveling S&D team members would experience and how the London, Zurich, and New York offices would interact. SOLUTIONS was set to test the application in the process of developing training materials. In mid-July everyone on the S&D team in Zurich and in London started the European ritual of three weeks' vacation. The whole team would not be together again until September. At this time, Steve John left SBC Warburg to join a Big Six consulting firm as director of human resource planning and development. Our plan for a summer 1996 implementation faded.

August 1996

Meine Bruhin assumed the role of project leader for the S&D team and became the liaison between SOLUTIONS and Otto Jaggy. We, at SOLUTIONS, had several conversations with and received frequent e-mails from Bruhin that identified tasks related to the training and implementation. Since John was no longer involved, we requested that at least one team member review the application from a team process and procedure perspective before we developed the training materials.

September 1996

October was chosen as the new training date (as opposed to June, the old training date). SOLUTIONS was concerned, however, that no one from the project team had seen or reviewed the application. Fortunately, as a result of a phone conversation and follow-up e-mails with Bruhin and Jaggy, the decision was made for me to attend the team staff meeting in Zurich on October 1 to demonstrate and review the proposed system with the team. The agenda for the meeting clearly stated that the purpose of the meeting was to perform a system walk-through, with a goal to make procedural decisions, such as whether comments would be made within the document as annotations or separately appended items. We knew that process and procedure changes might affect the application design and possibly the training design.

October 1996

I flew to Zurich for the staff meeting, scheduled to run from 11 a.m. to 1 p.m. A heated discussion ensued on how approval and document distribution would take place. Another serious question centered on team members making annotated comments and edits in the original document. For example, the team questioned whether changes should be made to the document itself or if separate comments should be procedurally instituted (as recommended by SOLUTIONS and the developer)? At 1 p.m. Jaggy left the meeting. The team continued the discussion. At the end of the meeting, Nils Mehr (global leadership development program [GLDP] project leader) stood and said, "Based on what I've seen, I don't see how this system will add value. I would vote to stop development now." Lynne Fisher (Performance Management and Measurement process [PMM] project leader) responded that there were advantages of having the documents in one central place and being able to track document history, especially when team members were located in different offices or were traveling. Bruhin was left with the responsibility to discuss the issues with the team, build consensus, and advise SOLUTIONS of the team's decisions.

After the team meeting, I met with the information technology (IT) group in Zurich. We scheduled the training for October 31, with October 30 as a set-up day. We created the training guide as a Notes data base so that it could also be used as online training and documentation. We believed that as the team learned together they would produce new knowledge and ways of doing things that were not part of the original design [2].

Jaggy intended to be an equal participant in the training experience. However, since he had unique approval functions, we suggested and received agreement to train him the day before the S&D training. He was prepared to provide ongoing support if required and integrate the new collaborative process in the team's work processes. As the team grew throughout its life cycle, we anticipated that the collaborative team process would become the norm [3].

October 31, 1996—Training Day

The S&D team was polite but seemed harried. Bruhin had defined teams of two to work together at one workstation. I began the application training with the agenda and goals for the training program.

As soon as the teams began the first exercise, they were engaged and appeared to be learning. As the day progressed, a to-do list of technical and procedural issues was developed. Open issues would be addressed at the team meeting the next day.

By 3 p.m. the group seemed spent. We did a wrap-up, summarizing the open issues. The S&D team members agreed they were ready to use the system.

They planned to discuss the open issues and identify changes at the team meeting the next day. SOLUTIONS prepared the list of open issues.

November 15, 1996

A conference call with Bruhin and Jaggy ended SOLUTIONS' direct involvement in the project.

Jaggy proceeded to identify Information Technology London as the main contact for technical issues and Bruhin for team process and procedural ones. Jaggy believed the system was operational and met the S&D team's requirements. It would be the team members' challenge to learn to use it in a collaborative way. He said, "We need to pick up the ball and make it work," a task to be accomplished with SBC Warburg resources. We concluded the conversation with agreement that the test system would be turned into a production system by deleting all the test documents. The team would be encouraged to work with the system by starting 1997 planning and projects in the system.

Both Authors' Perspectives

Lessons Learned

SBC Warburg had set its sights high when its senior leadership publicly stated its intention of being in the Top 5 investment banks by the year 2000. In addition, the HR Department had a formidable challenge in supporting the business units during their transformation. As described earlier, the way investment banks were designing products and services and delivering these products and services to clients was changing in fundamental ways. Vision, values, and cultural norms were in flux or, as some employees expressed, in chaos. Line units were deftly modifying business processes and now they recruited, developed, rewarded, and promoted people to leadership positions. Some HR professionals were accepted as business partners, while others were not. Some line units were more successful at transforming their business units. Unfortunately, the transformations were occurring in silos either bounded by product and service or by geography.

If HR could create a collaborative team process within its own function, it could utilize this process to design and implement key HR processes that would be needed to create a world-class global investment bank. We moved the initiative to Lift Off, but couldn't sustain the energy level needed to successfully implement the collaborative team process into S&D, much less into the business units.

S&D reflected the entire organization—newly formed with team members from all over the world who knew little about each other professionally or personally. In addition, S&D lived in a complex and chaotic culture valiantly trying to clarify its vision, values, and norms. Finally, S&D had the same technology and organizational infrastructure issues that all the business units were facing. We have focused our lessons learned around these three areas: (1) technology, (2) team processes, and (3) cultural issues.

Technology. The bank's information technology (IT) strategy was very much in flux. The decision to provide a standard software platform with a PC workstation was conceptually agreed to; however, NeXT machine users were fighting hard to keep their machine as the standard. Most IT professionals realized that the NeXT machine environment could not be a global standard. Steve Jobs, CEO of NeXT Computers, had stopped producing these machines in the early 1990s. Clones were available but at substantial price increases over standard PC workstation configurations. In sum, efforts to standardize the IT environment were being met with stiff resistance.

In a similar vein, Lotus Notes was used by SG Warburg, and since SG Warburg had been the acquiree, not the acquirer, there was some doubt that it should become a standard in SBC Warburg. Courageous IT executives as well as senior leadership realized the untapped potential of Lotus Notes in the bank and fought hard for its acceptance. These brave souls were starting to win the battle.

Finally, a split occurred between IT and HR that is only being resolved as this chapter is being written. IT had focused entirely on providing service to the business units and the back office, which is where transactions the business units produce are finalized. As a result, HR had formed its own human resource information system (HRIS) function to develop systems for HR Department use. These systems for the most part didn't "speak" to the IT group's system. These separate IT functions are now being integrated to provide seamless service to everyone in the bank.

Team processes. S&D saw itself as a role model for the bank in the way teams were formed, did their work, and reformed into new teams as new assignments or business conditions required. S&D found itself moving erratically through the forming, storming, norming, and performing stages of team development [3]. Trust and professional respect levels were relatively high on the team. On several occasions, the S&D team discussed how close it was to becoming a high-performing team. The general consensus was that the team had quite a way to go toward becoming a high-performing team, although most team members were pleased with the team's progress toward this goal.

As S&D delivered on the performance management and leadership development initiatives, team members were being added, and others were leaving, either for different positions within the bank or to join new organizations. During 1995 and 1996, there was not a month that the team didn't experience a change in personnel or responsibility for projects or deliverables. This continuous change of team members added to the overall unstable environment that followed the SG Warburg acquisition.

From an implementation standpoint, we also learned several lessons that are relevant to HR professionals, internal IT professionals, and external consultants who are implementing systems in a global organization [4]:

☐ Get users involved in the decision-making and development processes. Let them own these processes from the beginning. Listen to their input. Get buy-in from the beginning.

☐ It is essential that at least one team member is included on the project team. A significant detriment to the project was Steve John's leaving before the system was tested and training developed. The role of the team member(s) included describing processes, reviewing specifications, testing the system, and participating in developing and delivering the training. A walkthrough of the system, with the entire team if feasible, and final consensus on how the application will work are critical requirements before implementation.

☐ Test, test, test. Make sure everything works as planned before you roll it out. Thorough testing to ensure the code meets the specifications is important. Before training team members, the system must operate successfully in the team's environment. The user community should test that the processes associated with the application are effective. To contain costs, against our better judgment we agreed to test the system and create training materials simultaneously. This was a significant mistake since the system was constantly changing as the training materials were developed. In the end, it probably took more time, rather than less, to do the functions in parallel rather than serially.

☐ Train, train, train. Insufficient training is often identified as the reason for slow acceptance or nonuse of applications. The training team should include users and members of IT who will support the application. The users should be involved in developing the training case study and delivering the training so they will be available for ongoing support after the initial training session. The training should include an overview of why the application has been developed, how it will be used in the environment, and procedures and examples of how to perform specific functions. Training participants should complete a case that follows the process from beginning to end. A team of two users at one machine was an effective means of delivering training for this application. The two users helped each other learn by discussing problems or issues and resolving them before moving forward in the case study. Training should include quick-reference materials and resources for coaching and support.

Cultural issues. During this initiative, the bank had been valiantly trying to integrate at least four organizational cultures while continuing to grow the business at a furious pace. In addition to the differences in values and ways of doing business found in these four organizations, there were also other profound cultural differences at work in the bank's environment, for example, traders versus investment bankers [5]; business unit specialties, such as foreign exchange currency specialists versus bond and stock specialists; and, finally, a regional focus particular to Europe, Asia, or the Americas. Taken together, all these powerful differences tended to drive people toward preserving their present system versus taking the risk to support a new way of working. Vision and value messages were lofty and inspiring but targeted at the 25,000-foot level. Work processes, tools, and development and reward systems didn't support the vision and values articulated by senior management.

Reflecting on the Initiative

Using the 20/20 vision of hindsight and the process of critical reflection, we produced the following list of what we wish we had done:

1. Searched for a business development opportunity that had to be structured by utilizing a cross-functional and cross-regional team

2. Enrolled the appropriate business leader in the role of champion (that is, a visible supporter and ideally a participant in building a global collaborative team process)

3. Enrolled the chief technologist or, at the very least, a high-level technology executive in paving the way for infrastructure and technology support

4. Staffed the business development team with specialists committed to working across specialties as well as regional cultures

5. Clearly articulated the rewards available for the individual and team when they succeeded and also provided a communication process that spread the word after success and reward had been accomplished.

By taking these five actions, we would have clearly defined the business benefit of the collaborative team process, as well as connected HR processes to work team processes. Our approach to the initiative required that HR be a true business partner. While HR had a seat at the board of directors' table, it still hadn't proven itself to line executives. Many line executives saw HR people as paperwork and transaction specialists and not strategic business partners. By having S&D take the lead role, we were asking for respect and trust that HR had not yet earned.

Conclusion

The collaborative team process initiative is still alive. HR is gaining credibility at the line executive level. Several key hires from Top 5 investment banks are adding strategic capability, both in fact and in perception. Many existing SBC Warburg HR executives are strategists and consultants; however, the chaos and turmoil in the bank frequently hides this. Line executives demand that transactions be done now, while having a strategic business focus is viewed as only nice to have in your HR professionals. This is changing rapidly for the better.

S&D has gone through a major restructuring. Glenn Satty, a managing director, is now in charge. He is a hard-hitting, no-nonsense executive who heads up recruitment and education. He has responsibility for *all* education—technical, technology, and leadership development. He carries significant weight with line executives and has a long string of successes in the bank.

Some of the original S&D team members who are still on the team believe in the initiative and are working to present it to Satty for approval and funding. The bank still needs cross-functional and cross-regional teams to do global business deals, and the window appears more favorable at this point to refine and then implement the process we designed. Collaborative team work processes are needed to build the global business teams. HR people must work on teams that are internal to HR as well as having a role directly on a business unit team. This is our dream—that HR professionals will be thought of as business professionals who happen to specialize in HR. Maybe 1998 is the year SBC Warburg will make our dream a reality.

Successful implementation of collaborative technology requires both a careful assessment of the fit of technology to the organization and a well-designed training program that can introduce this technology and describe its potential benefits to the organization. One of our going-in assumptions was that HR professionals would understand and act on these requirements intuitively. Our experience is that, when it comes to technology, many HR professionals react like other first-time users. They are busy and perhaps believe, "I am smart and learn quickly, so I don't need to spend time on training." Ultimate success, measured by adoption of the system, depends on a team's acceptance of the system as a work process that will improve the efficiency of its work (at a minimum) and, it is hoped, its effectiveness too. Our collaborative team application with the implementation plan had the potential to improve efficiency within the S&D team as well as to provide an effective work process for the business units.

Groupware offers the potential to transform organizational functioning. Achieving that transformation requires significant effort and skill. HR professionals can play a significant role in integrating technology into business processes. Transforming their own department using groupware can be a good first step.

The technology implementation literature [6, 7] offers four prerequisites if the introduction of collaborative technology (groupware) is to be successful in fostering collaboration:

1. *A need to collaborate must exist.* This was true in the S&D team.

2. *Users must understand the technology and how it can support collaboration.* This was addressed in the implementation plan as two-phase training: first generic Notes, followed by a case-study hands-on training session of the document management application.

3. *The organization must provide appropriate support for the introduction and ongoing use of the technology.* Arrangements were made with the internal SBC Warburg IT staff to support the application after initial training.

4. *The company culture must support collaboration.* Because the S&D team was already collaborating on producing documents, we assumed the culture would be open to a work process tool that would aid in creating the global investment bank.

The technology implementation literature also provides pitfalls that we were aware of when we began the project. Our plan included interventions to avoid these pitfalls and to ensure successful use of the system. Examples of these pitfalls and our responses are in Table 7-1.

Despite the fact that we explicitly addressed the prerequisites and pitfalls, culture and policy did become significant issues within the team. This was the most powerful lesson we learned. The entire team agreed on the business problem that had been defined—to provide a more efficient and effective way to create, review, edit, approve, and publish documents within the S&D team. Collaboration was viewed as a necessary condition for the team to become a high-performing team. However, members of the team had different visions of how they would function as indi-

TABLE 7-1.
PITFALLS AND INTERVENTIONS.

Pitfall	Intervention
Systems more often reinforce existing structures and practices than introduce new ones.	We planned to introduce the system in the context of live work and not modify structures or practices. The system would be a new tool using existing structures and practices to make more efficient the sharing of information. We would not change the basic authoring tools, such as Microsoft Word, Excel, and Microsoft Project.
There is a need for an appropriate framework for understanding the technology, and a fit between the technology's underlying premise (such as collaboration) and the organization's structure, culture, and policies. A major question is: Can the technology provide benefit if it is implemented in the organization as it stands? Or must the technology or organization change for the implementation to be a success?	Since the leader of the S&D team believed that the application would improve efficiency of existing processes, the structure, culture, and policy issues did not seem relevant to this technology project. The collaborative technology application could be implemented in the organization without structural, cultural, or policy changes.

viduals and as subgroups. The criteria for senior management review became a major issue because there was some concern that the ultimate purpose of the system we were trying to implement was to provide a vehicle for senior management to function as Big Brother.

Almost a decade ago, Zuboff [8] cautioned us that computer-mediated work had a fundamentally different feel to it than current work processes. She forecasted that profound social and cultural issues would arise out of integrating computers into work processes. Earlier, Deal and Kennedy [9] started discussions on organizational culture and its impact on people and work processes. It appears that technology and organizational development theory and practices must intersect as organizations restructure their work to achieve their business strategies. Yet even savvy HR professionals who have organizational development and technology experience find this intersection difficult to make sense of and deal with in rapidly changing cultures.

The role of organizational development specialists in providing effective change practices is more important than ever. However, it is also much more complicated now. The technology itself adds a major body of expertise that organizational development professionals as well as other HR professionals must now master. Finally, cultures in chaos have surfaced a paradox for everyone in an organization but especially for HR professionals who are attempting to transform themselves, their departments, and the business units—all in the same time period. The chaos can make it incredibly difficult to make sense of situations and apply the appropriate processes and tools to positively change the situation(s). At the same time, this state of chaos can present the opportunity to make deep systemic change a reality. Collaboration between senior and line leadership, technology operations and support, and HR professionals is critical to making these systemic changes a reality. It is our hope that this case study sheds light on the roles and responsibilities of all the above constituencies in the organization. An American Express television commercial tells us, "Don't leave home without it." Our experience in SBC Warburg tells us that "you don't leave home without it"—technology-enabled collaboration, that is.

References

1. Hammer, M. and Stanton, S. *The Reengineering Revolution: A Handbook.* New York: Harper Business, 1995.

2. John, S. G. "A Study of Team Learning in a Professional Services Firm," Unpublished doctoral dissertation, New York: Columbia University, 1995.

3. Tuckman, B. W. "Developmental Sequence in Small Groups." *Psychological Bulletin,* Vol. 63, No. 6, 1965.

4. Gorelick, C. K. "Toward an Understanding of Groupware and Organizational Learning: A Case Study of Structuration and Sensemaking in Virtual Project Teams," Unpublished dissertation proposal, Washington, D.C.: The George Washington University, 1997.

5. Auletta, K. *Greed and Glory on Wall Street: The Fall of the House of Lehman.* New York: Warner Books, 1986.

6. Bjorn-Anderson, N., Eason, K., and Robey, D. *Managing Computer Impact: An International Study of Management and Organizations.* Norwood, N.J.: Ablex, 1986.

7. Orlikowski, W. "Learning from Notes: Organizational Issues in GroupWare Implementation." *Proceedings of the ACM Conference on Computer-supported Cooperative Work,* Toronto: Oct. 31–Nov. 4, 1992, pp. 362–369.

8. Zuboff, S. *In the Age of the Smart Machine: The Future of Work and Power.* New York: Basic Books, 1988.

9. Deal, T. E. and Kennedy, A. A. *Corporate Culture.* Reading, Mass.: Addison-Wesley, 1982.

8

Career Dynamics in a Major Commercial Bank Exposed to Downsizing and Strategic Reorientation

HENRIK HOLT LARSEN, LILIAN MORGENSEN,
AND TANYA RYTTERAGER OLSEN

This case describes changes in a major bank in Denmark. The organizational changes stem from the forces affecting many organizations around the world—increased competition, new technology, and deregulation. The firm merged with several smaller banks, downsized, and in the process, introduced a series of human resource initiatives to develop managers and help them adapt to the changing organizational circumstances and expectations. The changes affected career paths, changed the nature of job security, and increased employees' responsibility for their own development. The HR Department introduced a number of creative programs for new and different career opportunities.

Corporate Profile

Den Danske Bank is an international financial-services organization based in Denmark. It is the leading purveyor of financial services to Denmark's corporate sector and the first choice for other financial institutions, public authorities, and foreign companies looking for banking services. The bank counts nearly one third of the Danish population as its customers. The bank was created in 1990 by the merger of three banks, and it is one of the leading banks in Scandinavia. The bank's head office is located in Copenhagen, and the rest of Denmark is covered by a network of 432 branches. At the end of 1996, the bank employed 11,100 full-time staff members.

Environmental Influences on Internal Reorganization and Development

In recent years, the Danish financial sector has seen many changes, and these changes have not abated. A number of external factors have affected the bank's organization and presented considerable managerial challenges. These factors have provided the bank with new opportunities but have also set certain restraints. The most important external factors impacting the bank were the national economy, profitability, competition, legal regulations, customers, and new technology.

A financial institution the size of Den Danske Bank is strongly affected by cyclical fluctuations in the national economy. This is a well-known challenge to management. Particularly in banking, the quality of management is really on trial during a recession. In the late 1980s and early 1990s, the recession in Denmark led to a large number of bankruptcies and forced sales—and a sharp fall in employment. This seriously affected the sector's business potential, and core earnings fell. It also put pressure on the bank to enhance the efficiency of its operations to sustain profitability; and even though the economy is now undergoing healthy growth, the requirement for greater efficiency still exists.

Expectations of keener competition from foreign banks also proved correct; competition has been heating up in the last few years because new technology makes the physical location of a bank less important. Within the Scandinavian market, for example, cross-border business is increasing and is now aimed at both corporate and retail customers. Foreign banks, however, are not Den Danske Bank's only competitors. Other Danish banks are also becoming stronger competitors. Although Den Danske Bank is the largest bank in Denmark, it is experiencing competition from niche banks, special-purpose banks, and regional banks, as well as from new types of players, such as finance companies.

The legal regulation of the financial sector, or more precisely, the deregulation, has meant that banking, mortgage credit, life insurance, and general insurance, which were previously provided by separate companies, are increasingly being provided by the same company or encompassed by various cooperative agreements. This has been a significant factor in the shift made by Den Danske Bank from providing traditional banking services (deposit taking and lending) to becoming a financial supermarket, providing banking, mortgage credit, life insurance, and general insurance services.

The demands and needs of customers are of course essential to the bank's development—no customers, no profits. And today's varied customers are far more critical of and less loyal to the bank than they used to be. In general, social trends have altered customers' savings habits. The recession in the late 1980s and early 1990s has made customers more cautious when it comes to borrowing money. The bank has therefore found it more difficult to generate earnings from the traditional banking services.

The conditions of contact with customers are also changing markedly. Previously, all contact with customers was made at the bank. New technology, however, means that customers no longer have to come to the bank as often. And when they do come, they place other and higher demands on the bank's advisory services to meet their special needs. This in turn places greater demand on the bank to deliver customized service, while the traditional banking products, little by little, become standard goods.

With respect to both customers and the bank, technological developments have led to a higher use of resources for more and more complex problems. New technology used to be applied primarily to making production processes more efficient, whereas new possibilities exist today. For example, the bank now sells banking software and has new distribution channels. And in the future, the bank will market new financial products and services electronically—on the Internet—which will simplify and build communication lines directly between the bank and its customers.

By virtue of its size and financial strength, Den Danske Bank has played an important part in the development of Denmark's financial sector. But continued development is required for the bank to maintain and expand its position and to ensure satisfactory core earnings by providing customers with the right services at competitive prices. The bank has therefore been undergoing constant reorganization since the merger. At the end of 1996, yet another reorganization process began to change the bank fundamentally from an administrative organization to a competitive marketing enterprise that focuses persistently on sales and customers. The ability to reorganize is therefore an essential core competency required for the bank's success.

Internal Reorganization and Development on Many Fronts

Overall, the following four organization components are the focus of the bank's current reorganization effort: structure, tasks/objectives, tools/technology, and employees.

The employees of Den Danske Bank—and also its customers—have slowly become accustomed to a steady flow of changes. This does not mean that everybody is delighted about them. In fact, this is far from being the case.

One of the most important structural changes that has taken place since the merger has been combining the three banks into one. It was not easy at the beginning, but it gave the bank good practice in reorganization and organization development from the outset. The bank's major objective was to get the structure right as soon as possible and to achieve economies of scale.

Other things being equal, the merger may be regarded as a structural merger. The focus was on the bank's new tasks, new products, and new business objectives—while attending to the new structure. The cultural factors were thus not in the spotlight. Not until 1993—three years after the merger—were new measures initiated to integrate the three different banking cultures into one new culture.

On the technology side, it was important to focus on introducing a common system for the bank as quickly as possible, establishing efficient internal operating systems and smooth systems for customers.

Finally, reorganization is still under way as the bank's strengths and weaknesses are discovered. The most recent instance of this was the shift to a sales-oriented organization. In general, there is the realization that it is very important to continually assess whether the bank's structure is optimal in relation to the tasks that must be performed.

These structural reorganizations have greatly affected the bank's tasks, the need for new technological tools, and employees. The focus of the bank's tasks has shifted toward international business development, particularly in the Nordic countries. Furthermore, technological developments, combined with an expansion of the product range, have meant moving away from heavy administration to a focus on sales, advisory services, and product development and service. And in sales and advisory services, there has been a shift from supporting traditional bank products toward a full-service concept in financial services. This places new demands on employees and drives the bank's HR objective, which is quite simply that employees and managers become so willing to change and show such great adaptability that the bank will be able to respond constructively to unforeseen developments. The ongoing challenge to Human Resources has been to handle the dilemma presented by the business reality described above: employee development and downsizing at the same time, during a period when all employees are finding their bearings after the merger.

Human Resource Initiatives

When the first wave of excitement after the 1990 merger had passed, the bank announced in 1992 that the number of employees was to be involuntarily reduced by 20 percent over a three-year period. This was a significant change. It resounded throughout the entire financial sector since it was a break from the previously enjoyed job security that existed in the financial sector. The shock waves spread even further, creating ill will among the Danish population—resulting in a loss of image for Den Danske Bank. This reduction was later followed by voluntary early retirement programs; however, by the end of 1996, it was ascertained that voluntary retirement was not sufficient, so additional involuntary cuts were made.

Since the merger, reductions have cut the number of employees by just over 25 percent. A combination of external factors drove the reductions. As mentioned above, general economic trends led to a slowdown in the growth of the bank's traditional business. At the same time, competition has lowered profit margins. To sustain and strengthen the bank's core business, it has quite simply been necessary to reduce costs. To a bank, this inevitably means a reduction of payroll costs, since payroll represents about 70 percent of a bank's overall expenses.

The bank has regularly said that employee downsizings will continue. Some of the reasons for this include the development of new technology, rising internationalization, and keener competition. Although the bank has cultivated new business areas, they have not been sufficient to maintain the same level of employment. Moreover, new business areas often require different competencies, which current employees may not possess.

Obviously, the ongoing reductions have given rise to a feeling of insecurity among employees, a feeling that has no doubt grown since the merger.

Career Development

Before the merger, in the "old bank," the criteria for success within the bank were well known. A relationship of trust existed between employees and decision makers about job rotation and appointments, which depended both on accomplishments and, because of the size of the organization, personal networking. Career plans and agreements were made and kept. This gave employees a feeling of security and a clear idea of their own possibilities—as well as the limitations faced in the organization.

The merger and reductions blurred this picture for employees, thereby rendering it difficult for them to find their bearings and assess their worth in the organization. The new values, measuring sticks, and criteria of success were neither visible nor communicated clearly. Furthermore, the organization grew and became harder for the decision makers to comprehend. Old networks were breaking up. Finally, the criteria of success were dynamic because they were greatly influenced by external factors, such as competition and customer demands.

Employee job uncertainty curbed development and growth—of both the individual and the organization—and this affected productivity and, ultimately, earnings. This kind of uncertainty also created the risk that many competent employees would seek new opportunities in other companies. To avoid this, an *in-house recruitment data bank* was established at the time of the merger; it was used to register employees with managerial and specialist potential. Special career plans were made for such employees. To retain them, they were given special treatment. These career plans were different from those of the "old bank" because these were more goal-oriented. In the first rounds of downsizings, special attention was therefore paid to these employees: they were told by their managers that the bank had plans for them. The bank wanted to increase the feeling of security for the employees it considered high-potential employees.

With the purpose of making the objectives, values, and policies of the "new bank" more visible, a *training course* was held for all employees. It focused on the company of Den Danske Bank. It emphasized quality and cooperation and, most of all, focused on dialoguing with employees about the bank's new values. At the same time, HR kicked off a more targeted *competence development program,* recognizing that employees' competence and qualifications are important competitive parameters for a business in the services sector. Of particular concern was the need to develop workers with knowledge rather than those with strong administrative skills, who were primarily accustomed to supporting manual work routines.

Finally, to make tomorrow's job requirements also more visible, a *job handbook* was published for employees. This handbook described the various types of jobs at the bank, listed skills and personal requirements, and outlined career paths and opportunities.

The development of competence and targeted planning were supported by a new *employee interview policy* introduced in 1993. The purpose of this initiative was to ensure that a more precise dialogue would take place between managers and employees about the bank's needs and demands in relation to the employees' career plans, qualifications, and potential. The interview has two components: a status section and a development section, and the latter includes an action plan for the employee's professional and personal development. The status section provides the opportunity for each employee to receive general feedback about his or her accomplishments and potential on the basis of the past year's results. As a result of this status discussion, the manager and the employee must come to an agreement on the required development of the employee and the creation of an action plan. The action plan is thus a kind of career plan the employee should follow on a daily basis. If the manager finds that the employee has managerial or specialist potential, that employee may be registered in the in-house recruitment data bank. The employee interview is thus the foundation for all career planning at the bank. And at the bank employees may pursue careers on vertical, diagonal, and horizontal courses—and also downward, when appropriate.

Management Development

A new *management policy* was released in 1994. The policy outlined the expectations for and demands on group executives. Overall, it specified that senior managers must be capable of achieving business results; focusing on the customer and increasing customer satisfaction; achieving profitability in daily operations; and developing their own organizations, employees, and themselves.

Issuing this policy was a major attempt to make clear to managers at Den Danske Bank that they themselves must be able to contribute actively to the bank's readiness to change, particularly in how they relate to customers and how they develop their organizations and their people in times of change. The policy also made clear that a manager's own professional competence was no longer enough in itself. Personality as well as skills became essential factors to be taken into account when appointing managers. This approach to staffing was a break with a long tradition at the bank of appointing managers chiefly on the basis of their professional qualifications.

But this new management policy alone was not enough to change. It was therefore underpinned by a comprehensive training and development program: *the management development program*. The main purpose of this program was precisely to strengthen the individual manager's ability to manage changes in how he or she goes about the day-to-day work. This involved, among other things, seeing the necessary connections between the environment, business opportunities, and possibilities for reorganization and development. The management development program was thus a way of securing the bank's future in that the bank's managers would be better equipped to play a more active role in future reorganization and ongoing organization development processes. The program combined theoretical learning and practical learning, and in the latter, the daily manager took on the role of mentor.

Our experience with the management development program demonstrates so far that the bank's managers obtained greater insight into the external and internal factors involved in the reorganization process, and they also expanded their contacts in the larger network of managers across the bank. These results have already helped initiate large and small changes, which have further moved the bank in the right direction.

Besides the management development program, another comprehensive process has now begun that should help ensure the reorganization and ongoing development of the bank: a *total quality program*. It is a long-term organizational development process that concentrates on involving employees, managers, and if possible, customers in the ongoing development of a more customer-oriented organization—in short, the program concentrates on creating more and more satisfied customers. At regular intervals, customers as well as employees share their perceptions, captured through questionnaires and interviews, of the current quality level of the bank and areas they think should be improved.

Driven by these customer satisfaction measurements, a number of activities have been initiated in every department to contribute to the following:

☐ Making the branch or department more customer-minded

☐ Making internal work processes in the individual departments and across the organization more effective

☐ Improving internal collaborative relations among specialists

☐ Increasing the employees' engagement and motivation

☐ Creating a more visible and goal-oriented management.

The total quality program will, without a doubt, shake up the bureaucracy and the sometimes-too-formal organization. Employees will have greater responsibility, influence, and involvement in the process of change. As a result, they will help ensure that resources are used as well as possible—for the benefit of the customer, as well as for themselves.

For a service organization like Den Danske Bank, intellectual capital is a strategic asset. Through the management process that this total quality program constitutes, HR can help ensure that the bank will capitalize on its resources as it pursues its business opportunities.

Impact of the Changes

This section is based on information collected during interviews with fourteen members of Den Danske Bank. The interviewees were employees, managers of employees, managers of managers, and senior managers, and these interviewees represented the head office as well as the branch network. The purpose of these interviews was to determine employees' attitudes toward career development in light of the transformation process following the merger. We begin with a discussion of the interviewees' ideas about careers in general and of their attitudes toward the merger.

The career concept is understood in various ways at the bank. According to our sample, two definitions of *career* exist: a wide definition and a narrow definition. The wide definition of a career is that a career is a working-life process in which individuals strive for something they would like to do and in which they reach their own goals, improving their qualifications in the process. This career definition focuses on personal and work-related development in a direction determined by the individual in order to reach specific goals; it is not associated with certain positions, titles, or authority. By this definition, a career is a "path in your working life" or "how you manage your time in the labor market," according to interviewees. In this way, there is no difference between pursuing a career and having one or several jobs. "A career is probably something that we all have," one respondent said.

The narrow definition of a career is that a career is a planned, and often managerial, working-life process in which individuals advance in a hierarchy and in which their careers are defined by how far they get. Interviewees described those who progress in this model as people who strive for power and responsibility and who have a natural gift for making it (climbing the ladder of success).

However, several interviewees considered it difficult to define the career concept in the first place. They confused the wide and narrow definitions, as is evident from the following remark, in which one person in the same sentence states that he *has* but does not *pursue* a career: "Having a career is to advance in the hierarchy; it is also something planned. I haven't done that because I haven't planned my career."

Our sample of employees largely agreed that pursuing a career does not necessarily involve climbing the ladder of success. "It may be a horizontal move as well as a vertical move. And across business sectors and national borders," one interviewee said. If pursuing a career is to strive to reach individual goals, then a career does not have to entail an upward move. But as another respondent put it, it may "take a strong personality" to move in directions other than up or down. "It is difficult to pursue your career while descending the ladder," one interviewee said, but pursuing a career should, in principle, mean moving in all directions with respect to levels of activity, commitment, and influence.

Yet several employees suggested that it is not always socially acceptable to move in directions other than up, particularly if you are well known in your local community. Another issue is that the pay structure—although it reflects the hierarchical type of career—may seem illogical: "After all, it is a paradox that you are on the highest pay scale when you retire," a respondent pointed out.

As we discussed earlier in this chapter, employees have experienced many changes since the merger started, and this has put great demands on employees and managers. For example, one interviewee stated, "The bank is a mirror image of the outside economic reality and the economic situation of the country. We are affected by what happens in society, and you never know what might happen." Despite this, all respondents generally considered the reorganization an exciting, but tough, process that was an inevitable consequence of merging three major banks. As another employee put it, "Quite a number of people were laid off, and it wasn't funny, but most of the people laid off were the right ones to go. The number of people working in the banking sector was too high." Another said, "If your attitude was negative at the time of the merger, you would probably not be on the payroll today. If you have chosen to join the new bank, it's full speed ahead and don't look back."

Our interviewees agreed with the need for and the inevitability of the merger. They saw it as removing a good many dysfunctional aspects of the three individual banks involved in the merger and creating one bank better capable of operating on contemporary business terms. Yet the merger was as painful as it was right and necessary, and it put great demands on individuals for tolerance, respect, the ability to free themselves from a sheltered life, living with massive press coverage, and the ability to work with colleagues who came from entirely different cultures. On one hand, the drastic measures of recent years have created fewer career opportunities—mostly the result of downsizing—thereby reducing the number of vacancies, including managerial positions. On the other hand, the new activities in the bank (combined with an economic recovery) and greater employee turnover have stimulated mobility: "When you expand your activities, you also expand your opportunities. If one thing is possible, then so is another, but it will take a greater effort," an employee told us. The spectrum of tasks is wider, so "you will not be caught up in one type of company," another said. One interviewee commented, "Pursuing a career at the bank today is not the same as it was in the mid-eighties. The bank is making other demands today. The bank used to attach importance to specialized qualifications, which it still does, but it is now considering personal qualities as well. Yet this is still not enough. Today you must be quick, competent, accurate, and honest to do business with, and this is what counts."

The merger involved many dismissals and made employees somewhat insecure, but those who remain on staff have now accepted the fact that they must continue to improve their skills, as the bank keeps only the most competent employees on its payroll. The merger is therefore considered a great milestone in the daily life and work of all employees. But the merger also brought new opportunities for career development. Opportunities now exist in the form of new job types, giving employees a larger spectrum of job opportunities. Opportunities, as well, are now greater for specialists since the bank has increased in size and since the chances of working in other branches and departments are better than before. More importantly, many employees think they have learned quite a few lessons from the merger and its consequences; in other words, they have increased their abilities to tackle problems. The downside of the merger is that it also introduced limitations to career development, which the staff members meet in the form of a new culture, a nonexisting network, and rationalizations as a result of new technology. On balance, however, employees consider the merger a positive one because it has brought about a wider spectrum of opportunities for personal development, new challenges, and career moves.

Most of the employees interviewed agreed that the bank gives career development a rather high priority, and they pointed out that in the last three to five years they have seen a sharp boost in career development. "Rationalizations have made people realize the importance of having the right person for the right position," a respondent said. Before, chance and personal willpower determined people's careers, but today the bank is pursuing a totally different policy of employee interviews, training, and commitment from senior management. This policy has increased employees' opportunities since "it is possible to move around the entire organization," although it may be necessary to stay in the same function for two or three years. But another interviewee said, "If you don't study and take courses, you shouldn't expect to get very far. The choice is yours alone." One employee put it this way: "Career development is given high priority at the bank on the assumption that you will do all the legwork by yourself. It is all at your feet— all you have to do is choose from the many opportunities."

Generally, the bank's employees are benefiting from this new development environment. The vast majority of the people we interviewed said that if individuals display initiative, opportunities will abound for them. They have every chance, and if they have the desire, the bank is willing to spend the money. One respondent simply put it like this: "It's easy and simple to pursue a career at Den Danske Bank." But some people also described the culture as a barrier, citing "the very correct habits, the defensive routines, the suppression of bad news and the consideration of good news only, the appearance as a winner, the banking facade, and the reluctance of staff members to ask others for help" as problem areas.

The bank offers two types of *career paths*: managerial and specialist. This is not said in so many words, but it can be read between the lines. Our interviewees largely agreed that many opportunities exist for a specialist career if an individual does not want to become a generalist. "Opportunities are available to every taste," one person remarked. Even though a career at Den Danske Bank may not be of a truly specialist nature, a huge number of specialist functions exist within the branch network and at the head office. And the bank tends to "promote specialists by rewarding those who strive to become super-specialists instead of encouraging them to become managers if they have no potential in this respect. Yet this does not take place systematically. It is all done on a subjective and individual basis," said one respondent. Several people, however, think the management training program is given higher priority than the specialist training program. But employees at the bank are generally satisfied with the specialist career training program. Yet a few believe that specialist careers should be given as high a priority as managerial careers.

Finally, the size of the bank means that opportunities for employees are abundant, but our sample believes that the cultural characteristics of the bank have put a check on many of the initiatives taken. They also feel that the merger has brought about positive cultural changes but also say that a total change in the culture will be long in coming.

As discussed earlier in the chapter, the process of change and the ever-changing world of finance have caused employees to feel somewhat insecure about their jobs and careers, and this is clearly reflected in our interviewees' attitudes toward the future. They believe that the future will entail the following:

☐ Fewer managerial positions and thus fewer managerial opportunities

☐ Fewer jobs and more staff cutbacks, but better and more opportunities for the remaining staff

☐ More use of specialists and less use of generalists

☐ Fewer, but larger, branches

☐ Fewer opportunities for the traditional banker.

Since the bank is progressing at an accelerating speed, few of the people we interviewed have a concrete plan for their futures. Yet most of them have ideas of their aspirations in life, their future jobs, and so on. Generally, they predict that jobs in the financial sector will be scarcer in the future but also that the remaining employees will have many opportunities open to them.

Conclusion

The case of Den Danske Bank leads to a good many interesting conclusions:

1. The case presents and argues for the contextual dependency that is and should be present in career development. Before, during, and after the merger, the business environment, including the bank's business opportunities, has largely dictated the need and opportunities for career development. Adapting a company's career development program to its surrounding environment is thus not just a textbook exercise. Career development is actually one of the tools used by the bank to secure itself a place in the future world of finance.

2. The case demonstrates that nothing is so bad that it is not good for something. Tougher conditions of existence, sharper competition, and higher expectations from customers and society in general were so severe that no one questioned the necessity of taking fairly severe measures. Simply realizing the gravity of the situation brought about an understanding as well as a kind of energy within the system to do something: intimidation will promote understanding. As a matter of fact, the easier conditions of existence for the bank and the comfortable economic situation that prevailed before the merger did not help the bank maintain or develop its readiness for change. On the contrary, it created an illusion of peace and tranquility.

3. The many dramatic changes introduced at the merger and the consequent cutbacks meant that many taboos about career development were overthrown. The concept of job security was given a new meaning, career plans were changed, new demands were made on managers and employees, and career development opportunities were improved and radically changed in the process.

4. The merger was a crash test of the organization's and employees' abilities to change; knowing the ins and outs of the orga-

nization, being familiar with existing routines, and knowing how matters of a similar nature used to be solved no longer conferred status and authority. The organization was now adapting to deal with new routines, and matters were often being solved in new ways. This was putting large demands on employees because part of their "heritage" was in fact of no use or perhaps even detrimental in these situations now involving other new demands and methods of working. Similarly, the organization had to not only merge three units (and cultures) into one but also had to strengthen its ability to do banking business on new and different grounds in an ever-changing society. It is thought-provoking and exciting that the bank distinguishes between working out general strategic plans and simply strengthening its ability to change by setting new goals.

5. The case shows that the merger and the turbulence of recent years (including the layoffs) have actually improved career development opportunities instead of curtailing them. New types of jobs have emerged, new career paths have seen the light, dogmas about the necessity of sticking to a certain process of development have been weakened, and the speedy development of job tasks and working conditions makes the daily work an intensive learning process. Despite the staff cutbacks and the shedding of a large number of managerial positions, opportunities for training, job rotation, and promotion have improved. Yet this assumes that each individual has the necessary qualifications and background, and is committed and willing to help create opportunities for development. Career development has largely become a buffet of choices and opportunities, but employees are expected to help themselves.

6. Employees reacted rather positively to the changes, including the layoffs, that were a consequence of the merger. The people who remained and who are still on the bank's payroll feel that the measures were not only necessary but also largely implemented in a sensible way. They also say that it is now time for

employees to look ahead. They feel that the dramatic measures taken have strengthened the bank's position and have made further growth and financial success feasible. In other words, the bank is now a better place to work!

7. The bank is characterized as a good place for learning and personal development, with undreamed-of opportunities, provided that employees are aware of these opportunities and know how to make the most of them. The introduction of new business activities, the high number of development projects, the growing cooperation across the organization, the training programs, the management development program, and the staff interview policy are all considered "boosters" to the career development of employees and thus create a perception that anything is possible if employees know when and how to make their moves. This being said, the bank's culture is considered an important factor. This means that the hierarchical structure impedes the emergence of alternatives to the traditional, vertical promotion; that the banking way of putting everything in boxes puts a check on the willingness and ability of an individual to experiment and test new methods; that the conservative and prudent banking attitude tends to have a behavior-controlling and unifying effect on the staff; that the structure of power and respect for authority curtail the free exchange of information on, say, problems and mistakes; that too much energy is wasted on keeping up appearances instead of working with specific job tasks; and that status, pay, and opportunities for promotion make traditional virtues persist instead of rewarding new behavioral patterns. In other words, a certain degree of repression exists that helps keep the bank locked in the past but that is also being bombarded by inside and outside influences and, not least, by the growing external recruitment of employees for managerial and other key positions in specialist functions.

8. The case demonstrates the schism, present in most other companies, between the wide and the narrow career concepts. The

majority of the employees we spoke with are strong advocates of the view that a career is and should be a full-life process—regardless of its direction, form, and goal—and *not* just a vertical organizational climb. Yet the collective self-knowledge at the bank is typically characterized by the narrow definition of a career: climbing the ladder of success is good. Moving in other directions requires a specific reason and is less attractive to many staff members. Moreover, the bank is not able to offer alternative career-development possibilities (with respect to status, title, and pay). Yet there is a major breakthrough in this respect, as the specialist career is becoming a legitimate alternative to the managerial career. Not least, as a result of difficult and complex business conditions, a need exists for a large number of highly qualified specialists, and since many employees do not necessarily strive for managerial careers, the bank must create career paths in a number of functional specialties.

9. The case presents a company that has chosen to embed and support career development in a number of coordinated but independent activities that have been launched within a short period of time. Part of the explanation for why the bank is perceived as an active environment for employee and management development is probably the synergy emerging among recruitment, training, employee interview and assessment systems, pay, and in-house training. These systems are all based on the same organizational reality and support and depend on each other. One clear example is the interplay between the in-house recruitment data bank and the management development program; earmarking employees for managerial jobs assumes there is something to earmark them for, while a development program like the management development program presupposes initial screening and selection.

10. The case demonstrates the central role line managers play in the development of employees' careers. Nearly all career development methods depend on the active participation of line

managers in their own development. In fact the management development program is targeted to train managers for this role. But although line managers are largely responsible for employee career development, the belief is that that line managers are seldom rewarded handsomely for these efforts. The general view is that many managers continue to be promoted—or are allowed to remain in their present managerial positions—by virtue of their professional banking qualifications.

11. The opportunities for career development are almost unlimited. Yet individuals must realize and seek these opportunities for themselves, communicate their wishes to their managers and the system, be willing to take on new challenges, participate in training, and neutralize active or passive resistance from a manager who may not be particularly talented or interested in employee career development. This proactive, even aggressive, style suggested for employees, however, conflicts with the classic pattern of banking virtues and probably makes it difficult for those who are not as good at drawing attention to their track records.

12. The case describes a company that clearly subscribes to the earmarking of potential candidates for managerial and key positions. The purpose of the in-house recruitment data bank is to provide a basic list of qualified employees from which to pick to fill managerial vacancies in the organization. Supported by the employee interview process and staff assessment systems, employees are able to make up their minds about the development of their own careers, to discuss this with their managers, and to apply for other positions within the company. Yet it appears from the interviews that many people have the opinion that the in-house recruitment data bank is often not used when vacancies are to be filled. The informal network, contacts within the organization, and being in the right place at the right time are all still regarded as common and efficient methods to fill vacancies.

In summary, the case described a bank that changed its relationship with its external environment as well as its internal organization because the conditions for its continued existence changed radically. In specific, it had to drastically alter its approach to career development to adapt to these changing conditions. In view of an entire renegotiation of the psychological contract in accordance with these new conditions, the enthusiasm for and satisfaction with the career development opportunities remain strong. But to ensure the bank's long-term success, it is still necessary to improve career development methods, to adapt the opportunities to a wider perception of the definition of *career,* and to change the bank's culture to support career development more than it does now.

9

Today's Special: Career Development in a Spaghetti Organization— Think the Unthinkable in a Dynamic Network Organization

HENRIK HOLT LARSEN AND STINNE MADSEN

Introduction

This case deals with career development processes in Oticon, a Danish high-technology company with about 1,500 employees. The company produces hearing aids and hearing-care products

229

and is one of the world market leaders in this industry. The headquarters is located in Copenhagen, and the production takes place
in several locations in Denmark. The company also has sales
offices in most parts of the world.

In 1990 through 1991, the company underwent extensive organizational changes, which, among other things, introduced a pro-
ject-oriented, loose organization structure, an open-office plan
with mobile workstations, and a paperless information system.
These—and other organizational initiatives—not only led to radical renewal of the firm but also altered career development
processes and employees' career opportunities.

Here we present a brief description of the company's development, a description of organizational changes that started in the
early 1990s, and the implications of these changes for perceived
opportunities for employee growth as well as barriers to career
development. The case is based upon personal interviews with
twelve managers, including the firm's president.

This case demonstrates how introducing new, innovative organizational structures and processes can affect human resource
issues, such as career growth and advancement opportunities. Like
other examples in this book, the case shows the tie between organizational change and human resource issues. Unlike other cases,
however, neither a human resource department nor HR professionals played a dominant role in the design and implementation
of the change. Indeed, Oticon didn't even have a traditional
human resource department. Nor did it call on external HR consultants to help with the change. The initiatives described here
were introduced by the firm's CEO, who was the driving force
and principal change agent. The case shows how new ways of
doing business can affect employees' attention to human resource
issues. Moreover, it shows that traditional human resource
processes, such as career planning and development programs, do
not necessarily fit with new organizational designs. Theory and
practice do not provide much guidance on how organizations like

Oticon can handle employees' needs for career growth and advancement. In this instance, most if not all employees felt that the new flat, flexible organization structure and the absence of bureaucracy and hierarchy were empowering. Some missed the support for professional growth that can be fostered by training and human resource departments and the opportunities to advance one's career within the firm by moving up a corporate hierarchy.

The Company's Foundation and History Prior to 1988

The Beginning . . .

Oticon is a Danish hearing-aid producer, the world's third largest. Since its establishment more than 90 years ago by Hans Demant, the national and international market for hearing-aid equipment has expanded tremendously. After the death of Hans Demant in 1910, his son William took over the company as managing director. At this point, Oticon was merely importing hearing-aid equipment produced in the United States. This continued until the mid-1940s, when the lack of reliable supplies, due to World War II, made William Demant start the first production of Danish hearing-aid equipment in 1946.

Oticon As a World Market Factor

The growth of Oticon and other Danish hearing-aid companies was helped by the Danish government's decision that hearing aids should be available to the public free of charge. This increased demand considerably. In 1958, William Demant retired, leaving the firm in the hands of a board of four senior managers. This was a somewhat untraditional move. When the new management team members, who were all in their thirties, took over, the company still had a craftsman culture. Little new technology had found its way to Oticon, and most production processes were carried out by hand. During the following years, Oticon expanded by establishing subsidiaries in many countries, including New Zealand, Spain, Japan, England, and France. An increasing focus was also placed on research. As a result, Oticon became one of the most proactive companies in the industry, launching a number of better and smaller products. An engineering culture emerged in the company as it focused on becoming a leading-edge technology company. Production increased as well. However, marketing was given short shrift.

Oticon in Trouble

In 1986, Oticon began to have financial problems. This started with the drop in the U.S. dollar exchange rate. This was a major problem because the U.S. market accounted for a large portion of Oticon's sales. Also, despite the advice of its own marketing department, the firm focused on developing technically better behind-the-ear products, while customers wanted in-the-ear equipment.

Oticon at a Crossroads

During 1986 through 1987, Oticon's top managers realized that something drastic had to be done. Oticon had put its stakes on the safer and more traditional products, which resulted in a lack of market development. It seemed clear that the managers who had by now been in charge of Oticon for almost four decades had to be replaced. Fresh ideas and new ways of looking at the business were needed. The board of directors informed the board of managers that it would start looking for a replacement. This time Oticon chose to have only one CEO instead of four.

An Upheaval in Company Culture

The Coming of a New Generation

Lars Kolind, forty-one years old with an engineering background, was hired as Oticon's CEO in 1988. One of his initial steps was to cancel employees' authority to conduct financial transactions that exceeded a certain amount without his personal authorization. If employees wanted money for an idea or a project, they had to conduct a feasibility study, which would assure Kolind that the money would be well spent. During 1988, Kolind fired 10 percent of the administrative personnel; he also worked with the board to cut costs, improve efficiencies, and enhance profitability. Four months after starting his new job, Kolind wrote a memo to all employees outlining the firm's new strategy: "All activities in Oticon are aimed at one task—becoming the most attractive partner for the world's most professional dealers and clinics of hearing-aid equipment." Early in 1990, he announced the birth of Project 330, to convey the goal of 30 percent growth in three years. He also announced that a number of fundamental organizational changes would occur to make the goal a reality. He encouraged employees to "think the unthinkable." The organizational changes were to take effect on August 8, 1991, thus giving the firm 1½ years to develop and implement the changes.

Needed Changes

According to Kolind, Oticon needed vital changes to have the lowest possible costs, ensure ongoing innovation, and still provide world-class quality and an intensive understanding of the customer. First of all Oticon needed new office facilities that would help the company overcome rigid organizational structures and a lack of constructive communication and cross-functional innovation. The new working conditions were supposed to emphasize and encourage working in cross-functional project teams. This would be facilitated by open office landscapes, flexible furniture, no titles, individual salaries based on what employees contributed—not on their positions—and total access to information of all kinds. These changes were intended to create and enhance communication and innovation. This meant employees would be working in an office environment where their personal belongings and all their papers could not exceed what could fit into a little cabinet with wheels on the bottom. This was done to ensure the most flexible working conditions possible. Literally, an employee could move every day based on his or her assignments and projects. The idea was that an employee might work on more than one project at a time. Table 9-1 outlines Oticon's new philosophy of management.

Second, the idea was to cut down paper use to an absolute minimum. All incoming papers were to be read, thrown out, or scanned into the network system before they were shredded. Creating the paperless office enhanced the idea of mobility and forced employees to get to know the computer system inside out. Every single employee, including Kolind, had a rolling cabinet and a password, which gave that person access to the network wherever he or she was seated. In 1993, the company won a prize for the most innovative information technology in Denmark.

To ensure that the vision became a reality, a committee was established to spearhead the new organizational processes. In April 1990, Kolind held a company-wide meeting in which he described to all employees the organization changes and the plans for unifying the departments. He told the employees about the rolling cabinet, about shredding all paper, about the new computer system, and about the 1,000 birch trees on wheels that he had ordered to make it possible to change the office environment from day to day. He also introduced the concept of multijobs.

TABLE 9-1.
OTICON'S MANAGEMENT PHILOSOPHY.

Oticon's Fundamental Human Values	How Do We Implement Them?
We assume Oticon employees want to take *responsibility* if they get the opportunity.	Whenever possible (especially within a project), employees choose tasks, work hours, and places of work.
We assume Oticon employees want to develop and *grow in their jobs* and experience new challenges within the company.	We make it possible for employees to assume several tasks at the same time, if interested and qualified—possibly with the support of colleagues.
We assume Oticon employees want the greatest possible *freedom* but at the same time accept the necessity of having a clear and structured *framework*—chiefly in the form of an accepted strategy and approved plans.	This freedom is possible because Oticon has the fewest rules possible and because we encourage employees to use their common sense instead of slavishly complying with the rules.
We assume Oticon employees want to have qualified and *fair* feedback for their work and a salary corresponding to their contribution.	All levels of management—technical, staff, and project managers—are required to give honest feedback to their employees. Each employee participates in an annual talk with his or her mentor. To achieve a fair salary assessment, Oticon considers the evaluations of relevant project and technical managers.
We assume Oticon employees want to be *partners* in Oticon, not adversaries.	At intervals, we offer Oticon shares at a favorable rate so employees benefit financially from the success to which they have contributed.
We assume Oticon employees want the *security* that derives from improving themselves in their current jobs so they are able to get another job if they—for one reason or another—should leave Oticon.	We make it possible for employees to improve themselves in their jobs and to assume other tasks in the company wherever relevant. We expect employees to take the initiative and to be willing to make an effort—possibly by participating in courses in their spare time.
We assume Oticon employees want to be treated as *grown-up, independent people.*	Oticon's entire way of operating supports this value.
We assume Oticon employees want to *understand* how their own tasks fit into the *context* of the whole company.	Oticon is an open company where all employees have access to as much information as possible. The limits are set partly by the data protection law and partly by the fact that certain pieces of information are so sensitive that we cannot run the risk of them getting into the wrong hands. When Oticon is quoted on the Copenhagen Stock Exchange, we shall have to respect the stock exchange rules of conduct, which set limits to openness concerning certain types of information.
We assume that Oticon employees are more interested in challenging and exciting tasks than in formal status and titles.	We have a minimum of titles and no formal career planning. We seek, however, to give each employee the possibility of personal and professional development through varied and increasingly challenging tasks.

The Concept of Multijobs

One of the profound changes anticipated at Oticon was the move to what was called multijobs. Having a multijob meant that an employee would have more than one job function. The idea was to capitalize on the employee's multiple competencies and give the employee an opportunity for continuous self-development. One of the best-known examples was the story of the accountant, who was fluent in the English language as well as Danish. Since the work load in Accounting was mostly concentrated around the beginning and the end of the month, the accountant would also be assigned to translate material into English for the marketing department during other times of the month.

The multijob concept meant an employee would be assigned to more than one project at a time. So, due to the reduction of administrative support work, administrative personnel would also take part in more innovative and creative assignments by participating in various project teams.

Thus, jobs in Oticon would be built around two different concepts, the project team and the multijob. While holding a multijob, employees would be involved in different projects and often more than one project at a time. Employees, however, could transfer themselves from one project team to another based on their time and interests. In this way Kolind succeeded in enhancing flexibility, innovativeness, and responsibility.

Supporting Initiatives

In the spring of 1990, with almost 1½ years before the actual implementation of the changes, employees were having a difficult time. Some were excited, some afraid, but most seemed to think that all these crazy ideas would never become reality anyway, and so they chose to wait and see. During this time the employees were offered the opportunity to purchase shares of Oticon at a favorable price. To communicate that he was serious about making the changes work, Kolind attached his own private fortune to Oticon by buying so much company stock that he would suffer a financial catastrophe if his plans failed.

During this time, Kolind stated, "Hearing aids are not the core of what this company is about. It's about something more fundamental. It's about the way people perceive work. We give people the freedom to do what they want."

The Spaghetti Organization

The structureless "structure" meant that a lot of assimilation was needed by employees. Employees had to develop new competencies, such as networking and interpersonal skills, to be able to make their way around an organization based on electronic and informal communication.

Now any employee could propose a project and could become the leader of a project. Project leaders were free to manage the project group as they deemed suitable. There were hardly any rules in the game, no job descriptions, no titles. Project leaders recruited the workers they wanted on their teams. As one employee said, "It's social Darwinism." The freedom to choose one's own methods meant that some project groups met every day, others once a week. Every group had to set its own goals and operating procedures. The only demands from the company were to honor the agreed-to deadlines and to keep costs within the budget. How, where, and why the groups worked was of no particular interest to Kolind as long as the results were there.

The Company's Development Since the Cultural Revolution

In 1992, Kolind hired a second-in-command, Niels Jacobsen. Kolind was the visionary, the man with all the ideas, the heart of the new Oticon, and the one who wanted all projects started right away. Jacobsen was the more traditional economic- and budget-minded type who would balance all Lars Kolind's "wild" ideas.

Oticon was on the right track. New products were developing and employees were getting used to the new organizational format. During the first years of the revolution, one might have expected a lot of people to leave the company due to the drastic changes. It turned out, though, that few employees left. Moreover, the publicity the company received about its new style of management led to numerous applications for employment.

By 1994 Oticon had launched fifteen new products, new-product lead time had been halved, revenue grew 20 percent per year, and profit grew from close to $0 in 1991 to $14 million. Oticon also bought several companies in both Switzerland and the United States.

Career Development: Possibilities and Limitations

The absence of management structure meant that project management was loose. It was a democratic form of management; in principle everyone had a chance to become a project leader and serve as a team member. However, it turned out that some projects were viewed as more important than others. Also, some projects were more successful than others in terms of how well the team members worked together and the outcome of the team effort. So employees competed with each other to be part of the projects they perceived as most desirable.

There was also the growing recognition that project management was not professional enough. This led to an intensive project management development program. This program included establishing and defining the function of the project manager, implementing a systematic selection procedure for project managers, offering courses in project management, and externally recruiting project management professionals.

Despite the professionalization of project managers, Oticon distanced itself from the traditional concepts of management, organization, and personnel administration. Employees could not speak openly about management development and about moving up in the hierarchy. "We don't distinguish so much between management and nonmanagement," one employee said. "Traditional management views have become practically taboo. However, traditional management problems still exist." Another person said, "Oticon *does* need management, but it is odious to speak of management." Others spoke about "the hierarchy that isn't there but naturally is there anyway." One person said, "Functional managers—well, we don't call them that, of course. We call them technical leaders for development and economy and marketing, et cetera, but in fact they are functional managers."

Employees had mixed emotions about this. On one hand, some found it pleasant not to have to compete for limited promotions. On the other, some found this frustrating in that few obvious ways to advance in the company existed. Yet some people were promoted to the few higher-level positions that existed or that were newly created, but it was not clear how this happened.

Career Development = f (Challenge, Responsibility, Project Management, Visibility, Prestige)

The possibilities for career development in Oticon were closely linked to the work situation itself. Everyone recognized that opportunities existed for independent work, challenge, influence, and responsibility. Generally, employees were greatly satisfied with this, even though not everyone felt they had the opportunities for development that they would have liked. Career development was not just a question of the challenges and the responsibilities one held. It was also a question of whether one was involved in project management, was visible to others, and enjoyed a certain amount of prestige. Generally speaking, career development for most people requires "more of everything," in that success seems to be measured by factors such as fields of responsibility, budget, closeness to the top management, which department one belongs to, and personal status.

The concept of career was viewed broadly at Oticon. Development didn't mean promotion or taking classes but rather participating in as many ways as possible that added value to the company. Some employees reacted positively to this while others did not. As one interviewee expressed it, "My guess is that for approximately half of the employees, the concept of a career has little meaning. That is, they are not worried about their career advancement. The other half do worry about this. They think that there are too few career opportunities in the company. They have trouble understanding or accepting that a career in Oticon means something other than advancement along a traditional organization hierarchy. They feel uncomfortable with the 'informal career scoring board' of who gets on what projects, who has the most personal influence, and who is most visible to the top executives." Traditional criteria for managerial success don't exist at Oticon, and there are not many status symbols a person can display to others that indicates his or her level of success. With the exception of mobile telephones, the company is nearly free of material status symbols. There are simply no traditional career paths.

On the face of it, Oticon was a textbook example of the learning organization. The possibilities for professional and personal development were proclaimed to be—and to a vast degree were—unlimited, and if one knew how to exploit these opportunities, he or she was able to develop competencies the organization valued. However, what in principle was an arena for professional, personal, and managerial development was seen by some as an arena with unclear roles and decision-making processes that lacked systematization and plans—or maybe even an anarchic arena. Some felt the vagueness and the lack of planning were not only inescapable consequences of the chosen way of organizing the company but that they were part of, maybe even the catalyst for, the learning process! Others pointed out that limited learning possibilities created lagunas of unexploited resources, caused insecurity, and furthered competitive, aggressive behavior. What for some was "the good career" entailing individual, flexible personal-development possibilities became a struggle, a limitation, and a barrier to development for others. Project management was not a viable career ambition. It didn't count for enough in Oticon.

Career development in Oticon (just as in other companies) was widely characterized by social processes. Personal contacts were critical for getting a good project idea accepted or for becoming part of a desirable project team. With a flat hierarchy, however, there was uncertainty about who had to be won over to get a project accepted. The project structure and importance of networking also fueled aggressive, competitive behavior. "You must have a lot of self-confidence in order to make it here," one person said.

Rounding Off

Kolind did not feel that the absence of traditional career development opportunities created a problem at Oticon. He stated, "I must say that there's room for improvement. Some people may feel that we don't pay enough attention to developing their potential. But this doesn't mean that they miss having a chance to move up an organization hierarchy. People want to do what they are best at. Top management needs to be more aware of what people really want to do."

Conclusion

There are pros and cons to a spaghetti-style organizational structure when it comes to career development. The unthinkable proved to be not only thinkable but also realistic. The firm showed that it could be successful and have an exciting, dynamic organization. However, some modifications were made. For instance, the idea of the movable workstations was realized, but the desks on wheels are only moved a couple of times a year now—not several times per day. Project groups have been retained but are now supported by a professional project-management organization. The free-and-equal access to projects still exists, but a discreetly informal project hierarchy and personal status variations send (in)visible signals about where one can turn to tap resources and secure good tasks. The CEO is still on board, but he has hired a co-CEO, who supplements the CEO rather than resembling him. The vision and the fundamental human values regarding the employees are still unflagging (see Table 9-1). The nearly religious conviction that management should not be personified and hierarchically rooted is undiminished, but some employees experience unsatisfactory career development opportunities. The CEO maintains that personal and professional development is just as good as a promotion. However, about a dozen employees have been promoted to key positions in the subsidiaries. It is a declared principle that pay should reflect individual performance and contribution to the firm, but the pay level is considered both too low and without a pay differentiation that mirrors individual work effort. The firm maintains that every employee—despite education, job assignments, and position in the organization—has a career and may shape a career, but still a minority of shy employees consider themselves outside the Oticon mainstream.

IO

Transformation in the Pharmaceutical Industry: HR's Prescription for Success

JAMES B. SHILLABER, PSY.D.

Introduction

Transformative change has affected nearly all industries in the United States over the last three decades. Not only have we seen the fundamental assumptions governing the conduct of business change in industry after industry, but change itself has become the only constant. One by one, heavy manufacturing, steel, automotive, and financial services industries have been yanked out of relatively stable environments and transformed by domestic and global economic forces.

The pharmaceutical industry has until recently been sheltered from some of the pressures experienced by other sectors of the economy. A relatively small tail on the healthcare dog, pharmaceutical companies enjoyed fairly stable manufacturing, regulatory, and selling environments right into the managed care revolution of the 1980s.

This chapter examines the more recent pressures and changes in the pharmaceutical industry over the last two decades and the choices made by one company about how to compete. This chapter will also look in detail at the role of the HR Department and the initiatives, programs, and processes it helped champion to support the company's future success and transformation in strategic direction.

Healthcare and the Pharmaceutical Industry

Thirty years ago the healthcare delivery system in the United States was relatively simple. Independent hospitals and physicians were the mainstay of this system and made choices about care in conjunction with patients and knowledge of the latest available technologies. Pharmaceutical agents were brokered by physicians and hospitals and became increasingly valued components of healthcare through the pharmaceutical heydays of the 1950s and 1960s.

Pharmaceutical companies sold drugs to wholesalers, retail pharmacies, and hospitals, which then sold their products to the consumer (see Figure 10-1). New pharmaceutical agents were highly desired, as they expanded the physician's treatment options. New entrants in the marketplace always captured a premium price over existing drugs, even when they offered no real new therapeutic outcome.

In a stable environment, drug companies were incited to develop as many new products as possible because new drugs could command premium prices. According to one study, 57 percent of the new drugs introduced between 1979 and 1988 were priced at premiums above existing market leaders despite the fact that many offered no real therapeutic advantages. Then, in an eigh-

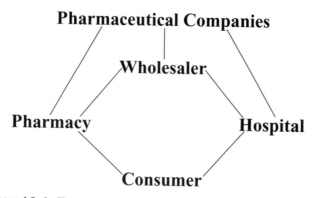

FIGURE 10-1. THE PHARMACEUTICAL PRODUCT DELIVERY CHAIN.

teen-month period in the early 1990s, not a single new drug commanded a premium because of increased pressures in the new managed care environment [1].

The only problem with this patient- and technology-driven approach to healthcare was that it was expensive. In 1970, healthcare costs were roughly $75 billion, or less than 8 percent of the domestic gross national product (GNP). In 1980 they were $248 billion, in 1990, $647 billion, and by the year 2000 it's estimated we'll spend more than $1.6 trillion, or approximately 15 percent of the GNP, roughly twice the 1970 percentage [2].

Several factors are driving the cost escalation, but two clear ones are the increasing longevity of the American population and the increasing cost of high-tech medicine. When we prolong lives by using more and more expensive treatments, it doesn't take long for the total healthcare bill to escalate dramatically.

Healthcare Reform

In the 1970s and 1980s the reform started. Both the HMO Act of 1973, which set the stage for the formation of a new kind of healthcare delivery, and the Prospective Payment System, which emerged in 1983 and allowed for reimbursement based on statistical averages for all different classes of disease, really threw the healthcare industry into high-speed change.

Suddenly the gates opened for a new form of competition. Of course there always was competition among providers, but rarely was it cost-based. Now different organizational structures were popping up to compete for patients based on controlling or managing costs. These organizations have continued to evolve over the last twenty years and show no signs of stabilizing soon. Health Maintenance Organizations (HMOs) were joined by Preferred Provider Organizations (PPOs) and now are being swallowed up by Accountable Health Plans (AHPs) and Integrated Healthcare Networks (IHNs). The trend toward larger, more integrated provider organizations has brought more scrutiny and control to the practice of medicine throughout the United States.

The Impact on the Pharmaceutical Industry

But what of the pharmaceutical companies? How have they been affected? As with most changes, there is good news and bad. The good news is that pharmaceutical agents represent a relatively small portion of total healthcare spending, between 5 and 8 percent [3], and so they have been subject to less scrutiny and pressure until recently. The further good news is that, relatively speaking, pharmaceutical agents often are the preferred treatment for many disorders because they are either inexpensive, easy to administer, or both. The cost of orally-administered acid-blocking stomach medications is far cheaper than treating a bleeding ulcer in a hospital. Healthcare payers (increasingly the decision makers) are eager to exploit new pharmaceutical treatments if they feel such treatments may lower their overall cost profile for treating a specific disease.

The bad news, though, is that competition in the industry is severe. Two major forces, and several smaller ones, have been driving the increased pressure—the introduction of generic drugs and the increasing bargaining power of larger and larger managed care organizations.

First, imagine you have been eyeing a new Porsche automobile. Now imagine someone tells you you can have a car that is functionally equivalent to the Porsche in every single way—virtually identical—for about 40 to 60 percent of the cost. That's what happened in the pharmaceutical industry. Once a patent expires on a drug, competitors are free to manufacture and market the same compound at whatever price they wish. Typically the price of a new drug includes costs the company has had to incur for research and development—both for the product being introduced and for the hundred or so other compounds that didn't make it. Since generic manufacturers typically don't have extensive drug development operations, they don't have to recoup those costs and thus can introduce their products at a significantly lower price. Generic drugs now make up between 10 percent and 35 percent of pharmaceutical sales in the United States [4, 5].

The impact of managed care organizations (MCOs) on the pharmaceutical industry has been less obvious, though probably more powerful. HMOs and other MCOs came about as mechanisms to control escalating healthcare costs. Simplistically, these organizations manage the business side of healthcare delivery by organizing large groups of providers into networks, offering fixed costs to employers for covering their employees, and—of particular interest to the pharmaceutical companies—managing the purchase and distribution of medical supplies and drugs. Whereas in the past each hospital or drugstore might purchase pharmaceuticals from each individual company (or their wholesalers), suddenly larger and larger buying groups were coming to the table asking for contracted price concessions, rebates, and higher service and support levels.

MCOs also impacted the selling process. Pharmaceutical sales representatives had been accustomed to talking with physicians about the medical benefits of their products. If the pharmaceutical company could prove a drug worked (efficacy) and the sales rep could show it to physicians and get them comfortable with it, the physicians would write prescriptions, which would result in sales. To control costs, however, the MCOs limited the number of different drugs their physicians could write prescriptions for, thereby driving higher volume in those selected drugs, called the formulary, and consequently allowing the MCOs to ask for larger price concessions from their suppliers. Suddenly individual physicians were saying their hands were tied and that they were not the decision makers for which products were prescribed, and pharmaceutical companies were rushing to give price breaks to gain a larger market share with their products.

Not only did this shift put tremendous cost pressure on pharmaceutical companies, but it also changed completely the way business was done in the industry. Pharmaceutical companies found themselves establishing managed-care sales and contracting units to try to keep up with the changes in healthcare. They started to bundle their products together and offer value-adding programs, such as patient or practitioner education campaigns. For those drugs with clearly identified competitors, an all-out price war had begun. The only drugs less affected by the MCOs' cost pressures were those that were unique in their clinical profiles, offered new advances over existing products, or had no competitors at all.

In summary, the impact of generic competition and managed care along with other forces in healthcare have transformed the pharmaceutical industry. Companies have found their margins increasingly destroyed by these forces—with little recourse. Now profitability is increasingly provided by sales growth. But it is not uncommon to see companies with double-digit sales growth encounter significantly less growth in profit over time.

Berlex Laboratories

In 1980, looking to establish itself in U.S. businesses and markets, a large German chemical and pharmaceutical company acquired Cooper Laboratories, a $30 million diversified pharmaceutical and consumer goods company. At this time the parent organization created a holding company in the United States and developed a diverse portfolio of operating companies, including its pharmaceutical business, renamed Berlex Laboratories. Right at this time the previously mentioned business changes were taking the industry by storm.

During the next decade or so, Berlex executives would see first hand how some of the forces outlined above would affect their business. The impact was dramatic. In the early 1980s, Berlex had no formal rebate programs for any of its products, but by 1993 discounts and rebates amounted to tens of millions of dollars per year. The average actual selling price of some Berlex products dropped as much as 30 percent as a result of government and contracted discounts and rebates. Berlex executives were left scrambling to make up the shortfall.

In the late 1980s, as the turmoil in the industry was really heating up, Berlex (with headquarters' approval) began paring down its operations and divesting its nonpharmaceutical businesses. Berlex and its parent had decided that to win in the pharmaceutical industry required an exclusive focus on pharmaceuticals. This afforded the opportunity to step back and ask critical questions about how to compete in the U.S. marketplace. Several strategic possibilities presented themselves. Some companies had made a shift to generic drug production. Others were moving into specific therapeutic areas or treatment modalities to dominate the market for one particular product or disease state.

Strategy

Berlex management determined that neither of these strategies would work for its small company. Generic drug production requires sophisticated, low-cost manufacturing technologies, which Berlex hadn't developed. Also, Berlex's product portfolio and development pipeline were too broad to support domination in just one disease state or therapeutic area. Instead, in the early 1990s Berlex set out to examine the healthcare and pharmaceutical marketplaces and identify a better way to compete.

In some respects the answers came easily. If it couldn't compete on mass alone, it would need to be quick; the company would need to be opportunistic to identify and seize emerging product possibilities and quick to form business alliances and partnerships when they met long-term needs. Because the only products less subject to cost pressures were those that were new or had few competitors, Berlex needed to identify new drugs in areas where no existing treatments were available. The company would need to be flexible in changing priorities and thinking when needed in order to pursue and capture the most promising of these opportunities.

The imperatives of opportunism and flexibility came out of the executives' strategy meetings in the early 1990s and then fell to the organization to implement. Until this time, despite its relatively small size, Berlex behaved traditionally. In a heavily regulated industry, it was functionally organized and somewhat bureaucratic in its thinking and actions. There was not a lot of teamwork across departments, and decisions typically went up through the chain of command—not an environment favorable to seizing opportunities and maximizing flexibility. Change had to occur in all aspects of the operation—from thinking to behavior. The challenge facing us all was how could we, in fact, develop a different mindset and the related behaviors around our work?

The remainder of this chapter details the approach taken by Berlex's Human Resource Department to take stock of the company's current situation and systematically modify its systems and programs to support and, at times, lead the changes needed to realize the new strategy.

Congruence Model

Before changing systems or implementing new programs, it is vital to understand where the organization stands relative to where it needs to be and to use that information to plan a comprehensive change strategy. Our HR department thinks systemically, using a modification of Nadler and Tushman's [6] congruence model to understand how organizations function and to plan how to intervene. Briefly, this model states that an organization's environment, history, and resources shape its competitive strategy. The organization's effectiveness is measured by the extent to which its formal structures and systems, the work that people do, the individual knowledge and skills possessed, and the organization's culture and informal practices are aligned with (or *congruent with*) that strategy and each other.

Other things being equal, the greater the total degree of congruence or fit between the various components, the more effective will be the organization, effectiveness being defined as the degree to which actual organizational output at individual, group, and organizational levels are similar to expected output, as specified by strategy [7].

For simplicity we say that the company's structure, systems, capabilities, and culture must support the strategy [8], and the HR Department's job is to look at each of those components and work to bring each more into alignment with the needed direction. This is, of course, an ongoing process. Below we will look at a summary of this analysis at Berlex and the actions taken by the HR Department and company to initiate and support change. Although it may appear quite rational and planned here, the process was of course an evolving one. In practice, companies prioritize, identify "hot spots," measure where tthe greatest influence can be attained, and then use whatever vehicles are at their disposal to leverage for change.

Organizational Analysis

The strategic imperative faced by Berlex in the 1990s had dramatic implications for all aspects of the organization—in short, the structure, systems, capabilities, and culture all supported a traditional hierarchical organization, not the flexible and opportunistic company it needed to become. The question became how to launch a manageable campaign to initiate change.

Structure

Berlex was organized functionally—drug development, marketing, sales, finance, and so forth, all reported to different executive committee (EC) members. Spans of control were relatively small, and few organizational structures were in place to support the new strategic imperative.

Systems

The HR systems in the company did not support opportunism and flexibility. Job descriptions were static instruments, typically created by the manager to justify a specific compensation grading. Performance management was a retrospective analysis of behavior along four dimensions, which may or may not have been relevant for the work an employee performed. Numerical performance appraisal ratings were calculated to two decimal places, and compensation increases were determined using those appraisal ratings (five categories) and position in the salary range (three categories).

Readers familiar with such an approach know that, instead of using the performance appraisal process to give genuine feedback to employees, managers will use it to justify the compensation increases they want to give. Rounding an employee's rating off to the nearest hundredth gives an illusion of objectivity, but most managers readily admitted to using the system to get the raises they wanted for their employees. Describing jobs, managing performance, and compensating employees were systems that needed to change if the company was to change.

Capabilities and Culture

In such an environment it's not surprising that the culture and capabilities that were needed to exploit the opportunism strategy were in short supply. For the size of the company, the culture was surprisingly bureaucratic—it was easy for managers to toss responsibility over the fence to the next department if the work couldn't get done or to HR if managers didn't like the size of raises they were able to give. Specific skills supporting accountability, risk analysis, risk taking, relationship management, and flexibility were not reinforced in the culture.

Time to Act

As the executive committee was introducing the new direction in 1992, it made a significant structural change in support of the strategy. Berlex organized its drug development and marketing efforts into three different strategic units, allowing for greater focus on product area and independent growth and development. Each group had its own core medical, marketing, and development staff, and they all shared resources that were not specific to any individual therapeutic or product area.

But as we know, changing an organization's structure is not enough to change the way its people think and work. Although in this chapter we address the role that HR systems and processes played in supporting the new strategy, the real question we debated was much broader than that—what do our *people* need to face the challenges of a new marketplace, a new organization, and the ever-raising bar? This is what drove the systems and program changes.

What HR Did

An organizing or unifying theme is a good place to start a change effort. If HR just worked on the individual systems or programs through which change is implemented, it would run the risk of employees not seeing the interconnectivity of the parts. Understanding strategy and what's required to implement it are critical precursors to introducing the systems and programs that employees ultimately will use to implement the change.

The theme at Berlex was "relationship." Opportunism, or how Berlex would succeed in the outside world, required good connections between key Berlex employees and the right external people and organizations. Our physicians needed to have good relationships with the medical centers where our studies were conducted. Scientists needed good relationships with potential collaborators.

Salespeople needed good relationships with the increasingly complex array of people and businesses that bought our products.

Flexibility, or how Berlex succeeded internally, depended on managers' relationships with employees and employees' relationships with each other. To change direction quickly, seize opportunities, and explore new areas for the company, we needed to have good communication and high trust with those who gave direction.

Good relationships became the key to flexibility and partnership, both inside the company and out, and became the cornerstone for the development of HR systems and programs. Fortunately "relationship" was a theme consistent with our small-company approach and the more paternal culture we had both developed and imported from our German parent. It was appealing from a personal point of view and relevant strategically. The next question became how to operationalize it. We needed more tangible outcomes to focus our efforts and decided to use a company-wide training program to introduce the concepts. Our initial focus was on internal relationships while recognizing and stating that the same critical principles and skills applied to success in all relationships.

The Berlex Outcomes

In early 1993 I had the opportunity to ask our executives and a number of employees what would be happening within Berlex if

TABLE 10-1.

STRATEGIC LEVERS FOR TRANSFORMATION AT BERLEX.

Strategic Demands	Means	Theme
External: Identify drugs for unmet medical needs, develop them quickly, capitalize on collaborations	Innovation	
		= "Relationship"
Internal: Become less bureaucratic foster teamwork, take more risks	Flexibility	

we were doing a great job of managing our relationships. The answers, called the Berlex Outcomes, became the foundation for our internal relationship development efforts:

1. People are in jobs that match their skills and interests
2. People know what is expected of them and how their work contributes to organizational strategies and goals
3. People know how they are performing
4. People are developed for their current and future jobs
5. People feel recognized and equitably compensated for their contributions
6. All employees contribute to business success.

Training

The Outcomes are compelling enough but tough to achieve. These Outcomes are obviously the long-term goals to be reached by working at our internal and external relationships. Few would argue with their desirability or the way they ultimately influence our success in the marketplace. In those same meetings with employees, I asked where we should be devoting our internal training efforts, and four areas were identified:

☐ Individual one-on-one relationships
☐ Team relationships
☐ Managerial relationships
☐ Global relationships with our parent organization.

As a result of this input, the first product to help introduce a new culture and develop skills was a two-day course on individual relationships, called One-on-One. The course focused on the Berlex business environment, key elements of an effective relationship, obstacles to forming good relationships, and relationship skills, such as listening, feedback, and performance problem solving. Although the course initially was targeted for managers, all the early participants said the principles and skills were critical for everyone to have. The course was then opened to all employees. Each of our executives made the course a requirement in his or her unit, and all employees participated in training in 1993 and 1994. Now the class is run for all new employees four times a year.

Subsequently, programs for team development and management have been introduced, each with the central theme of understanding and improving a particular kind of relationship. The courses have been developed and delivered primarily by internal people and are steeped in Berlex's business context. Why these skills are critical for our business success now is emphasized, and how these processes (teams or management, for example) work at Berlex drive the programs. They are directly connected to the company's strategic imperative. Training builds on the core message, the programs relate to and progressively build on each other, and all work together to create a core set of values for the company (see Figure 10-2). Over time we have also introduced courses aimed directly at improving external customer relationships.

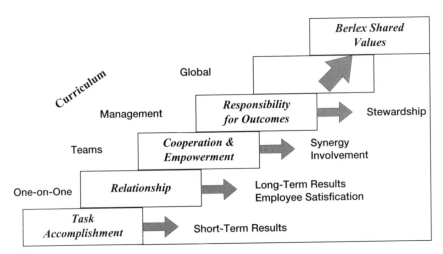

FIGURE 10-2. BUILDING PRODUCTIVE WORK RELATIONSHIPS.

Performance Management

Training programs are good vehicles to introduce cultural ideas and train or reinforce skills, but they are often seen as not directly related to one's job, especially if the material being trained is somewhat foreign to an employee's way of thinking or doing things. Participants consistently said they liked the relationship training but they thought it would be difficult to apply to their day-to-day jobs. In a culture focused on task and function, it would seem out of character to focus on the development of relationships.

Berlex needed a tool to help employees translate the strategic concepts (both the content, or *what* needed to be done, and the process, or *how* we ought to behave) into meaningful objectives at the individual level. Human resource organizations know the importance of examining the performance management and compensation systems to be sure they support the strategic direction of the business.

Performance management at Berlex was anything but relationship-focused. First, it wasn't really performance management, but performance appraisal. There was no forward-looking performance planning as part of the system. Instead, four major areas, job knowledge, management capability, initiative taking, and human relations, were each broken down into five to eight individual statements, which were rated on a scale of 1 (does not meet job requirements) to 5 (exceeds all job requirements). In addition, 100 weighting points were distributed among the 28 total items. Those weighting points were allocated according to the manager's perception of the relative importance of each item. An example of a completed section for job knowledge is depicted in Table 10-2.

The end result was a scientific-looking performance appraisal. Each of the four major categories had subratings for relative importance, average evaluation, and the total weighted evaluation (for example, job knowledge has 21 of 100 importance points, an average evaluation of 4.24, and a total weighted evaluation of 89.9 in the example shown). An overall evaluation rating was calculated by taking the grand total of the weighted evaluation points

TABLE 10-2.

**SAMPLE JOB KNOWLEDGE SECTION OF THE BERLEX
PERFORMANCE APPRAISAL FORM.**

Relative Importance	I. Job Knowledge	Performance Evaluation	Weighted Evaluation
4	Demonstrates knowledge of job requirements, skills, techniques, and principles	4.5	18.0
3	Understands company, divisional, and/or departmental policies and procedures	3.9	11.7
6	Applies specialized knowledge and skills	4.5	27.0
4	Identifies and uses internal and external resources	4.2	16.8
4	Expands knowledge and keeps current with developments in the field	4.1	16.4
	Other		
21		Avg 4.24	89.9

and dividing by the 100 relative importance points to yield a number between 1 and 5. This rating was displayed to two points past the decimal. The final rating scale is described in Table 10-3.

Good managers may have asked employees for input and spent time discussing the ratings, but many employees told us they either never saw the appraisal form or simply received a copy of it from the manager with no explanation. For most, "performance feedback" came in the form of the salary increase at year-end, but often that came without explanation as well. The system was hierarchical, activity-driven (versus outcome-driven), and in most cases not conducive to the development of relationships. Employees played no role in the process, and although Human Resources

TABLE 10-3.
BERLEX PERFORMANCE APPRAISAL OVERALL RATING SCALE.

1.00–1.99	2.00–2.49	2.50–3.84	3.85–4.64	4.65–5.00
Does not meet job requirements	Meets some job requirements	Meets all job requirements	Exceeds most job requirements	Exceeds all job requirements

received the appraisal forms at the end of the year, it played no strategic role in the process either.

As soon as the One-on-One program was up and running, the challenge fell to the HR group to do something with performance management. In the early One-on-One classes, it was difficult to stand in front of a group of employees and tell them that top management supported the development of productive relationships when the performance management system sent such clear messages that employees were not part of the process.

In 1994 a task force was formed, led by HR, to redesign the performance appraisal and management system. Its goal was clear—help the organization achieve the Berlex Outcomes. Work with the strategy messages, not against them. Put more responsibility in both managers' and employees' hands for developing relationships that contribute to business success.

The task force met to review the current system and make plans for an overhaul. By the time they were done, the new approach bore no resemblance to the old. The new employee performance development process (EPD) was *defined* as:

☐ Effective two-way dialogue in manager-employee relationships

☐ Mutually defined and understood goals and standards

☐ Developing better performance in our current roles.

Many shifts in thinking were required to understand the new approach and get comfortable with it. These shifts included going from a one-time event to ongoing dialogue, a focus on the past to a focus on the future, evaluation to development, forms to business tools, HR ownership to line ownership, one-way approach to a mutual approach, and from relationship and trust diminishing to relationship and trust building.

EPD involved a mutual clarification of role and performance expectations followed by ongoing dialogue during the year about performance successes and development needs. There were no required forms to fill out, no set time cycle across the company, and no HR oversight of the process. Each unit set its own implementation schedule and made decisions about when and how EPD would be done. Sounds simple, doesn't it? Have a dialogue to achieve clarity about expectations, and then follow up and give feedback about successes and failures.

We emphasized that the specific structure or format of the process was not important, but what was important were the outcomes. HR's role was to design the process and useful tools, provide training, and measure the success. We said we would have been successful if significantly more people knew what was expected and knew how they were performing at the end of the first year. The Berlex Outcomes (specifically Nos. 2 and 3: people know what is expected of them and how their owrk contributes to organizational strategies and goals, and people know how they are performing) then became the critical measures for how we were implementing key human resource programs and processes.

In fact, we do use the Outcomes as measures in a very direct way. Instead of a traditional attitude survey, we simply ask employees once a year to what extent each Outcome applies to them. For example, we ask, "To what extent are you in a job that matches your skills and interests?" (Outcome No. 1). Employees use a 1 (to no extent) to 7 (to a great extent) scale. We compile the data by unit and compare year-to-year results. Indeed, there were significant changes in the Outcomes relating to performance management from 1994 to 1995. While other items were relatively unchanged, these Outcomes showed gains of from 6 to 13 percent in overall percent favorable. In addition, that year 88 percent of employees reported they had created written goals and objectives with their managers, 70 percent felt their managers were committed to establishing an open dialogue, and roughly half felt the process helped them make progress toward relationship and trust building broadly in the organization.

EPD rapidly became the vehicle for further implementation of the strategic imperatives around innovation and flexibility. It was extremely helpful in our ongoing training activities to have a relationship- and outcome-focused system like EPD to rely on for supporting the messages delivered through training and for acting as the primary implementation vehicle for relationship-focused ideas. Employees could no longer point to the chasm between what we said we wanted and the systems or tools we provided to help people get there.

Compensation

Right behind the performance management system came the need to redesign the compensation system. Because in the old system annual compensation increases were "hard-wired" to the performance appraisal rating, we didn't have much time before we had to turn our attention to compensation. In fact, the team considered this issue during the design of EPD.

The old system (see Table 10-4) relied on a grid based on a person's position in salary range and performance rating. Once both of those items were known, an increase could be selected from a narrow range within each cell in the grid. A manager might have the discretion to raise or lower an increase by one half of 1 percent in any particular cell in the grid.

By eliminating the performance rating through the implementation of EPD, we stripped away one axis of the grid. At the same time we were examining our salary grading approach to see how it continued to meet the company's needs. Grading jobs within specific salary grades implies that work is static. We tended to

TABLE 10-4.
SAMPLE BERLEX COMPENSATION GRID.

	Position in Salary Range		
Performance Rating	Lower Third	Middle	Upper Third
1.00–1.99	0.0	0.0	0.0
2.00–2.49	2.0–2.4%	1.5–1.9%	1.0–1.4%
2.50–3.84	4.0–4.5%	3.5–3.9%	3.0–3.4%
3.85–4.64	6.0–6.5%	5.5–5.9%	5.0–5.4%
4.65–5.00	8.0–8.5%	7.5–7.9%	7.0–7.4%

grade jobs when they were first created and then ignore the grading until an issue arose. In fact, the work of most employees was fluid—it changed as technology, business demands, and the skills of the incumbents changed. The roles our sales reps or even HR people play today are quite different than they were even five years ago.

Locking jobs into grades also hampered career development for key individuals. For example, if the product manager job was graded lower than the sales manager's, what incentive did the sales manager have to come in-house and learn the product marketing side of the business? Yet that may be the best thing for the manager and company.

Ed Lawler has described a shift occurring in industry from a focus on job to a focus on person [3]. He noted that as that shift occurs, the entire human resources infrastructure needs to change to support it. Systems for describing and paying for work, developing skills, assessing potential, and selecting employees all need to evolve to reflect a new balance between the work that needs to be done and the people who will do it. Unfortunately, he noted that legislation, tax codes, and a host of other supports in the larger environment are slow to catch on. Berlex needed new flexibility with its compensation approach but also needed to maintain some sense of internal and market equity.

The company investigated broad-banding and other systems but ultimately found its strategic solution in using differently the systems it already had. Actual compensation levels need to reflect both the job and the incumbent, and the salary grades give us information about where jobs rank relative to other jobs. It's not this system that is limiting, per se; it was how rigidly we were using it.

As a result of this investigation, Berlex moved to a two-step process for setting compensation levels. We now begin with external "market referencing" to understand and value a particular job and then add another step to consider how we want to compensate a particular individual. If there are reasons to compensate an individual above or below the market data, managers have the flexibility to do so. Practically all of our salaries fall within the market ranges, but for those cases in which something innovative needs to be done, we have the flexibility to do it (it would seem that such a market reference approach could only be taken in a company small enough where HR knows its jobs and people, however).

Another aspect of compensation is setting annual increases. Making salary grades guidelines and not absolute boundaries eliminated the meaningfulness of the second axis of our compensation grid. Employees feared that the absence of the grid would result in subjectivity, favoritism, and systematic abuses. We didn't find that to be true, although a great deal of education needed to occur to help managers learn how to use the compensation tools more strategically. We taught that performance should be the major driver of one's annual compensation increase but not the only factor to consider. Managers needed to learn to weigh factors like someone's overall level of compensation for his or her role, the effective contribution to the company, and of course the limited budget they had to work within. Their ongoing performance review discussions with employees set the stage for their choices about compensation. The truth of the matter was managers had always used their judgment to differentiate increases; they had just had the performance and salary grids to hide behind when delivering the messages.

In addition to providing training and support, HR's role in compensation is to measure outcomes, not dictate the process. After the first round of salary administration, we analyzed the increases given. Most groups came in on target for total compensation increases (expressed as a percentage of total compensation in the unit), but we were interested in how far individual increases deviated from the mean. In other words, were managers using salary to differentiate performance by giving some people no or very low increases and others much higher increases? Our strategic imperative required us to better link rewards to the appropriate performance and outputs (Berlex Outcome No. 5).

Not surprisingly, the first year showed little differentiation in some units. Salary increases ranged from 0 percent to 9 percent with a standard deviation of 1.4 percent. This means most of the salary increases given that year were within 1.4 percent of the mean. One unit had a deviation of only .26 percent, about one quarter of a percent, suggesting almost no differentiation of salary increases. Most high-performing employees won't hesitate to say that receiving a pay increase only a percent or two above lower-performing employees is decidedly *not* motivating. Although most managers had previously told us (and their employees, too, unfortunately) that the grid hampered their ability to reward top performers appropriately, when given the opportunity to distribute increases any way they wanted, they didn't differentiate any more than the grid would have. They learned that giving the top performer a 10 percent increase in a zero-sum system such as ours meant giving one or two employees no increase.

The problem was we gave managers exactly what they asked for. Responsibility is great in theory, but in actuality many people would rather not have to deal directly with the feedback and salary increases given to their employees. The HR systems at Berlex now had placed that responsibility squarely with the manager. Help was provided in the form of job aids, training, and coaching, but the implementation was up to the manager and employee. Over time we've seen the annual salary administration process used more aggressively to support the needs of the business. The data for the 1998 process, just being compiled at this writing, show the range of increases to be from 0 percent to 17 percent, with a standard deviation of approximately 3 percent. The individual unit that posted the .26 percent deviation two years ago has its average increases deviating 2.14 percent from the mean this year—a significant increase.

Another compensation vehicle at Berlex used to support the changes in strategic direction (and supporting Berlex Outcome No. 5) was a peer-nominated recognition program called CITE (for the values of creativity, initiative, teamwork, and employee development). CITE works in the following way. Employees nominate other employees based on those values, and selection committees composed of all managers in the company review the nominations and select the final awardees. The cycle is run twice yearly and has an annual target of 15 to 20 percent of all employees. CITE recipients receive "shares" linked to Berlex's sales growth. These shares are at a target amount of either 6 or 10 percent of annual salary, depending on the level of the award given. A portion of the award is paid out immediately, and the remainder of the shares pay out in five years at whatever value they have accumulated to. This is a significant award.

Berlex also was able to use the CITE nomination and selection process as another mechanism to send messages about the importance of relationships. Although nominations typically had been made for outstanding task achievement (sometimes at the cost of relationships), we added relationship as another consideration in the award. It was no longer sufficient to accomplish a task, but the manner in which the work got done also became important. Getting managers in the selection committees to talk about how work gets done sent a powerful signal to Berlex employees.

Over time, other programs have been created or adapted to support the evolving needs of the business. We have modified the new employee orientation to include explicit messages about the strategy of the company and what is required of employees to achieve it. We've brought in additional training programs to support various aspects of the message. And an innovative career planning and management program was developed for our field sales force that accompanied dramatic changes in the field structure and included bold new messages about what is required for career success.

Beyond Systems and Programs

In short, the HR Department modified nearly every one of its systems and programs to ensure the department supported the strategic direction of the company. But we in HR had to look beyond the systems and programs we deployed. We also needed to look at the many day-to-day transactions we were involved with and ensure that they, too, supported the strategic messages. Too often HR departments can be split by HR function or organization development staff who create new programs that the front-line HR generalists don't understand, implement or support.

At Berlex, the results of our analysis of the structure, systems, capabilities and culture became a filter through which the front-line HR staff members could, and would, view their work. When opportunities arose to influence a unit's structure, they asked how they could help the organization become more flexible. When employees or managers talked about skill gaps, HR held up the "new" skills around communication, work process, and relationship. Similarly, whether through the annual attitude survey or their day-to-day work, the HR staff members have helped shift the culture of the company's different units to support more flexibility and innovation.

In addition, we've structured HR at our east coast facilities to model the approach our client organizations must take with their own internal and external customers. We provide a high-level internal consultant as the lead HR person in each unit. This person is responsible for the organizational integrity of the client unit including organization and job design, human resource planning, talent acquisition and development, and the full range of human resource transactions. When these people operate as consultants and not HR-function employees, they must use and develop skills in communication, partnering, and relationship building.

Lessons Learned

Berlex has made many changes since the strategy meetings and restructuring in 1992. The executive committee has continued to make company-wide changes and to create tools to communicate the messages that it believes are critical for success in the new competitive environment. The Human Resource Department has played, and will continue to play, a critical role in translating messages about strategy and its implications for employees and inb helping implement those messages through its systems, programs, and day-to-day activities. In summary, several lessons have emerged from our work at Berlex.

1. Support strategy, not initiatives. HR staff members are fully aware of business pressures and in an effort to show their value to top management, may be too responsive to programs or initiatives. It is important to step back and ensure that HR efforts are linked with the larger business strategy. One way to find out if you're working on the proper level is to ask what time frame applies to the work your department is doing. If it's measured in months or even one or two years, you may be more initiative-based than strategy-based. We knew that the work to foster innovation, flexibility, and relationships at Berlex would take many years to make substantial progress on and that it wouldn't change or become less relevant over time. If anything, the need to excel in these areas has increased.

2. Lead, don't follow. Wherever possible, HR should be closely involved in the setting of strategy because of its intimate knowledge of the organization's capabilities. But as strategy is emerg-

ing, HR needs to lead the process of internal analysis and change management to shift and develop the internal capabilities where they are needed. Employees may be resistant or confused, and executives won't understand why it's taking so long, so if HR looks to others for direction the job will never get done.

3. Go deep *and* broad. To make significant change, a broad range of systems and programs need to be engaged, but these mechanisms all must build on each other and send the same messages. At Berlex we used all of the systems and programs at our disposal, but we ensured that every one of them had a similar texture and feel, and we sent the same messages.

4. Leverage wherever possible. Don't just look at the world through HR lenses. Piggyback onto other programs, and get managers and employees to send the strategic messages through their own initiatives. Not everything has to be made in HR—in fact, initiatives may be more powerful if they start somewhere else. At Berlex we were able to tap into development efforts that were under way with our field sales force and a major customer service program to ensure they sent the strategic messages.

5. Finally, recognize that real change takes time. We in HR have the tools and knowledge to create significant change, but we also need the patience and perseverance to design it thoroughly and implement it consistently.

References

1. Boston Consulting Group. *The Changing Environment for United States Pharmaceuticals.* Boston: Boston Consulting Group, 1993.

2. Management and Marketing Corporation International. *Trends Shaping United States Pharmaceutical Industry Strategies: A MMC Strategic Report.* Stanford, Conn.: MMC International, 1994.

3. Lawler, E. *Strategic Outsourcing and HR: Leveraging the Business Impact of Human Resources,* Conference, New Orleans: Linkage Inc., Mar. 25–27, 1996.

4. IMS. *Retail Perspective: Market Research Reports for the Pharmaceutical Industry,* Plymouth Meeting, Pa.: IMS; 1997.

5. Pisano, G. *The Development Factory.* Boston: Harvard Business School Press, 1997.

6. Nadler, D. and Tushman, M. "A Congruence Model for Diagnosing Organizational Behavior," in *Organizational Psychology: A Book of Readings,* 3rd ed. Kolb, Rubin, and McIntyre (Ed.), Englewood Cliffs, N.J.: Prentice Hall, 1979.

7. Nadler, D. and Tushman, M. *Change/1: Concepts for the Management of Organizational Change.* New York: Delta Consulting Group, 1988.

8. Schiemann, W. "Supporting Strategy: Tools for Total Organizational Alignment." *Catalyst* (company newsletter of Wm. Schiemann & Associates Inc.), Spring 1992.

Index